MW01102406

CENTRAL MONTANA ROCK

2nd Edition

Central Montana Rock 2nd Edition by Jake Mergenthaler
©2022 Sharp End Publishing, LLC
All rights reserved. This book or any part thereof may not be reproduced in any form without written permission from the publisher.

Published and distributed by:

Sharp End Publishing, LLC
PO Box 1613
Boulder, CO 80306
303-444-2698
www.sharpendbooks.com

ISBN: 978-0-9657079-5-4

Cover Image: Kim Mergenthaler on *California Dreamin'* 5.12c | Photo by Garret Smith

Opening Page Image: Taylor Fragomeni on *The Thimble* 5.12d | Photo by Jules Jimreivat

Table of Contents Image: Henry Schlotzhauer on *Best Before 5.14a* | Photo by Ben Herndon

Printed in South Korea

READ THIS BEFORE USING THIS BOOK: WARNING!

Climbing is a very dangerous activity. Take all precautions and evaluate your ability carefully. Use judgment rather than the opinions represented in this book. The publisher and author assume no responsibility for injury or death resulting from the use of this book. This book is based on opinions. Do not rely on information, descriptions, or difficulty ratings as these are entirely subjective. If you are unwilling to assume complete responsibility for your safety, do not use this guidebook.

THE AUTHORS AND PUBLISHER EXPRESSLY DISCLAIM ALL REPRESENTATIONS AND WARRANTIES REGARDING THIS GUIDE, THE ACCURACY OF THE INFORMATION HEREIN, AND THE RESULTS OF YOUR USE HEREOF, INCLUDING WITHOUT LIMITATION, IMPLIED WARRANTIES OF MERCHANTABILITY AND FITNESS FOR A PARTICULAR PURPOSE. THE USER ASSUMES ALL RISK ASSOCIATED WITH THE USE OF THIS GUIDE.

It is your responsibility to take care of yourself while climbing. Seek a professional instructor or guide if you are unsure of your ability to handle any circumstances that may arise. This guide is not intended as an instructional manual.

HELENA CLIMBERS' COALITION

Helena Climbers' Coalition (HCC) started in 2019 after several years of late night conversations, scheming sessions, and a Facebook group that seemed to be yearning for more. We are a group of Helena area climbers that are passionate about our climbing but are really just after a grand-old-good-time. As our town and climbing community grows, we aim to meet the evolving needs of the land and its people to ensure longevity as well as enjoyment at some of our favorite places. We think this is done best by bringing people together, building lasting relationships, and promoting ethics that encourage both new and weathered climbers to invest in the climbing community. Mostly, we think we live in a pretty rad area for climbing and we want folks to enjoy it and take care of it.

If you are new to town and looking for partners—let us know! We'll hook you up. If you are traveling through and want some beta—we've got some talkers that will help you out. If you are new to climbing, climbing-curious, or want to try something outside of the gym but don't know where to start—help out at one of our events or come to a meeting and meet like minded folks. Or if you just think this whole thing is pretty sweet—donations are always welcome. This book is a direct extension of our mission to foster a thriving, welcoming, diverse climbing community. We hope you find enough information to get you out there, with enough freedom to explore for yourself.

Helena's Local Climbing Resource

the BaseCamp
Gear for the Great Outdoors

HELENA · SINCE 1975 · BILLINGS

5 West Broadway · 406-443-5360 · thebasecamp.com · f

Mon-Fri 9:30 am - 8:00 pm · Sat 9:30 am - 6:00 pm · Sun 11:00 am - 5:00 pm

TABLE OF CONTENTS

Metolius
Super Chalk

Jonathan Siegrist on Spank the Monkey 5.13d, Smith Rock

Metolius
Super Chalk
4.5 ounces / 127 grams

America's #1 Climbing Chalk
La magnésie la plus populaire pour
l'escalade en Amérique

www.metoliusclimbing.c

Blackleaf
Canyon

Bynum

N

89

North Fork
of the
Teton River

Choteau

Helena

287

Rocky Mountain Front

Beaver Creek

15

Trout Creek
Canyon

Blackleaf Canyon &
North Fork of the Teton River

Hellgate

Avalanche

Blue Cloud
Spires

Helena

Mount
Helena

287

Missouri River

Sheep
Mountain

Clancy

Google Earth

15

Indian Creek

Helena Area

WELCOME
by Megan Helton

Welcome to the Second Edition of Central Montana Rock, the Helena area climbing guide. This book covers the large and diverse landscape united under the Helena Climbers' Coalition stewardship area.

What you hold in your hand is a community effort. Just as there is no one developer, there is no one author. Each area's climbs have been compiled by a local enthusiast who relied on others local knowledge, both published and unwritten, to capture the current snapshot and past history of known routes. As you use this guide to explore the area, your experience will contribute to the uniqueness of these places, to the campfire tales yet to be told, and to the history of rock climbing in and around Helena.

The Helena region is, in many ways, the middle child of Montana outdoor recreation. Situated between the megaplex of the Gallatin Valley and the sprawl of the Bitterroot Valley, Helena is often described by that inbetweeness—it's a stopover between Yellowstone National Park and Glacier, it's between Butte and Great Falls on I15. It's overlooked as a place on its own. Those of us who have chosen Helena as a home like it that way. We are proud to be out of the limelight.

You will see that pride in our local lore, as we celebrate people within these pages who are prolific route developers and fast-charging hard-people, yet they may have no Instagram account or outside acknowledgement. They are just as likely to be found top roping with their kids as they are to be pushing grades and training for the next obscure objective. Those local legends are the gatekeepers of two fundamental principles of this region: climb for the joy of it, and don't take yourself too seriously.

So it is with a little trepidation at calling attention to ourselves that we update this region's guidebook. We hope that by sharing these places, we can also share excitement, adventure, friendship, and whatever personal lessons climbing is likely to bring. We ask visiting climbers to acknowledge the effort we've put into caring for these places, the risks we take by sharing them, and to take the time to read the following before heading out:

ROUTE DEVELOPMENT
This guide does not include a number of routes and a handful of areas that are currently under development. Given the long history of development additional routes that have probably gone up over the years have undoubtedly been lost to time, although pitons and tat may remain. Climbers should not be surprised to encounter both old and new routes not listed in this guide. In several cases we have noted unfinished projects. Many of these have been included for reference only and some may not yet be suitable for leading. If you want to try these lines, be cautious of loose rock and be prepared to lower or bail off a single bolt. Contacting the person who established the climb might be prudent to better understand the nature of the route.

For those looking to add their own routes, please consider the following. The ethics and best practices for development of limestone sport routes have been covered extensively in other resources and developers should look to these before authoring anything. Limestone, like all rock, can have dangerous blocks and other objective hazards, please minimize or eliminate these when establishing routes. Remember not everyone will have the experience to know to avoid loose rock, and accidents have occurred in Montana on routes established without adequate cleaning. Our rock can be soft, so not all cracks take or hold gear and judicious use of bolts may be appropriate near these features. Also please consider using bolt types that are easy to maintain and made of long-lasting material such as stainless steel.

As recent controversies in Ten Sleep and the Bitterroot Mountains have shown, several issues are currently at the forefront of access and development. First, there is a difference between developing a route and manufacturing a route. Please do the former not not the latter. Second, sport climbing areas can receive quite a bit of traffic. When considering bolting near trails or other areas used by non-climbers, please think long and hard if the route is worth the potential impacts on these other user groups and the access we enjoy. Third, bolts, hangers, and anchors can be an eyesore, camouflaging your hardware is imperative. Finally, remember that routes will likely be repeated by others, so strive to put up clean and safe lines that will be enjoyed by others and not present objective hazards to the climber or others below the cliff on roads or trails.

If you are developing, consider a donation to the Helena Climbers' Coalition, as your masterpiece is our maintenance.

BE NICE

I know, you're expected to be nice. And maybe that is for good reason, we can use more niceness in the world. Consider following this rule as if it is your good-karma deposit for each time you climb, and one day it will come back to you as some glorious send. The Helena climbing community is small and people tend to know one another. We like to have friends. If you are new to town, new to climbing, or from out of town, more than likely you will be asked your name and your story at the crag. We are, for the most part, excited to see a new face, but we do expect that new face to be able to flash a smile and be able to muster a genuine exchange of pleasantries. You might be teased for your license plate number if you act like you can't take a joke, but you will be encouraged on your climb and get actual answers to beta questions. So be nice. We're nice.

SHARE SPACE

There are plenty of climbs at our crags to pick from and we are lucky enough to rarely wait in line. If another party beats you to your project for the day, just follow rule number one, you may end up sharing ropes and routes and beers back at the truck. But we still have to share, which means:

- Don't dangle an unused toprope all day.
- If another party wants to climb the same route, work together so everyone gets their climb in.
- Don't clean loose rocks off a new route with other parties around.
- Yell "ROCK" if you do send loose rock (or a quickdraw or a nut or a carabiner) plummeting to the ground.
- You probably want to wear a helmet belaying, climbing, and in mountain goat/bighorn sheep habitat.
- Don't climb with your Bluetooth speaker.
- Don't share un-requested beta.
- Leave the wildlife alone and respect closures due to bird habitat and other protections.
- If you open a gate, close the gate and leave livestock alone.
- Don't mess with someone else's project.
- Report hardware issues to Helena Climbers' Coalition.
- Respect private property access restrictions.
- Make sure someone in your party knows how to use your equipment, tie your knot, and build an anchor before climbing outside.
- Helena doesn't have "climbing only" locations. We share our space with mountain bikers, runners, hikers, hunters, 4 wheelers, ranchers, pack trains, and picnickers. In fact, most Helena climbers also fit into at least one of those other categories, too. No one group has authority over another and we value the diversity of user groups in our climbing areas.
- If your dog is going to run up to every person and get caught up in their ropes—leash your dog.
- We don't have designated parking areas at a lot of the crags, so please take a moment to park in a manner that allows others to get around you or to be able to park, too.
- Remember Rule #1: Be Nice.

LEAVE NO TRACE

Climbing is a sport that leaves an impact on the environment, through bolts or chalk or belay pads or dog crap. Helena, and Montana in general, is growing and so is the traffic at our climbing areas. So far, the Helena area has not seen climbing area closures or access limited due to climbers impacting and degrading an area. We would like to keep it that way and we can always do better, even if you roll your eyes and think you know how to keep a crag clean. We ask that climbers educate themselves on actual Leave No Trace practices by visiting either LNT.org or accessfund.org. For those of you who want it spelled out right here, right now, please practice the following:

- Be considerate by keeping trails open and accessible to other users.
- Only camp in designated areas.
- Park in areas meant for parking, not in meadows meant for habitat.
- If you have to poo, use toilets when they are available. If they are not available, do not leave your toilet paper flapping in the wind and make sure the dogs are not going to dig it up.
- Stay on trails whenever possible. If there is no trail, try to use access points that are already impacted and do not cut or prune trees.
- Place gear and pads on durable surfaces.
- Respect wildlife, sensitive plants, soils, and cultural resources.
- Clean up chalk and chalk spills and tick marks.
- Pack out all trash, crash pads, and gear.
- Use, install, and replace bolts and fixed anchors responsibly.
- Volunteer at events to maintain and clean climbing areas.

A NOTE FROM JAKE MERGENTHALER

In 2006 I had the great pleasure of writing the first guidebook to Helena rock climbs. Since then we have continued to bolt new routes and the sport of climbing has grown wildly. The fact that we kept bolting made the old book antiquated and since it was out of print it was very hard to acquire. A new book was needed. While writing the first book was rewarding, making another one seemed too daunting to me.

In 2018 the Helena Climbers' Coalition came to me with a plan: They would do all the heavy lifting if I would help write the book. Some of the proceeds would go to them to fund conservation of these areas, helping keep Helena climbing areas thriving and sustainable. They would also provide more modern equipment to make our new routes even safer.

Since I knew most of the routes, I felt this would be easy. I was wrong. Countless hours have been spent making this book informative and fun. This endeavor has been a labor of love for the HCC, my wife, and me. We are very proud of how it turned out. I honestly could not have made it happen without the and other contributors.

The format of this book is different from many others. Members of the HCC have been assigned to write different chapters. Assignments were made based on passion for the areas. Since I was still bolting in Hellgate, Avalanche, and Blackleaf, I took those chapters. Bob Goodwyn and Megan Helton love the granite of Sheep Mountain, and since that is a very expansive area, I was glad to let them have it. Martin Kazmierowski lives near Blue Cloud and is tough enough to frequent the approach. Dan Bachen had been bolting in Beaver Creek so that was a natural fit and since Andrew Schrader worked out towards Townsend he ended up (and fell back in love) with Indian Creek. The unofficial leader of this rag tag group was Brad Maddock. He handled Mount Helena and much of the photos and editing. Sarah Maddock, with two kids in tow edited, rewrote, and reworked much of the book. The HCC let me put my name on it, but this book belongs to the Helena climbing community. I thank them for their support and hard work.

Instead of making a long list of others who have contributed we mention them in their respected chapters. Of course our talented photographers, along with their amazing models, deserve special consideration. Most photos are donations, the photographers receiving only credit and sincere thanks.

ROUTE DEVELOPERS
Randall and Theresa Green, Bill Dockins, Kristen Drumheller, Scott Payne, Chris and Van Alke, Bill Bucher, Ron Brunkhurst, Kevin Huchison, Martin McBirney, Jamie Johnson, Meg Hall, Jim Wilson, Rob Hagler, Cameron Lawson, Frank Dusl, Mike Best, Wayne Harney, Kyle Perkins, Jennings Anderson, Brad and Sarah Maddock, Ted Sims, Whit Magro, Henry and Mariam Schotlzhauer, Luke Evans, Kyle O'Meara, Taylor F, Brad Hornung, Hermes Lynn, Josh Apple, Andrew Schrader, Terry Cowen, Pat West, Dan Bachen, Daniel Noonan, Aaron Lefohn, Jackson Wetheril, Kyle Redberg, Ian Whorral, Zach Bushilla, Ron Pedraza, Chester Carlson, Klemen Mali, Martin Kazmierowski, Joe Benson, Brandon Alke, Kevin Bellington, Jim Semmelroth, and Pat Wolfe.

BOOK CONTRIBUTORS
Martin Kazmierowski, Andrew Schrader, Bob Goodwyn, Megan Helton, Dan Bachen, Terry Cowan, Dan Frazer, Mark Plante, and Bradly and Sarah Maddock.

DISCLAIMER ABOUT GRADES
The original route developers have given me the difficult assignment of bringing the grades into the 21st century. We have tried to do this conservatively and respectfully.

Climber Owned
Dirtbag Frequented

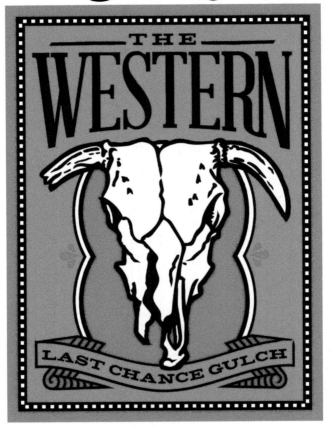

Helena's Premier Dive-Bar

Serving MT grass-fed burgers, craft cocktails & cold beer

406 Last Chance Gulch

Tim Mergenthaler on *Black Lung 5.12a*
photo by Jake Mergenthaler

WELCOME to Mount Helena. The limestone cliffs can be seen from almost anywhere in town. For Helena locals looking to get their climbing fix, the simplicity of commute and a great mix of both moderate and harder routes makes this a great spot to end your work day. Although the time it takes to get to the trailhead is essentially non-existent, depending on which part of town you live in, the hike always takes longer than you think. By the time you get to the cliff, sweaty and tired, the roadside climbing of Avalanche, Hellgate, or Indian Creek starts to sound really nice! Nonetheless, you will probably forget about the hike and find yourself once again hiking the 30-40 min up the historic 1906 Trail to the base of the cliff the next week.

Mount Helena offers a small selection of fun limestone sport-climbing routes ranging from 5.6 to 5.13. It is also host to one of the most concentrated beginner walls in the Helena area, making it a great place to take new climbers. Although the smallest crag in the book, Mt. Helena might be one of the most popular and it's no wonder. You can walk, ride your bike, or take a short drive to the Mt. Helena Trailhead, meet fellow climbers, get in a few routes after work, and end your day at one of Helena's many breweries or eateries. What's not to like!?

HISTORY AND ROUTE DEVELOPMENT
There is physical evidence and lore of climbing by the military on the Mount Helena cliff many years ago, but it has sat mostly silent until recently. The cliff runs along the most popular trail in Helena to the top of the town's namesake peak. In 2016, a group of climbers connected by the recently opened Stonetree Climbing Center, started throwing around the idea of developing the cliff for climbing. A few brainstorming sessions and a couple of trips to the cliff later, a proposal was submitted to the City of Helena Open Lands Division by Brad and Sarah Maddock, Hermes and Emily Lynn, and Jake and Kim Mergenthaler on behalf of the Helena Climbers' Coalition. Route development began in the spring of 2017 and there are now 25 routes on the cliff with room for many more. Much work and coordination has been done with the City of Helena on this area and as of the writing of this book, there have been no complaints or user conflicts. LET'S KEEP IT THIS WAY! Please respect all other users, keep your dogs under control, pick up your trash, and keep a low profile. With your cooperation, we will be able to expand and enjoy this "backyard crag" for many many years to come.

There is NO BOLTING or new route development without permission from the City of Helena and Helena Climbers' Coalition. The HCC has planned work—and route—development days to keep other trail users safe from rock fall during route development. If you wish to develop routes on the cliff, please don't go rogue, instead contact the HCC at helenaclimberscoalition@gmail.com. They are more than happy to help when the time is right!

GETTING THERE
From the Blackfoot River Brewing Company or the Lewis and Clark Public Library head south on Park Avenue for a little more than a ¼ mile. Take a right into the Reeders Village neighborhood (Carriage Lane). Take your second right onto Reeders Village Drive. Bear right at an intersection to stay on Reeders Village Drive (you can see the trailhead at this point). Follow the road up the hill until you reach the popular trailhead. The trailhead has a kiosk with a trail map, and a pit toilet.

From the trailhead, hike up the popular 1906 Trail staying straight at all intersections for 1 mile and 700' elevation gain to the base of the crag. The hike takes 30-45min moving at a leisurely pace. The first routes are uphill to either side of the obvious trailside cave known as "Devil's Kitchen" but the most popular way to access many of the climbs is by hiking a few steps farther up the trail to a big yellow sign stating the dangers associated with rock climbing.

NOTE
Though mountain bikes are allowed on the 1906 Trail, it is not recommended due to the steep grade and heavy use of the trail by hikers. Please obey all park policies. No camping. Dogs are required to be on a leash within 200 ft of the trailhead.

Routes are listed from left to right as you first approach them from the trail starting to the left of Devil's Kitchen and ending at the upper end of the Sunset Slab.

**MOUNT HELENA
PARKING**

**MOUNT HELENA
CLIMBING**

Climbing Area

Parking

Downtown Helena

Mount Helena

Mount Ascension

N

Google Earth

Water Streak Area

Kitchen Wall

Devil's Kitchen
Cave

1906 Trail

gilante Wall

Red Slab

Sunset Slab

Whit's Wall

1906 Trail

KITCHEN WALL

Routes are to the left of the large cave to the side of the main trail known as "The Devil's Kitchen" and features the fantastic two pitch climb *Get it While It's hot!* Routes are listed from left (farthest up the hill) to right (closest to the cave).

1. PAN HANDLER 5.10c ★★

Farthest route at the top of the hill in a small alcove. Start up easy terrain to a high first bolt. After an early crux on good rock, route rambles up past a dirty ledge and back onto the face finishing up a steep corner to the chains. Named after the long time cooking equipment store in downtown Helena.

105 ft, 11 bolts to chains
FA Brad Maddock, 2021

2. DINNER BELL 5.9 ★★ (Not Pictured)

Sustained 5.9 climbing. Between *Get It While It's Hot* and *Pan Handler*. This route is a bit dirty but will clean up with time.

110 ft, 11 bolts to chains
FA Hermes Lynn, 2021

3. GET IT WHILE IT'S HOT! 5.10c

Fantastic 2-pitch route with an alpine feel a short hike from downtown! First climb to the left of the Devil's Kitchen cave.

P1: Chains at a semi-hanging belay (110 ft, 5.10b)
P2: (100 ft, 5.10c)
Descent: Rappel the route
210 ft, 15 bolts to chains
FA Andrew Schrader, 2021

WATER STREAK AREA

This area is found most easily by following the cliff wall up and right from the Devil's Kitchen cave. *Pay Dirt* and *Cadillac Desert* will soon be on the left. The water streak is a low part of the cliff where a red/orange lichen streak forms. It is in-between both *Oasis* and *The Prospector*.

1. PAY DIRT 5.10d ★★
Work up the chimney to a ledge. Move through the steep section on big holds to hero jugs.
45 ft, bolts to chains
FA Dan Bachen, 2021

2. CADILLAC DESERT 5.11c/d ★★★
Boulder up a calcite streak to a sloping ledge. Rest up and stem and thrutch through the crux corner. Short, pumpy and technical in places, this thing packs a punch.
45 ft, bolts to chains
FA Dan Bachen, 2021

3. DRY WELL 5.10d
Awkward clips and strange movement, luckily it's only 3 bolts long and over quick.
30 ft, 3 bolts to chains
FA Hermes Lynn, Andrew Schrader, Brad Maddock, 2018

4. OASIS 5.9 ★★
Unlike the climb next door, this one is actually quite fun but similarly over too quick! Just to the left of the water streak.
30 ft, 3 bolts to chains
FA Hermes Lynn, 2018

5. THE PROSPECTOR 5.9+ ★
This is a good moderate route to the right of the water streak with a distinct crux and a tricky clip giving it the "+" rating. Easier if you are tall. A bit chossy, but cleaning up nicely with traffic.
70 ft, bolts to chains
FA Dan Bachen, 2018

water streak

Megan Helton on *Vigilante* 5.10b
Photo by Bradly Maddock

VIGILANTE AREA

To get to these routes, leave the 1906 Trail at the yellow "Climbing is Dangerous" sign and take the left trail up and past the Red Slab. If you are already at the Water Streak Area you can simply continue along the wall downhill from *The Prospector.*

1. BAT CRAZY 5.11c ★★

To the left of the obvious arête. This climb is relatively sustained and has great movement. Named for a bat that flew out from a crack while bolting. Easier if over 6ft.
70 ft, bolts to chains
FA Jake Mergenthaler, Kim Mergenthaler, 2018

2. VIGILANTE 5.10b ★★★

Up the obvious arête between *Bat Crazy* and *Sleeping Giant.* Steep and pumpy. A classic for the area, though if you're a rock snob you might not love it.
70 ft, bolts to chains
FA Hermes Lynn, 2017

3. SLEEPING GIANT 5.11c ★

To the right of *Vigilante* toward the small alcove. Engaging and fun.
70 ft, bolts to chains
FA Hermes Lynn, 2017

4. HAPPY TRAILS 5.11d ★★★

Steep and fun. Get your pump on. Just to the right of *Sleeping Giant.* Farthest route in the alcove/cave. Black anchors.
45 ft, bolts to chains
FA Jake Mergenthaler, Kim Mergenthaler, 2021

Paul Berry on *Bat Crazy* 5.11c
Photo by Bradly Maddock

RED SLAB

Approach these climbs directly uphill and left of the "Climbing is Dangerous sign". This is also the first place on the 1906 Trail that the rock meets the trail. Climbs are listed from left to right. It is best to have a 70m rope for these routes and don't forget to knot your end! Although nicknamed the "Red Slab," this wall has its fair share of vertical rock with a few mini roofs in the mix as well.

1. BIG DOROTHY 5.10d ★★
The farthest route up the Red Slab wall. This route has a steep start that slowly transitions into technical slab moves up higher. Named after the madam who ran a brothel in Helena's current Windbag restaurant building until her arrest in 1973.
110 ft, 14 bolts to chains
FA Jake Mergenthaler, 2017

2. DEVIL MAKES THREE 5.10d ★★
A long techy slab journey. Named for the three who were bolting and cleaning routes simultaneously on the wall.
110 ft, bolts to chains
FA Jake Mergenthaler, 2017

3. APPLE 5.10c ★★
This climb seems to be the easiest of the bunch but not by much. Long and sustained steep slab climbing with good edges and a few good rests.
90 ft, 11 bolts to chains
FA Josh Apple, 2017

4. BLACK LUNG 5.12a ★★
Long route with a thin and tricky crux high on the route.
110 ft, bolts to chains
FA Pat Wolfe, 2017

Jackson Wetherill on *Devil Makes Three 5.10d*
Photo by Jake Mergenthaler

WHIT'S WALL

Hike the 1906 Trail 20 feet beyond the "Climbing is Dangerous" sign and follow a faint trail up and left along the cliff wall until you get to a prominent alcove with good rock. Routes are listed from left to right.

1. WHIT'S WOBBLER 5.10b ★★
This route starts with 5.5 climbing through a short chossy section (tread lightly) to the high first bolt. After the 1st bolt, the climbing gets really fun with some great pockets! Worth the less-than-desirable start.
70 ft, 8 bolts to chains
FA Whit Magro, 2017

2. PROM NIGHT 5.13a ★★
Climb directly up the gut of the large alcove. A hard and sharp boulder problem. The appeal of this route is its proximity to town.
80 ft, bolts to chains
FA Jackson Wetherill, 2017

3. TOUR TRAIN 5.11a ★★★
This climb has a little bit of everything! Climbs easier than it looks with big holds when it gets steep, although it is still no gimme. Named after the train that tours around downtown Helena during the busy summer months.
70 ft, 8 bolts to chains
FA Brad Maddock, 2018

SUNSET SLAB
Follow the approach for Whit's Wall. Continue past Whit's Wall wall up the trail through the large scree field and along the base of the wall with many large steps. This wall gets blasted with afternoon sun and boasts 6 climbs 5.9 and under making it a great beginner area. The 3 farthest climbs up the wall can be easily set up as topropes following a short scramble adding to the allure. Routes are listed as you approach them from left to right.

1. ANSLEY'S WAY 5.6 ★★★
A fantastic location, moderate grade, and great rock make this a stellar climb! It has intermediate anchors and many do it as a 2-pitch route which makes it a great multi-pitch for learning. It can easily be done in 1 long pitch with 13 draws although it can be hard to communicate with your second due to the upper belay's position, so make a good plan ahead of time.
P1: (100 ft, 5.6)
P2: (50 ft, 5.6)
Descent: Walk right and along the top of the cliff band until you encounter a gully to the right. Follow this gully down and take the climber's trail back to the base of the route.
150 ft, 8 (13 if linking) bolts to chains
FA Terry Cowan

2. SUMMER SOLSTICE 5.7 ★★
Starts just right of *Ansley's Way* and follows an ever-steepening slab with a crack feature on the left. Stem and climb through interesting moves to the chains.
110 ft, bolts to chains
FA Hermes Lynn

3. MR. CLEAN 5.7 ★★
Great rock and a long 5.7 journey.
90 ft, 9 bolts to chains
FA Terry Cowan

4. GIGGLES AND GRENADES 5.7 ★★ TR
This route is on great stone. A toprope anchor can be set up on this climb and the subsequent two climbs by walking to the top of the gully and heading back (NW along the top of the cliff) to the anchors along the edge.
80 ft, bolts to chains
FA Terry Cowan

5. GOLDEN LIGHT GAINER 5.9 ★ TR
Climb up past the first few bolts to a small roof with techy feet.
70 ft, bolts to chains
FA Andrew Schrader, Dan Bachen

6. LAST CHANCE 5.6 ★★ TR
The last route up the gully just above a large tree. This short but sweet climb has been many folks' first lead and first climb! It is well bolted and has great holds on good rock.
60 ft, bolts to chains
FA Brad Maddock

Sarah Maddock on *Ansley's Way 5.6*
Photo by Brad Maddock

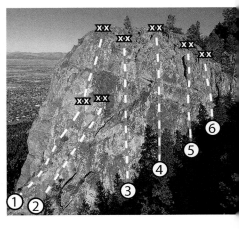

BLUE CLOUD BY MARTIN KAZMIEROWSKI

Dan Bachen on *One Step Beyond 5.10a*
Photo by Martin Kazmierowski

WELCOME to Blue Cloud. This is a quality granite crag just west of Helena offering an array of sport and trad routes. An easy scramble to the top of the spire accesses many of the anchors for setting topropes. The routes range beginner easy to challenging moderates. This Helena crag is rich in history with development going back into the 90's and home to classic routes like *The Road Goes on Forever.*

SEASON
Late spring to fall. During early spring and late fall the road can be a muddy mess. Deep snow can make the road impassable in the winter. A lot of the routes face south and west which may get pretty hot on summer days, but there are a fair number of routes on other faces of the spire so chasing shade is possible. Large pines shade the lower part of most climbs and belay areas.

GETTING THERE FROM HELENA
Head west out of Helena on US Hwy 12 for about 5 miles. Turn Right at the Baxendale Volunteer Fire Station onto Baxendale Dr. Shortly after passing the fire station turn right onto Blue Cloud Rd. Continue for a few miles, passing some houses. The road will pass through two gullies/creek bottoms. As you rise out of the second creek bottom in an aspen stand look left for a turn-out with green T posts blocking the track. This is the designated parking area. Please park at the green T posts and hike from there. The Helena Climbers' Coalition is working with the landowner to move this parking area farther down the road toward the green gate with the stile (fence ladder) to the left. Please keep an eye out for signage indicating if this change has occurred.

APPROACH
30 minutes. A moderate 1.5 mile hike from the parking area. Stay on the main two-track. The trail will bring you to the base of *Dos Amigos*.

CAMPING
Please respect the private landowners that generously allow us to cross their land to climb and **do not camp out at Blue Cloud.** This area is also tinder box so please refrain from having any fires. Thanks for your cooperation!

SPECIAL ACCESS NOTE
Parking and access is through private property and climbing is on public land. Please respect this private land, park only in the designated parking area, stay on the trail as you hike in, clean up after yourself, and please report any problems or vandalism to the Helena Climbers' Coalition.

**BLUE CLOUD
PARKING**

**BLUE CLOUD
CLIMBING**

WELCOME TO BLUE CLOUD

Protect America's Clim

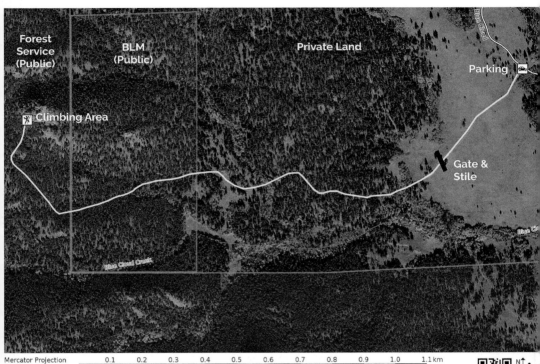

Forest Service (Public)

BLM (Public)

Private Land

Parking

Climbing Area

Gate & Stile

Blue Cloud Creek

Mercator Projection
WGS84
USNG Zone 12TVS
CalTopo

0.1 0.2 0.3 0.4 0.5 0.6 0.7 0.8 0.9 1.0 1.1 km

0.1 0.2 0.3 0.4 0.5 0.6 mi

Scale 1:6725   1 inch = 560 feet

ACCESS NOTES

- The route to the Blue Cloud climbing area crosses private property and we are grateful to be able to cross it to access our public land!

- Do not use and spur roads.

- Please stay on the yellow appraoch route/the most prominent road.

- Please use the stile/ladder to cross the fence.

- Pack out all trash and have fun!

Public access is offered in accordance with Montana's Recreational Use Statue. If you choose to use this area you are voluntarily assuming all risk of injury or death from your use. Numerous hazards exist on the property, some of which may not be obvious or apparent. Landowners and the Helena Climbers' Coalition do not maintain any fixed climbing hardware, including bolts and anchors, and make no representations or warrenties regarding the safety, reliability, or suitibility for use of any fixed climbing anchors or other hardware currently existing or installed in the future at Blue Cloud.

THE LANDING ZONE

JEDI WALL

SOUTH BUTTRESS

LA CANTINA

OLD MAN BLOCK

SUNSET WALL

LA CANTINA

A west-facing wall that lies past and above the Old Man Block. Turn the corner at the Old Man Block continuing past *Dignity* and then scramble up 3rd class ledges to the wall. There is a faint trail that breaks off at the start of the Sunset Wall that loops around lower from the formation around the side to La Cantina. This eliminates a lot of scrambling with the exception of the last bit. Look for cairns. Routes are listed left to right.

1. MY FRIEND FLICKER 5.8 ★
Left most route on the La Cantina Wall. Climb a slabby pillar with knobs and horizontal cracks.
40 ft, 4 bolts to chains
FA Randall Green, Theresa Green, 1998

2. GREEN VELVET 5.7 ★★
Crank up steep jugs on a cool green face. Shares chain anchors with *My Friend Flicker*.
40 ft, 4 bolts to chains
FA Randall Green, Theresa Green, 1998

3. VELVET RABBIT 5.5
Climb discontinuous cracks.
35 ft, gear to 2.5", no anchors
FA Laurent Huber, Randall Green, 1998

4. WALK THE LINE 5.11c ★★★
Steep and sustained with a thin start. Originally rated as 5.11a, but some of the better edges have broken off.
40 ft, 4 bolts to chains
FA Paul Travis, Randall Green, 1998

5. PLEASURE AND PAYNE 5.8 ★★
Look for a vertical plumb-line crack liberally sprinkled with knobs.
40 ft, gear to 2.5" to chains
FA Jake Mergenthaler, Randall Green, 1998

OLD MAN BLOCK

This west facing wall is just left of the open book corner and *Book of Payne*. Routes are listed left to right.

6. DIGNITY 5.10c ★

Left most route. Starts up a thought-provoking off-balance arête.

45 ft, 4 bolts to chains
FA Randall Green, Ted Simms, 1999

7. RESPECT 5.10

Climb a discontinuous crack system. Shares chain anchors with *Dignity*.

40 ft, gear to 2"
FA Randall Green, Ted Simms, 1999

8. SCREWED, BLUED, AND TATTOOED 5.11b ★★

First route on the Old Man Block just left of *Book of Payne*. A beautiful blank face with a crack up the middle that ends in blankness. Grunt up a finger splitter and then switch to delicate face climbing past bolts.

50 ft, gear to 2", 3 bolts to chains
FA Jake Mergenthaler, Randall Green, 1999

Bradly Maddock on *Screwed, Blued, and Tattooed 5.11b*
Photo by Jake Hymas

SUNSET WALL
This west-facing wall lies just around the corner from the left side of the South Buttress. Routes are left to right.

9. BOOK OF PAYNE 5.8 ★★★
Farthest left route in open book corner. Starts in the corner crack and finishes on a steep upper wall. Great route!
85 ft, gear to 4" to chains
FA Randall Green, Jake Mergenthaler, 1998

10. ONE LESS TRAVELED BY 5.13- ★★
This gorgeous face takes a hard bouldery start for the first three bolts (stick clip) to wandering, broken crack climbing with a spicy traverse into the last few bolts of *The Road*.
95' bolts, small gear. Shares chains with *The Road*.
Equipped by Jackson Wetherill
FA Unknown

11. THE ROAD GOES ON FOREVER 5.11a ★★★
Classic! Must Do! Start in a crack on a shield to the right of a blank face. Lay backs and cracks lead to face holds, a roof, and an arête. This one has it all.
100 ft, 11 bolts. Shares chains with *One Less*.
FA Jake Mergenthaler, Randall Green, 1999

12. JAKE THE GRIPPER 5.11b ★
Right of *The Road Goes on Forever*. Steep crack to a tricky roof and ends on a 5.8 shallow groove.
60 ft, small wires and TCU's. 2 bolts to chains.
FA Jake Mergenthaler, 1999

13.TREE HUGGER 5.10b ★★
Farthest right route on the Sunset Wall. On the corner separating the South Buttress and the Sunset Wall. Start in a crack on a steep arête next to a pine tree. Make some cool moves to transition off the arête and over a small roof. Super fun route. The proximity to the pine makes the name very appropriate.
60 ft, 5 bolts to chains (optional hand-size piece)
FA Jake Mergenthaler, 1999

Paul Berry on *The Road Goes on Forever 5.11a*
Photo by Brad Maddock

SOUTH BUTTRESS

This is the first wall reached from the approach trail. It's the tallest wall at Blue Cloud and holds a variety of good trad and sport routes. It's south facing and gets sun most of the day. Most of the belay areas are shaded by large pines. Most of the anchors on this wall can be accessed from the top making it possible to toprope many of these routes. Routes are listed from left to right.

14. DOS AMIGOS 5.6 ★★★

First route when you come up the approach trail. A great easy 2-pitch sport route.
P1: Fun face climbing up a slabby pillar that ends on a big party ledge. (60 ft)
P2: Run up a less than vertical headwall to a juggy bulge. (90 ft)
150 ft, bolts to chains
FA Randall Green, Jake Mergenthaler, 1999

15. TRES AMIGOS 5.8 ★★

Right before press time this new route was put in during record warm December temps. It is said to be a fun route between *Dos Amigos* and *Blue Monday*. Route goes just left of the big roof at the top. Belay up your 2nd and walk off to the right or bring a second rope to rap the route.
160 ft, 12 bolts to chains anchors
FA Luke Evans, Maisie Evans, Scout Jenkins, 2021

16. BLUE MONDAY 5.7 ★★

15 feet right of *Dos Amigos* where a large block forms a short dihedral. Start on the dihedral and jam up a fun and varied crack. Anchors are below the top ledge.
75 ft, gear to 3.5" to chains
FA Paul Travis, Randall Green, Jake Mergenthaler, 1999

17. ONE STEP BEYOND 5.10a ★★

Just past a dirty overgrown crack. A cool climb up a series of thought-provoking bulges.
85 ft, 10 bolts to chains
FA Martin Kazmierowski, 2020

18. SAY IT AIN'T SO 5.11c ★★

Climb a featured slab to a ledge below a blank band. Pull delicate moves to an immaculate face. Final boulder problem below the chains is the crux. If you're under 6ft, it's probably closer to a 12 than 11, for taller folks it might feel significantly easier.
85 ft, 10 bolts to chains
FA Dan Bachen, 2020

19. LAST CARESS 5.9 ★★

Next route right of *Say It Ain't So*. Starts in the crack just left of *Come as You Are* and climb prominent weakness to the splitter hand/ fist crack at the top of the wall. Anchor for this route is accessible from the top and can also be used to TR *Come as You Are*.
85 ft, small to medium nuts/cams, with a few hand and fist (#2-3) size pieces for the top, ends at chains.

20. COME AS YOU ARE 5.8 ★★

Climb great face holds through a series of bulges. A low crux at a small roof might make you think a little. Well bolted for first time leads and a great warmup.
65 ft, 8 bolts to chains
FA Martin Kazmierowski, Dan Bachen, 2020

21. FANTASY SUCKS 5.10a ★★

On the upper half of the South Buttress. Start on the right side of a small pine tree close to the wall. Climb up cracks and horizontal seams through a series of bulges.
65 ft, gear up to 1". Rap ring anchors
FA Terry Cowan, 2012

Routes 22-24 share the same start.

22. ONE MOVE WONDER 5.7 ★

To the right of *Fantasy Sucks* and left of a large roof. Climb up a shallow corner moving left to a sweet arête with big holds.
75 ft, bolts to chains
FA Randall Green, Theresa Green, 1998

23. CRACK ATTACK 5.10a ★★

Left most of two cool routes under the large roof. Climb on blocks and horizontal seams under the roof. Pull and grunt over the roof to a slippery slab finish.
60 ft, 7 bolts to chains
FA Jake Mergenthaler, 2000

24. GRUNT FEST 5.10a ★★

Start on the first three bolts of *Crack Attack* and then move right to pull over the roof finishing on easier ground.
60 ft, 6 bolts to chains
FA Jake Mergenthaler, 2000

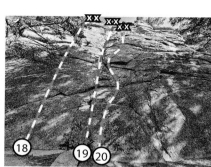

THE LANDING ZONE

This is a separate tower from the main crag that holds some great routes on bomber granite. The main wall is south facing with more routes around the corner in the shade facing north. Walk uphill along the South Buttress and go up and over a small hill. Follow the trail (usually marked with cairns) as it wraps around and goes down the backside and leads to a draw. Head up the draw to the left. You should see the wall when you turn the corner at the draw. Routes are listed left to right.

1. RAT KING 5.10d ★★★
Left most route on the south face at the Landing Zone. A must-do! Start with side pulls on big holds to a pumpy and awesome overhanging arête. Giddy up and stay out of the rat poop.
75 ft, 9 bolts to chains
FA Jake Mergenthaler, Lance Beckert, 1999

2. GAY MARTIANS 5.10a ★★★
Just right of *Rat King*. Another-must-do ! Climb bomber granite with large holds through some bulges to a pumpy finish. Watch out for rat poop.
75 ft, 7 bolts to chains
FA Jake Mergenthaler, Lance Beckert, 1999

3. DOMINO 5.10a ★★
Climb cool holds through some thought provoking bulges.
70 ft, bolts to rap ring anchor
FA Terry Cowan

The next climbs are on the north side.

4. TESTICLE FESTIVAL 5.11a ★★
Around the corner from the south side of the Landing Zone, in the deep shade of the north side. Go right past *Gay Martians* and *Domino* and scramble around the corner over some boulders to the North Side. *Testicle Festival* is the first route on the left. Short, pumpy, and thought provoking. Start on diagonal seams up this short but sustained route. Stay on the bolt line and don't stray left.
45 ft, 4 bolts to chains
FA Jake Mergenthaler, Lance Beckert, 1999

5. THE DUDE 5.10b ★★
Around the corner from the south side of the Landing Zone, in the deep shade of the north side. Pass *Domino*, scramble around the corner over some boulders. *The Dude* is in the middle of the wall just right of *Testicle Festival*. Short and pumpy. A gym rats' dream. Start on diagonal seams to a variety of cool holds. Super fun route leaves you wanting more. Get on it!
45 ft, 4 bolts to chains
Jake Mergenthaler, Lance Beckert, 1999

6. AFTER THOUGHT 5.10c
On the north side of the Landing Zone to the right of *The Dude*. Short, ornery, and tricky. Bouldery start and keep crankin'.
40 ft, 4 bolts to chains
Jake Mergenthaler, Lance Beckert, 2001

EXPERIENCE THE DIFFERENCE

TOP AND SIDE PROTECTION in our helmets. Various construction methods and quality materials of our harnesses. Reliable performance of our carabiners. These are the Petzl Differences worth justifying.

Access the

JEDI WALL

This short but steep wall is found on the north side of the main formation. Finding it is half the fun. From the top of the South Buttress trek left and north through a series of large boulders. The Jedi Wall faces NW and is one of the larger walls on the backside of the South Buttress although is only 25 ft, in length.

1. **DARTH CRATER** 5.10d ★

A steep climb up a cool arête. Some say it's dirty but use your head and the force. Soon you will be a Jedi.

25 ft, 3 bolts to chains

FA Jake Mergenthaler, 2000

SHEEP MOUNTAIN

BY BOB GOODWYN

Cody Cloepfil on *Rich Man-Poor Man 5.8+*
Photo by Bob Goodwyn

WELCOME to Sheep Mountain. In this new guide, no other crag is a better blend of the past & present. The following beta is a mixture of Jake Merganthaler's from 2006 and Bob Goodwyn's from 2020. What hasn't changed is the attitude of Sheep climbing. It's afterwork crag sessions, quick burns on legendary projects, living the history of first ascents, ridiculous stories, costumes at all night ragers, and the excitement of standing on top of Upper Rock for your first time. There's both—ground up and suck it up ethics, and rapbolting difficult projects. It's all here, beautiful, serene, and waiting for you, too. Sheep Mountain is a granite playground 20 miles south of Helena near Clancy. The area shines with great views of the Elkhorn Mountains and has an "old school" vibe to it. The earlier climbs were established in the 70s and 80s when the emphasis was on style and skill and not equipment. The newer climbs were bolted top down, accentuating movement and grace. The climbs range in height from 40' to 200' dotting the spires and crags across your field of vision, but many just out of it. The area abounds with cracks that split faces and run up corners, making some wonder "what's a Standard Rack, anyway?" (see next page) In between those features are bolts and face holds tempting you away from your security. And once you're done with that climb and you've climbed your way all the way around that spire, you'll be left wondering what's just over there?

One drawback to Sheeps is the distance between crags. But I won't be the last to ponder the logistics of a Sheep Traverse, covering just those distances in mere minutes. The approaches, often bemoaned by first timers, are slowly becoming etched into the hillsides by frequenters, and will always be well-dialed by the Sheep Lifers.

CAMPING

If you plan to stay, please abide by Bureau of Land Management's (BLM) regulations. There are plenty of places that are established near Haystack and the main parking area, but please be kind and considerate to those houses that are not far away, and other campers who might not share your same taste in techno music. The most important thing after Leave No Trace ethics is your safety with campfires. Abide by local restrictions and know that Sheep is prone to fires. We'd hate to see it damaged, or worse, a loss of homes.

SEASON

Sheep Mountain offers year-round climbing as most of the crags face south. The sun, zero wind chill, and dry rock make it perfect any time of year. Road conditions leading up to Sheep Mountain were once a limiting factor for winter climbing, but the development of private property nearby, road conditions only get hairy for the last 0.25mi to the main parking area. You can park on the main road and walk the rest of the way. This approach also conserves the condition of the road.

ACCESS

Every Sheep Mountain route described in this guide resides entirely on BLM land. We are lucky to recreate on these public lands. A word of caution, however, much of the area shares a border with private property, namely the approach to Happy Hour and the approach to Right Rock. Both are noted in their respective sub-chapters. There has also been a lot of new housing development along Sheep Road. We share the road with the landowners. Please be respectful, leave things better than you found them, and use caution when exploring the Sheep Mountain area. Do not take recreating on public lands for granted, make sure those who follow can enjoy Sheep Mountain too.

"STANDARD RACK"

Often noted, always debated, and mostly incorrect, this is the go-to for guidebook authors everywhere and first ascensionist with bad memories. Unfortunately, I'm one of those kinds of climbers. And as much as it would've been nice to have the person who can describe the exact off-set cam they used after the 2 and ½ finger lock at 89.23ft up their 3rd ascent of *Sting*, that person didn't volunteer. It's me. Therefore this guide will be no different. But, for the sake of later debates, I will try to better define, what I like to call, a "Sheep Standard Rack". … full of contradictions?

BOB'S SHEEP STANDARD RACK:

- ◆ ALWAYS a full set of nuts. Cams .3-#3 camalots, and 12 draws: 4 quickies, 6 single length alpines, and 2 double length alpine draws. Unless the thing is straight up, and relatively short (i.e. *Hangnail*), then I'll skip some of the draws.
- ◆ ALWAYS a good length of cord or webbing with locking carabiners for building anchors. You might get away with a shorter anchor sling or a couple of quickdraws but someday you'll get to the top of a climb only to be faced with a large tree or boulder and you'll be thankful you had the cord.
- ◆ IF the climb calls for more of a certain size, read: hand crack, I'll bring the Standard Rack plus Doubles in .75-#2. If I'm uncomfortable at the grade, I'll bring even another .75-#2.
- ◆ IF the climb calls for "protection to 4 inches" I'll throw in a #4, or two #4's if I'm uncomfortable with the grade.
- ◆ OR let's say the climb is 5.10 or harder and has the potential to get "butt-cracky." Then I might add an offset set of nuts and doubles of .1-.3 and/or offset cams in sizes 1/2—.4/5, if you have them. But mostly at this point you should understand that Sheep is old school and you might be in for a whooping good time that day. And instead of going home and complaining to your buddies because the guidebook said, "bring a standard rack" you're going to go to the Blackfoot and say, "Damn, what a good time." Now that's Sheep climbing for ya.

CLIMBING AT SHEEP FOR ME

I have a special place in my heart for climbing in all its forms. It's one of the few things that captures my full attention. The next hold, the next foot, pivot, pull this way, ease onto that one, or throw for that one—I think of nothing else while I'm climbing, and I'm sure that will keep me coming back. But there's another place in my climbing, when all of that is over. It happens on the top of any summit, but especially those Sheep spires. They are stand-alone plymouths of timeless granite, overlooking a picturesque valley, and I'm above it all. The fear is gone, the exhilaration subsiding, it's peace. I'm off belay, and all I have to do is breathe, bring up my follower, and dream of the next one. Those moments I will never live without.

- Bob Goodwyn

PAT WEST MEMORIAL

A memorial for Pat lies at the base of the east face of Haystack at Sheep Mountain. He was an inspiring climber who fostered many in the Helena area before his suicide in 2014. He will be sorely missed but his passion for climbing lives on in the folks that had the pleasure to climb with him. The following are some kind words shared in his honor.

Pat was one of the first people to introduce me to climbing and was my regular climbing partner for years. He had a profound influence on my love for climbing due largely to the passion he inspired it. I can remember the twinkle in his eye whenever a new climbing trip was posed or when some hard trad route was mentioned. I'd like to think I'm honoring his memory by sharing the passion he instilled in me to whoever else I climb with.

-Luke Michelson

While exploring Sheep Mountain, you might notice a small memorial at the base of Haystack Rock. This was placed in loving memory of Patrick Timothy West. Pat, a Helena native, was a quiet and shy man, and an avid and highly skilled climber. Introverted and humble by nature, he flew under the radar of many in the climbing community, but for those of us who knew him, he was a best friend, and the most solid, knowledgeable, and trustworthy of climbing partners. Pat started climbing as a reckless 18 year old, and bloomed in the sport with unmatched natural talent and athleticism. His passion for the outdoors made him a mountain man like no other, and there was no route be it sport, trad, alpine, or ice, that he couldn't do (or at least wouldn't attempt). He traveled and sent routes all around the Western U.S., but his love for Montana rock would never be matched. Pat died suddenly and tragically by suicide in September of 2014, but his spirit lives on in the Montana mountains he so loved, and in the hearts of those who had the honor of climbing and adventuring with him.

-Sarah Tomaske

HISTORY

The climbing history of Sheep Mountain is muddled before 1970, while a few routes were likely climbed they were not documented for our benefit. But in the early 70s, Bill Bucher and Dave Stiller, armed with Royal Robins' shoes and a rack of hexes, explored and documented some noteworthy climbs on Upper and Middle Rock. Soon after the young Alke brothers took climbing at Sheeps to a whole new level with ascents of the first 5.9s in the area. In the 80s Terry Kennedy, Jim Scott, and Sonny Stewart upped the Ante again by establishing the area's first 5.10s and 5.11s. *Intensive Care* and *Nemesis* were freed by Stewart in this time period and soon most of the obvious lines were climbed. In this decade bolts were used sparingly to protect the faces between cracks but it wasn't until the late 80s that the first very "sporty"
sport climbs were completed. Jim Wilson, Scott Payne and Jim Nymun put up several routes on Right Rock and Jamie Johnson and Mark Pearson added a few on the Devils' Thumb. More recently Randall Green, Luke Evans, and Jake and Kim Mergenthaler have added a handful of sport climbs on the Thumb making this the area with the highest concentration of sport climbs (5). Sheep Mtn. has the richest history of any crag near Helena and there is more to come with several blank faces awaiting routes in the 5.13 range. But whether these are bolted or not, Sheeps will continue to be an area defined by those who came before, those who put courage before bolts and emphasized skill before equipment. For this legacy we are indebted.

GETTING THERE

From Helena travel to Clancy on I-15 exit and head west on Lump Gulch Road for around 3 miles, turn right on Sheep Mtn. Rd. Start your odometer here, between mile 0.1 and 0.2 look for a wide spot in the road park here for Happy Hour or continue to 0.3 and turn left onto a BLM access road and bounce for 1 mile. At mile 1.2 and just after a steep grade park at a wide spot, the Thumb is a 10 minute walk south. To get to Right Rock and Middle Rock drive to mile 1.5 look for a brown sign and turn left. For Haystack drive to mile 1.5 and take a left at the junction travel 0.4 miles and look for a doubletrack that heads right. Follow this across a meadow it goes straight to Haystack

WHY DO YOU DO IT?

I guess it's different every time. I like my climbing like I like my music — all over the board. Sometimes it's metal. Sometimes it's classical. Sometimes it's jazz. Sometimes it's classic rock. Sometimes it's hip hop. Ultimately, it pushes me to expand in some capacity and whichever direction that's in doesn't matter so much. As long as I learn humility along with pride and fear along with confidence, it's a healthy form of expression for me.

- Justin Willis

I've always said it's the one thing I do that takes my complete focus. All my attention has to be there in order to perform my best. I often think clearest when I'm farthest from the ground.

- Bob Goodwyn

25 Years.

Still climbing strong.

Gold Leaf
PHYSICAL THERAPY

701 Helena Avenue
Helena, MT 59601

(406) 437 – 1917
GoldLeafPT.com

HAPPY HOUR

This short wall now has multiple routes—one bolted sport route, a couple of scrappy trad lines, and can all be toproped. They are fun, easily reached, and a great alternative to happy hour at your favorite watering hole—hence the name. Note—bring sufficient equipment to extend ALL anchors to avoid rope drag and the damaging of hardware. The anchor hangers are set far back from the edge of most climbs and just clipping quickdraws will not suffice. Routes are described right to left, starting with the west face. The obvious arête breaks the rock into a west and a north face, with routes #3 and #4 on the arête sharing anchors.

Please note that Sheep Mountain has seen a lot of housing development in recent years, and parking on the road is not acceptable. The road is private on both sides, but Happy Hour rock is on BLM Land. To honor our access to these public places, it is best to park at the Sheep Mountain kiosk, just on your left as you turn off of Lump Gulch Road. From the kiosk walk 240 yds up the road and turn left up a faint gully. Another 50 yds will put you at the base of the west facing routes. If you walk up the road and encounter a private driveway on your right, you've gone too far. There have been some land ownership disputes in the past, mostly due to parking, but this rock is entirely on BLM property according to modern land ownership GPS apps. Please be respectful and courteous to those you encounter, and have a happy hour drink on us!

Descent: Walk off the back side in either direction.

1. DOUBLE SHOT 5.11 TR ★★
This stout piece is just right of the bolted line *Fuzzy Navel*. There are a couple of ways to do it, both are engaging and hard.
30 ft

2. FUZZY NAVEL 5.9 ★★★
Crank past cool flakes in the middle of the wall.
35 ft, bolts to chains
FA Randall Green, Jake Mergenthaler, 2001

3. MAI-TAI 5.10+ TR ★
Dance up the arête on potentially tricky holds to a ledge breaking up the face. A couple of thin moves will gain the top.
40 ft
FA Randall Green, Jake Mergenthaler, 2001

4. TWO FOR ONE 5.9 ★
Climb the left side of the arête on steep jugs to a thin hand traverse and a tricky finish.
40 ft, TR or sparse gear
FA Randall Green, Jake Mergenthaler, 2001

5. WHISKEY DITCH 5.10 ★★
Start in a steep hand crack, then pull onto the face to find a good finger seam for gear. Finish through the flake or thin face holds to the left of the anchors.
40 ft, TR or sparse gear
FA Brad Hornung

HAPPY HOUR PARKING

HAPPY HOUR CLIMBING

PRACTICE CRACKS

This smaller outcrop is located on the side of a small valley above the frisbee golf course. Four short cracks split a slightly overhanging face. If the outcrop was any taller, these would be among the more classic lines at Sheep. However, these routes are just high enough for most folks to want a rope rather than a pad. All routes have bolt anchors to facilitate top roping, but they can also be climbed with a small rack of gear. If you are looking to get a lot of mileage on cracks without having to hike, this is a good spot to visit.

APPROACH

Pass the Frisbee Golf parking lot, and continue up hill. Park on the left side of the road after the road curves left or 100 yds farther up if your worried about frisbee damage. Hike downhill aiming for a point between the lower and upper rocky areas. The rock should be visible in a few hundred yards.

1. ALL OUT OF JAMS 5.11+ ★★

Steep and bouldery climbing up a finger crack leads to a flared crack with a few bad face holds. Hit the welcome cobble and finish up a thin crackm climber's left.

30 ft, light rack to chains

FA Unknown; anchor added by D. Bachen

2. MOSTLY HANDS 5.10 ★★

Slightly overhanging hand crack. Who could ask for more?

30 ft, light rack to chains

FA Unknown; anchor added by D. Bachen and A. Schrader

3. FISTS AND HANDS 5.10 ★★

Narrower than the previous line. Start above the wood rat nest.

30 ft, light rack to chains

FA Unknown; anchor added by D. Bachen and A. Schrader

4. BARS OVER STACKS 5.10 ★

Wide climbing with few options to cheat.

30 ft, a few cams between a #2 and #5 Camalot to chains

FA Unknown; anchor added by D. Bachen and A. Schrader

PRACTICE CRACKS PARKING

PRACTICE CRACKS CLIMBING

FAMILY FUN ZONE

This area, akin to those climbs of Haystack and Happy Hour, offers a chance to mix up your Sheep Climbing routine. There's a short approach, if you know where you're going, and it has 3 great topropes. Brad Hornung equipped these routes in 2019, although he was the first to admit, those who came before might have claimed the true first ascents. He will be listed here, to respect his equipment on the top of the routes.

APPROACH

Drive up the road past Happy Hour and park on your right just before the first guard rail, shortly after the disc golf course parking. Cross the road and head west, about 150 yards to the rock formation. The climbs are on the west (left hand side) of the face. This should be about a 5-minute approach, but "1 hour if you are with a 3 year-old" (- Brad Hornung, 2019). Scramble up the backside and you'll find 4 bolts for top roping.

FAMILY FUN ZONE PARKING

FAMILY FUN ZONE CLIMBING

1. YOU ARE GROUNDED! 5.8 TR ★
Climb on far left, up the slab, follow seam to roof, then exit left and up the slab.
40 ft
FA Brad Hornung, 2019

2. DON'T MAKE ME PULL THIS CAR OVER! 5.9 TR ★★
Up the slab, over the biggest part of the roof on big holds.
40 ft
FA Brad Hornung, 2019

3. MEANAGER 5.7 TR ★
Face climb the right hand side to the top.
40 ft
FA Brad Hornung, 2019

DEVIL'S THUMB

This great formation has the highest concentration of starred routes at Sheep. Ranging in height from 40 feet to 150 feet, whether you're cranking on jams or pulling on knobs there's a little something for everybody at this Sheep Mountain favorite. As Jake Merganthaler wrote in the original guide, "Bring your lycra and your high-top climbing boots to get the whole old-school vibe." Still true today. New and improved in this area are Totos, and Surf's Up. The same approach is used. Routes will be described starting with *Devil's Standard*, moving counterclockwise, to the right, around the spire.

To find this crag use the aptly named "Devil's Thumb Parking" pullout. Start your odometer at the bridge after turning off Lump Gulch Rd. After 1.3 miles, there will be a big switchback in the road as it turns from the northeast to the southwest. Park on your left below a large tree. From here hike due west, above the road, on a faint logging trail. This should take you over one small rise, and on the other side of that rise is the correct drainage for the approach. The correct drainage is often marked by a cairn on a stump, but not always. Continue north up this drainage following the path. This spire is difficult to see until you're very close and is behind the broken spire that can be seen from the parking area. The trail should put you right at the base of *Devil's Standard*, but you can cut west and around the southside of the Thumb for ease of access to the *Nemesis* area routes. You can also scramble right of *Devil's Standard* to access the routes near Hang Nail.

As of this writing, the approach was greatly improved by the clearing and cutting of the trail up the drainage towards the Thumb. These were scratched into the hill (including the novel switchbacks!) by the hard work, collaboration of Helena Climbers' Coalition member Andrew Schrader and his partnership with the Bureau of Land Management. Many thanks to all!

Descent: All routes that top out on the spire can be rappelled with a single 60m rope down Hang Nail. There are rappel rings on the Oz Wall if you peak over the edge and there are also clip-and-lowers on Beauty and the Beasties, where again, a 60m rope will get you back to the belay block for Nemesis. A 70m rope will get you to the ground using the same clip-and-lowers.

PARKING

CLIMBING

EAST FACE

Characterized by a grand steep slab above a shallow ledge, this is *Devil's Standard*.

1. DEVIL'S STANDARD 5.8 ★★★

P1: A couple of start options: One is to clip the first bolt of *Hamsters* and launch into the crack system. The true start is to grunt up wide crack with sneaky hands and feet to the sloping ramp below Hamsters. This does have protection and has the potential to make the climb harder. This section gives way to a ramp up to the right, enjoy a beautiful hand crack to a stance, sling the horn on the left for a belay. (5.8)

P2: Step up from the belay to either the thin lieback crack on your left, or the wide crack on your right with a block sticking out at 20 feet. From here you'll want to be in the right-hand crack. Grunt, finesse, or stem your way to the top where you can either go right or left, both are airy, strenuous, and worth the views. (5.8)

Descent: Rappel anchors of the Oz Wall or off of Hang Nail anchors with a 60m rope.

110 ft, gear to 4" and a gear anchor (as of 2020)
Doubles in #3, #4 if getting fisty is not your jam.

2. WHERE HAMSTERS DIE 5.10-

Start uphill of *Devil's Standard* then traverse left to the end of a sloping ledge, stick clip the first bolt and start up steep slab to a wide crack. Next, crank through two bolts and escape left to join *Devil's Standard*.

Descent: Same as Devil's Standard

100 ft, gear to 4", bolts to fixed anchor
FA Jamie Johnson, Mark Pearson, 1998

Megan Helton on *Devil's Standard 5.8*
Photo by Bob Goodwyn

OZ WALL

This wall is right of *Where Hamsters Die*, but before the ramp of *No Place Like Home* and includes the infamous *Yellow Brick Road*. Routes described left to right.

Descent: All routes on the OZ wall can be rappelled with a single 60m rope from the top of Yellow Brick Road.

3. TIN MAN 5.12c (or 12a) ★★
In Luke's words "excellent feasible climb for the Oz Wall." Enter your own definition of feasible. The 5.12c 3-bolt-slab start can be avoided, making it a 5.12a.
110 ft, bolts to anchors
FA Luke Evans, Klemen Mali

4. RUBY SLIPPERS 5.14a Open Project
Steep slippery slabby crux start with very small edges. Who has the slippers for this one?
110 ft, bolts to anchors

5. WICKED 5.14b/c Open Project
Climb *Yellow Brick Road* to the starting crux bulge and climb left into *Ruby Slippers*. It has been worked on toprope and would need a couple bolts to connect.
110 ft, bolts to anchors

6. YELLOW BRICK ROAD 5.14a ★★★
Bolts up a wild yellow face capped by a bulge in the middle. The words of the first ascensionist, "Sensational climbing more techy than pumpy…tap your heels together (really heels together for a move!) at the v10 crux bulge using intricate underclings and cryptic crimps to finish on fun moves to the top."
110 ft, bolts to chains
FA Luke Evans, 2006

7. TORNADO 5.13d/14a
Climb the cool tornado feature with a bolt to start then medium gear into the bolted crux and finish on *Yellow Brick Road*.
80 ft, bolts and gear to chains
FA Luke Evans, Benji Wiezel, 2009

8. NO PLACE LIKE HOME 5.8 ★★
Previously called "Ugly Crack," this one deserves the name upgrade and comes recommended by L. Evans. Climb the gully then finish up and left in a steep and stellar hand crack to the top.
120 ft, gear, no fixed anchor

9. OPENING GRADE 5.7 ★★★
This low-angle crack with a couple of bulges is a great way to get your feet wet at Devil's Thumb. You can also toprope *Intensive Care* from here.
45 ft, gear to 4" and a chain anchor

10. INTENSIVE CARE 5.11c ★★★
Thin left leaning crack on right side of the east face that leads to a sloping ledge. Can be painful for the uninitiated but is a hard-person classic. Belay by slinging the arrow-shaped summit.
Descent: Scramble to northeast face and downclimb.
45 ft, small-med gear to chain anchor
FA Sonny Stewart

11. DOUBLE DOWN 5.9
Just to the right of *Intensive Care* is this enticing inside corner with two cracks. Surely been done before but recorded here for the first time. Give 'er a go.
45 ft, small-med gear, no fixed anchor.

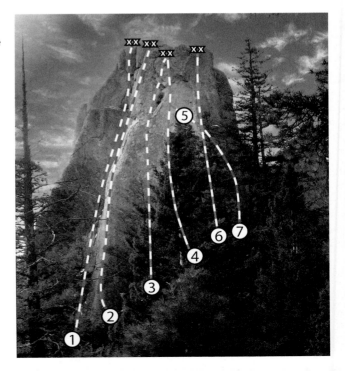

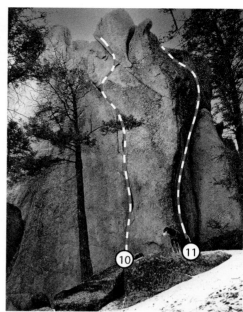

NORTH FACE

There is a block guarding easy access around the northeast corner of the formation from *Intensive Care* on your way to the North Face routes. You can boulder around it either right or left. After this boulder project, and immediately to your left, starts *Five Niner*. Between here and *Hang Nail* there are several short discontinuous scramble routes. They provide access to the summit if you so wish.

Routes are encountered just after the boulder moves to get around the northeast corner of Devil's Thumb. Listed as unnamed in the previous guide, they're named for clarity.

12. **FIVE NINER** 5.9 ★
A strenuous but fun flake just up and around the corner from *Double Down*. A hands start leads to a deep hand crack with solid jams and ends on the northeast shoulder.
Descent: Scramble to northeast face and downclimb.
45 ft, gear, no fixed anchor

13. **FIVE EIGHTER** 5.8 ★
Obvious wide hand crack splits main block of north face.
Descent: scramble left and downclimb blocks on left side of face.
35 ft, gear, no fixed anchor

HANG NAIL
Separated from the climbs *Five Niner* and *Five Eighter* by broken scrambling, this is the Hang Nail Area, the true north face of Devil's Thumb.

14. LIEBACK FLAKE AKA BOYS ARE BACK IN TOWN 5.10
A thin crack and flake that shares the anchors with its neighbor to the right *Hang Nail*.
45 ft, small-med gear to chains

15. HANG NAIL 5.9 ★★★
To the right of *Boys Are Back*, climb this classic hand and finger crack that splits the face and heads straight up to chains. A must do for the area, and it'll keep you coming back, again and again. Belay at the first anchors to your left or continue up the crack of your choice to the summit.
45 ft, .3-2" gear to chains

16. COOKIE MONSTER 5.8+ ★
Climbed more often these days, this crack was named out of respect for those who've got 'er done. It can be filled with debris; nevertheless, it is wide hands challenge with an exciting traverse to the chains of *Hang Nail*
45 ft, gear to 4" to chains

17. SISSY CRANKSHAW 5.10d ★★
Start on the southwest corner and get ready for action. The crux hits at mid-height, after that it's a cruise to the top. She's stout! If you've done *Beauty and the Beasties*, this is next.
90 ft, bolts to chains
FA Jake Mergenthaler, Randall Green, 2001

18. SPLIT SEAMS 5.10 ★
Just right of *Sissy Crankshaw* is this series of seams, split by some easy stances. It starts with a wide steep crack that you can jam or lieback, with decent feet. It shares the finish of *Nemesis* and anchors with *Sissy Crankshaw*. Done plenty of times before, recorded here for your afternoon sessions.
90 ft, gear to 4", chains

19. NEMESIS 5.11a ★★★
Can be done in one or two pitches.
P1: Step right over a chasm on the west face belay from a large flat block. Battle a thin crack and flake to gain a ramp to a low angle open book, belay on small ledge, or... (90 ft) **This pitch can be toproped from *Beauties* anchors.**
P2: Grunt up steep off hands crack to belay bolts on summit block. Often overlooked, don't miss this pitch. (30 ft)
Descent: Rappel the West Face.
120 ft, gear .3-#1 to chains
FA Sonny Stewart, 1979

20. BEAUTY AND THE BEASTIES 5.10c ★★★
From the same belay block of *Nemesis*, step across the chasm to clip your first bolt. Then pull down on beautiful edges and beasty horns to gain a gorgeous arête. Love it.
90 ft, bolts to clip-and-lower
FA Randall Green, Jake Mergenthaler, Kim Mergenthaler, 2001

21. BABIES ON FIRE 5.10b
(Pictured on East Face photo)
A fantastic voyage that takes you past a committing face protected with bolts and fixed pins to finally gain an arête and parallel crack system to the top.
120 ft, bolts, fixed pins and med gear
FA Jamie Johnson, Mark Pearson, 1998

Bob Goodwyn on *Hang Nail 5.9*
Photo by Megan Helton

TOTO'S TOWER

Just north of the often-visited Devil's Thumb, is this stoic pillar of rock. It will be recorded here for the first time. First climbed in 2012 by Luke Evans, he's continued to nurse this project bringing it finally to 7 routes as of 2020. In his words, "Unique and exciting climbing on airy arêtes with spunky top-outs make this little tower quite a thrill and charm to climb". With an opening grade of 5.11b and open projects yet to be done, you'll be dang proud to add this to your list of Sheep accolades. Many thanks to Luke and his partners especially his daughters, Maisie and Azaria, for their contribution.

Aapproach these climbs from the ground below *Nemesis* (the North Face). Or if this is your sole objective, on your approach to the Thumb, just before Devil's Standard can be seen, cut left off the trail to a small shoulder in line with Toto's and the Thumb. Weave up this shoulder to the south face of the tower. Go right for the East Face routes, go left for the West. Routes described left to right starting with the east face.

Descent: There are 3 bolts with chains for an anchor on top of Toto's, great for rappelling, but you'll need to bring a long chunk of webbing or cordage to extend the anchors beyond the lip of the edge for top roping. Remember, you gotta lead your way up there first.

EAST FACE
The first routes you come to.

1. SCARECROW 5.11c ★
This scary and airy arête climb is first viewed on the left skyline from the approach to The Thumb. It includes fantastic bouldery climbing as Luke says, "on the edge". After the 3rd bolt, stand on the ledge to clip the next high bolt on the edge.
60 ft, 6 bolts to chains
FA Luke Evans, Liza Cabizares, 2012

2. TOTO 5.11b ★
Climb the face and side pull the arête. Finish with a mantle up top and you've just climbed the easiest route up the tower. Shares start with *Somewhere*.
45 ft, 3 bolts to chains
FA Luke Evans, Maisie Evans, and Azaria Evans, 2012

NORTH FACE
Facing the south side of Devil's Thumb, these routes can be seen from *Nemesis* and *Babies on Fire*. From Luke Evans, "Many climbers standing at the base of *Nemesis* have been tempted by this arching crack… for years I sure was! I led up the center line run out on natural gear in 2012 for the FA of the tower. Finally, I rebolted the route to make it safer and more accessible.

3. SOMEWHERE 5.11c
Just left of *Over the Rainbow*, this climb shares the first 2 bolts of *Toto*, then transitions right to gain the arc and last bolt of *Over the Rainbow*. Confused yet? Some fun variations as where to enter…
45 ft, 3 bolts to chains
FA Luke Evans

4. OVER THE RAINBOW 5.11b ★★★
Traverse in on good gear and stoppers below the first bolt to enter the balancey crux to reach the rainbow arc off a key rock knob. "Classic," says Luke, "to say the least."
45 ft, 3 bolts, stoppers to mid-sized cams to chains
FA Luke Evans, 2012
Equipped by Luke Evans, Maisie Evans, Azaria Evans 2020

5. THUNDER DOG 5.12c ★★
Climb up and clip the first bolt of Over the Rainbow then clip the second on the arête from the key knob and finish on the arête, great climbing on small rock knobs.
45 ft, 3 bolts to chains
FA Luke Evans

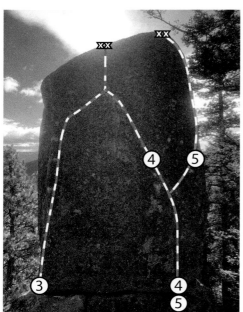

WEST FACE
Opposite side from the approach.

6. THUNDER STRUCK 5.12c ★
Stick clip the first bolt and climb the prow to gain the left arête joining *Thunder Dog* at the third bolt.
45 ft, 4 bolts to chains
FA Luke Evans, 2020

7. MONTANA MOONLIGHT PROJECT 5.12d?
Yet another Evans project to the right of *Thunder Struck*, stick clip the first bolt and climb the prow to gain the right arête, awesome exposed edge.
45 ft, 4 bolts to chains
Equipped by Luke Evans 2020

SURF'S UP AREA

Just east of Devil's Thumb and Toto's Tower stands this gem of a crag. Hosting new moderates and an inspiring project, they are spread between the main Pipeline Face to subsequent rocks to the right. Bring your tank top and flip flops to climb some rocks.

Follow the approach for Devil's Thumb, but just before you see *Devil's Standard* veer east (right) instead of west. It's close to Toto's, the Thumb should be visible in the background when looking at Pipeline. All routes should have bolted anchors on top and Surf's Up sports chains. All can be walked off easily or scramble up the backside to set topropes. Routes described left to right.

PIPELINE FACE

This is the most obvious face with Toto's and Devil's Thumb visible in the background. It hosts the routes *Pipeline* through *Rad*. Other routes are on the rocks to the right.

1. PIPELINE 5.9 ★
Climb the obvious chimney with big gear or clip the first bolts of *Longboard Lieback*.
50 ft, wide gear to chains
FA Luke Evans

2. LONGBOARD LIEBACK 5.10b ★★
Awesome lieback route.
50 ft, 7 bolts to chains
FA Luke Evans

3. LONGBOARD NATURAL 5.11 ★
Climb the crack all in gear with the crux to start.
50 ft, thin gear to chains
FA Luke Evans

4. THE TUBE 5.10 ★
Just to the right of the longboard.
50 ft, gear to chains
FA Luke Evans

5. RAD 5.10 ★★
Climb the featured face right by *The Tube*.
50 ft, gear to chains
FA Luke Evans

6. SURF'S UP 5.13+ Open Project
Climb the steep, unique granite tufa-like edge!
50 ft, bolts to chains
FA Luke Evans

7. HOLLOW COVE 5.7 ★
50 ft, 3 bolts to chains
FA Luke Evans

8. SURF SIDE 5.8 ★
50 ft, 3 bolts to chains
FA Luke Evans

John, Chris, and Van Alke at the base of Shoshone Spire, Blodgett Canyon 1978

AN INTERVIEW WITH CHRIS AND JOHN ALKE
By Bob Goodwyn

Bob: When did you brothers start climbing?
John: We started in 1974 & 1975, peak bagging in Glacier National Park. At this point we were climbing almost exclusively in Glacier, and didn't start what I call technical climbing until after we took a rock and ice climbing course in the summer of '76. Glacier would continue to be a place of inspiration for me. We started climbing harder and harder peaks until we decided we needed more technical skills.
Chris: Yep. And in 1976 we hired some instructors from the Trailhead in Missoula.
John: That's right. At that time Charlie Stevenson and his partner owned the store, and he had these guys working for him who would take people out.—Of the names I can remember there was Elliot Dubrueil, Dexter Hale, Don Scharfe, Todd Onken, and Randy Winner.

Two of these guys would become notable in the history of Montana climbing. Dexter Hale was one of the most prolific ice climbers and the originator of Big Horn Mountain Sports in Great Falls, MT. Don Scharfe was an accomplished climber and adventurer as well, and would open Rocky Mountain Outfitters in Kalispell, MT.

Bob: At this point, were you all still living at home? What did your parents think of your climbing?
John: We were out of high school, but we grew up on the base of Mt. Helena, over on Hauser Boulevard. Our dad was in the 10th Mountain Division. He had books all over the house about mountaineering, climbing, even books focused on Mt. Everest ascents. We drew our inspiration and some of our technical knowledge just from reading. We'd be on our way out of the house, headed up the hill towards Mt. Helena, and Mom and Dad would say, "Just don't play on the cliffs!" And of course, that's right where we were headed.

Bob: Dang, there are kids still doing that today I hope, getting their start on Mt. Helena.
John: To be clear, we didn't transition from playing on the cliffs of Mt. Helena to real climbing. At least in my case, we played on the cliffs when we were little kids, 4th grade probably through Junior High. All three brothers did team sports in highschool like cross country, track, and ski team. When we climbed Chief Mountain in Glacier Park in 1974, it was probably the first real mountain we had ever climbed. I was 23, Chris was 26, Van was 16. In other words, Chris and I started really late.

Chris: Yea, at that point it was the late 70s early 80s, I was working as a carpenter. And I was on such a tight budget that I'd save every dang receipt for every piece of climbing gear we ever bought. I still have a stack of old yellow receipts, most of them from the Basecamp. I figured at one point I should've just bought stock in some of those climbing companies. I was well known at the Basecamp, and Scott Brown hired me to do some of their remodel work, back when it was just on Jackson Street in downtown Helena. Then he hired me to do a remodel on his house later on. The former I'd do for a deal on climbing gear. But for his house he got to pay me. It all worked out in the end.
John: Chris and Van had the real talent, and were leading trad climbs at 5.7-5.9 by the end of 1977, mostly at Sheep. Although they didn't know how hard they were going at the time. This was the era where personal ratings on things like *Twinkle Toes* and *Rich Man* got their 5.7+ ratings.

This cued up the story of Rich Man Poor Man—*a classic Sheep Mountain test piece. Climbed in 2 pitches now, going at 5.9, it has thwarted many Sheep enthusiasts, or at least scared them out of their pants on either the bombay chimney or the thin smeary crux with only a blind undercling for comfort. On Chris & Van's first ascent, it took a series of 3 tries. They went after the first ascent finding they were short on large gear, so they went back to town to get some. Then on the second they realized they needed pins, or at least very small gear, and they finally put the whole thing together on their 3rd attempt. It stands today as a crowd favorite, and the standard for the variability of 5.9 climbing up at Sheep.*

John: In fact, the general rule was if Chris & Van could climb it it was 5.7 or lower. If they couldn't, it got a 5.7 or above.

Bob: Oh some of those routes are still out there today, just ripe for the uninitiated.

John: Van moved to Bozeman in the early 80s, and did a lot of hard rock climbing with the Bozeman crowd, including routes up Hellgate. Chris started to focus on ice climbing, and began his pilgrimages to Canada, usually with Dexter Hale. By the early 80's, my climbing ended up being one or two mountains a year in Glacier, and one new route a year in the Tetons. When I started paragliding in 1989, my climbing pretty much dropped to zero, although I started peak bagging again in Glacier after 2000. At this point I think I've done a little more than a hundred ascents on about 50 different mountains or high points in the park.

Bob: What internally, really inspired you both to climb?

John: I was all about mountains. Sheep and the other technical skills were just lessons to be learned and applied to the next biggest objective. Later on we started making trips down to the Tetons, where a lot of the hard climbing was taking place back then.

Bob: Were those climbs established, or were they first ascents too? Because everything you were doing at Sheep was all new. How did your tactics change for the Tetons?

John: No, the routes in the Tetons had already been done before, but we'd hear about them, get the word from Dexter or somebody, and we'd head down there to try them out. Don't get me wrong, there wasn't the info there is today. We'd hear that, "Ohh the grades in Yosemite are easier compared to Montana standards, or that the Tetons and Canada were a bit harder." So we'd load up the car and go. In 1987 Van and I did an ascent of the Enclosure Couloir. A month later Chris and Van went down for the Black Ice Couloir. Chris had quite the string of ice climbing ascents, from the Tetons to Canada. He and Dexter ticked off some of the Canadian classics; Slip Stream, Takakkaw Falls, and Polar Circus.

Chris: Yea I remember doing that Black Ice Couloir and it was a solid piece of blue-gray ice all the way to the top. You know the chockstone they talk about? That thing the size of a house that's often the crux now? That thing was encased in ice back then, just a dinner plate of rock was showing at the time.

Bob: Right, Chris, you became quite the ice climber at this point in the 80s. What internally inspired you to climb?

Chris: I was in it for the adrenaline, it was a rush. The way I see it, rock climbers are artists. And ice climbers are craftsmen. I was a craftsman. And you know, there's a good afterglow when it comes to ice climbing.

Bob: Between the adrenaline and your skills as a builder, your attraction to ice climbing makes a lot of sense. How did you all get into ice climbing in the first place?

Chris: It was those same guys from the Trailhead back in the 70s. They took us up to the Blackfoot Glacier to do some toprope ice climbing back in the day.

Bob: Dang that's amazing. That part of Glacier National Park has to look quite a bit different today, than it did back then. What was your first waterfall ice climb?

John: Oh that's a ridiculous story. We hit up somebody for a good piece of ice to climb, and they said Hyalite Canyon has some amazing ice, near Livingston, and when you get there you should try out Blue & Green Gully (he paused). Any ice climber in Montana that knows his or her stuff knows that Hyalite Canyon is in the Gallatin Range, south of Bozeman and nowhere near Livingston. Likewise Blue & Green ARE near Livingston but have nothing to do with Hyalite. So we take off for Livingston at least knowing where that is, start driving south down the Paradise Valley looking to our right, because we know those are the Gallatin Mtns where Hyalite Canyon is all the while thinking to ourselves, "S**** there's no way there's any ice over there." After driving up and down the road for a bit somebody finally sees a sign for Pine Creek, and says, "Screw it, let's head up that thing. Those are some real mountains." Low and behold we walked up Pine Creek and stumbled right into Blue & Green Gullies. It was a great day out, but an awful start.

Bob: HA! That is classic. It sounds like so many climbing adventures I've been on in Montana. You have to chalk every single one up to an adventure, you just don't know what's going to happen, and that's most of the fun. Do either of you recall any other stories from your travels?

Chris: I have one. I had this great dog one time, Yoda was her name, and I used to take the thing everywhere ice climbing. Dexter and I were up in Canada one time, climbing *Expert's Choice* (Grade III, WI6) around Waterton. This dog knew, if we were headed up, she would just sleep next to the packs, and usually I'd lay out a coat for her to stay warm. But when the ropes came out for the rappel, she also knew it was time to go home, and would often get a head start back for the car. Well we rappelled the route, which prompted Yoda to run all the way back to the vehicle. We could see her down there, sitting next to the truck, and she could see us. But when we started up a second climb, we watched as Yoda begrudgingly marched right back up the hill to enjoy the rest of the afternoon with us. And if any of you know the hill that I'm talking about, you'll know that's an approach you wouldn't want to do twice. Ha—she was a great dog.

John: You know, the only ascent I was proud of was the complete *East Face* of Going to the Sun Mountain in Glacier National Park. Norman Clyde, a famous Sierra climber, had done the upper part in the 1920s, traversing in from the Sexton Glacier. In 1978 my brother Van & I did what we thought was the first complete ascent of the face. This was chronicled by Terry Kennedy in the *Going to the Sun* Magazine. We left from the bottom of Baring Creek and did the entire face. It was a fun climb.

Chris: As far as climbs I was proud of, Dexter and I headed into Glacier Park one winter up the Many Glacier drainage. We were skiing in and ran into a park ranger. He asked what we were up to and we told him. He ended up giving us the keys to the ranger cabin there at Many Glacier. From there we skied to the south on whatever that mountain is, and did 5 first ice ascents over the course of our stay, each night coming back to the cabin to warm up, dry our stuff, and go again the next day. It was an amazing trip.

Bob: Damn, those are both amazing Glacier stories. And I can only say that the faces are up there are intimidating. To Chris, I've skied in there, in the winter to do the same thing, but I came way too late for the face you're talking about. That's awesome. To John, was your ascent of Going to the Sun in the summer or winter?

John: This was summer. I did most of my climbing in the summer with Van, who was the real rock climber.

Bob: Yea, he's the 3rd brother right? Tell me about him.

John: He turned into the real rock climber of our family. Here's a story on Van, if you'd like to hear it....

This story is from Don Scharfe of Kalispell, MT. He was nice enough to call and confirm it, but I'll continue telling it from John's perspective.

John: This was 8 or 10 years ago I'd guess. Our friend Don Sharfe was climbing up in Blackleaf some time ago. He and his son Kyle (Missoula, MT) were a couple of pitches up on "Zen & the Art of Bolting" (5.12a, 6 pitches) and looked over to see a single climber headed up next to them. After a minute the climber calls out to Don, "Hey, is that Don Scharfe over there!?" Don responds, "I think that's Van Alke!? How are ya?" Van waved a big smile and kept on climbing.

Chris, with a laugh: That sounds like Van. He wouldn't say shit if he had a mouthful of it.

John: Van wasn't free soloing but rope soloing. He self-belayed with a caming device, climbed up, put in pro, descended and cleaned. Then he'd re-ascend to start the next pitch. In essence, he climbed every pitch twice. Don and Van had known each other going back to the 70s first as climber and instructor, then as friends. They both met up at the base of the wall later that day, enjoyed dinner, and parked their Volkswagen vans next to each other. Don recalled how bold Van must have been to be climbing alone on that face.

Chris: Okay one more before we're outta beers here at the Blackfoot. We were down on a trip to the Devil's Tower back in the day. And we always enjoyed our beers after a day of climbing at the bar in Sundance, Wyoming. I can't remember what the bar was called, but I think there's only one. We still had our tape on our hands, because we were cheap asses and didn't want to re-place it every day. We slept with that stuff on! We weren't getting dirty looks from the cowboys in the bar, but stares of interest, or fear, or something. Finally after a couple of beers, one of the cowboys saunters over and asks, "Are you guys boxers?" We all got a good chuckle out of that one.

The Alke's and Bob were joined by Bob's brother, Lee that night. Many more words were shared and laughs were had, but these were the words that were captured according to the author. It was a brotherly affair over Blackfoot Brewery beers. We parted ways wishing Chris good luck with his upcoming knee replacement surgery. He and John had been walking below Mt Helena to keep him in shape and ready for the procedure. Lee and Bob were headed out to celebrate Lee's soon-to-be marriage. And all of them punched out their tickets at the Blackfoot that night.

THE IRISHMEN

The Irishmen is another great example of the many options and newer climbs that can be discovered out at Sheep. Like any newly listed climbs in this edition, they may well have been done by the hardy generation that preceded us all, but Brad Hornung is responsible for listing them here. Like all Sheep climbing, there's adventure in the approach, gearing up, and getting to the top. The Irishmen is no exception. Go find it, and have fun.

Use the Devil's Thumb pull out, and even if it's a little bit difficult to get to your first time, it'll be worth it. Instead of heading west as you would for the Thumb, head directly up the drainage in front of you heading northeast. The correct drainage will be on your left, but it's filled with deadfall, boulders and blowdowns, but you can bypass the worst of it by heading up right in a much clearer area. There may be a small rock cairn at the start. Do not follow the ATV trail that is too far right! Angle up and left, staying in this meandering drainage. The hiking and downfall hopping should never get too difficult, you should only have to step across a couple of logs. Keep a large blocky rock on your left (there are some short climbs on it). After about 10 minutes from the car, the drainage will spit you out on a nice shoulder with the the large block on your left, and the main hill on your right. Face the main hill, and start walking in about a 10 o'clock direction, north and west. You will have to step over a few logs at the start but then the angle steepens and you end up on a mostly sandy, rocky hill. From the shoulder to the base of the climb should only take about 3 minutes. Climbs are described left to right, all are trad, no top anchors as of Fall 2020, but plenty of natural stuff to work with. Walk off to the northwest of the formation.

1. HENRY FITZPATRICK 5.8 ★
Start at an obvious hand crack, below an obvious tree that grows on a ledge about ¼ of the way up. Follow this to the tree, then step left and head up the wide corner/off-width to the top. Brad's quote, and in fine Sheep style, "The more you want to protect it, the bigger stuff you will need."
60 ft, wide gear to #6 Camalot
FA Brad Hornung, 2019

2. PHIL M'CRACKIN 5.6 ★★
About 20 feet to the right of *Firtzpatrick* behind a fir tree, is a dish with a right facing corner. Head up this and to the left towards the tree on the ledge. From the tree head straight up the wide crack to the face and then back to crack again.
60 ft, standard rack
FA Brad Hornung, 2019

3. PATRICK FITZHENRY 5.7 ★★
Start just to the right of *M'Crackin* and head up the dish to a crack in the roof. Follow this up and to the right facing corner system, which will take you to the top. The dish to the crack is probably harder than 5.7, and you can't protect it. An easier variation is to start about 15 feet to the right in a series of broken, blocky rocks, directly below the corner, then head directly up.
60 ft, standard rack
FA Brad Hornung, 2019

PANDEMIC WALL

This is another one of those classic Sheep finds—once you find it, it'll be classic. These climbs were officially equipped with top anchors using a hand drill by the prolific Sheep climber, Brad Hornung. Although he is the first to admit they were routes possibly established in the earlier days, recorded here for your climbing pleasure.

The approach should only take 20 minutes from the car, but give yourself a time buffer the first time you go out looking… Follow directions for The Irishmen. Once at The Irishmen contour around to the east bumping over a couple of small gullies. 3-5 min of fairly easy walking/boulder hopping/log dodging should land you at this south facing rock. Once you get to the tower it is possible to set up topropes by heading up the right-hand side. Keep an eye out for a rock slab that you can scramble up easily. This will take you to a notch, with large boulders and the top ledge of the tower. There are two bolts at the top which will make it easy to toprope *Covid*. To toprope the other two climbs you will probably want a directional of some sort.

All three are essentially trad climbs but have a 20' slab section at the top that needs bolts before they can be lead safely.

1. PANDEMIC 5.8 TR ★

Sitting about 15 feet to the right of the deep notch starts this thin crack. Work your way up the crack, over a bulge to a ledge. Next, take the slab up to the obvious hand crack. This will take you to another slightly wider and easier crack system. Follow this until you reach the corner of the final slab. Head right into a wide crack for a little bit, then up the slab as the angle eases off, or take an easy wide crack to the top.
80ft
FA Brad Hornung, 2020

2. COVID-19 5.10 TR ★

This is an enjoyable climb that gets progressively harder the higher you get, with the crux being the slab at the top. Start up the wide crack in the middle of the rock formation and follow it to the roof. Tackle the roof if you want, or take the easier way by traversing out onto the block on the right-hand side. Regain the crack and follow this until it peters out, then up the slab.
80ft
FA Brad Hornung, 2020

3. COVID-19.5 5.7 TR ★

This climb follows the same line as *Covid-19* until you hit the roof. Instead of heading right, head up the left-hand crack. The crux is getting into the crack. Fortunately it is well protected. Once in, follow the double cracks until they run out. Step left and pick your way up the slab.
80ft
FA Brad Hornung, 2020

LEFT ROCK

With only one climb described in the previous guide, one would think this obscure sub area at Sheep Mountain wasn't much to see. Think again. New to this guide are some intimidating new lines and thought-provoking link ups, resulting in some 200' of continuous climbing. Throw in some of that classic Sheep Mountain grit that'll keep you walking back up that hill late into the season.

Long thought to be best approached from the main parking lot via Upper Rock, now most of these climbs are considered best attacked from the Devil's Thumb parking. You should bypass The Irishmen and The Pandemic Wall on your way. First, follow directions for the Pandemic Wall. From its base, traverse right at that same 2 o'clock direction, with directly uphill being 12 o'clock. This should take you up a small rise, then you'll lose some 60' of elevation as you continue to traverse to the right. After you lose that elevation a rock outcropp should pop up on your left. Keep hugging this outcropp as you traverse right, and you should soon (approximately 5 min from Pandemic Wall) have the *Lower Westside Block* on your left. Routes described left to right.

Lost to the ether since the previous guidebook, we are sure that many of these routes have been previously explored and established. Many thanks to Brad Hornung for listing them. Many apologies for the names and grades that were discarded.

1. LOWER WESTSIDE BLOCK 5.8

This obscure climb looks to provide you everything you ask for when you come to Sheep—grumbly wide, interestingly thin face holds and deep cracks. Start from a platform rock, squirm up a water trough, then starts the big stuff. It's worth it for the hand crack at the top though. No established anchor was available as of November 2020. Scrambled down off the backside.
60 ft, gear to 6"

CAVE ROUTES
The Cave Routes are up and right of the Westside Block. Go right 40yds, up another 40yrds, and you should be able to explore the cave created by a huge, toppled boulder on your left.

2. CAPTAIN OBVIOUS 5.10b ★★
This nasty, steep inside corner calls upon the love you have for your fingers and all the grit you've got in your gut. Start by bouldering onto a head-high slanting shelf, follow the endlessly steepening, tight inside corner that's tough to stem, but worth it in the end. Finish with low-angle slabs, wide cracks, and a 2-bolt belay on the right side of the first large ledge you come to. There were no chains on the bolts as of November 2020. This should be directly above Open Project.
100 ft, gear from .3-#4, doubles in .4-#1; bolt anchor

3. OPEN PROJECT 5.11+?
Just right of *Captain Obvious*, this climb has 3 bolts that lead you to a crack zooming up the face. Not much is known of this route. It looks hard, and it's waiting there for you. Continue to *Strikes Again* or pitch 2 of *Huck Berry*.
60 ft, 3 bolts, thin gear, to a gear anchor
Equipped by Luke Evans?

4. HUCK BERRY 5.11d/12a
P1: An arching finger crack broken by a small chockstone. Belay below the overhang above, or keep firing. (5.11d/12a)
P2: Fire this overhanging hand crack to a 2-bolt anchor on a ledge before the treed ledge above. (5.10d)
2 Pitches, gear from .2-2", gear, bolted anchor
FA Luke Evans, Paul Berry

5. LARGE, IN CHARGE 5.8 (Not Pictured)
Right of *Huck Berry*, this climb is in a deep wide crack, near-chimney status, with wicked flakes breaking it up.
100 ft, wide gear, to a chains

UPPER LEFT ROCK

These climbs start above the Cave Routes, on a large ledge that breaks up Left Rock. Best approached by climbing one of the Cave Routes, they're divided from Upper Rock by a steep boulder-filled drainage with some large trees in it. This is one of the descent gullies off of Upper Rock and is not recommended to ascend. *Bill's Crack* is seen on the east side of this drainage. Routes described from right to left, as they're encountered.

6. STRIKES AGAIN 5.10b ★★

Originally climbed as a continuation of *Huck Berry* by Evans and Berry, it is renamed here as a great link-up resulting in nearly 200ft of climbing. The sporty crux is down low with great face holds and sneaky gear leading to an amazing low-angle hand crack. Pull one more overhang, reminiscent of the one on *Book of Payne* at Blue Cloud, to a belay from a tree.

Descend the gully between Left Rock and Upper Rock.

70 ft, gear to #2, tree anchor
FA Luke Evans, Paul Berry

7. B.S. (BUCHER/STILLER) 5.7 ★

This climb starts left of *Strikes Again*, on a prominent ledge that crosses the crag. Scramble up and left to a chimney that tapers to a fist crack.

70 ft, gear to #4, tree anchor
FA Bill Bucher, Dave Stiller, 1970s

Chris Alke on *Sting 5.10*

THE ANT HILL

The Ant Hill is located in the gully between Upper Rock and Left Rock. Approach via the Devil's Thumb parking area. Begin walking on the northeast-bound two-track. When the two-track curves sharply away from the crags, head into the woods. Ascend the hill for about 20-30 minutes.

1. STRANGE NEWS 5.8 ★★★

Heading up The Ant Hill, this is the left-most bolt line on the larger face on the left side. Climb the short face to a wide horizontal crack. Move onto the main face above. Climb good edges until able to traverse left on a sloping ledge. Finish off on the arête.

60 ft, 7 bolts to anchors
FA Steve Ahlrich, Christy Meredith, 2021

2. THE GLASS BEAD GAME 5.10c ★★★

The second from the left bolt line on the lower east face of Left Rock. Start in the wide crack. Clip the first bolt and step out onto the face. Work through thin edges to easier climbing. Continue up through a steep section and finish left on an airy traverse.

65 ft, 8 bolts to shared anchors with *Strange News*
FA Steve Ahlrich, Tim Matthews, 2021

3. FOREST DWELLER 5.7 ★★

Right of *The Glass Bead Game* is a series of step-like, small, right-facing corners. Climb boulder to thin cracks in the right-facing corner. Work through the corners, exiting via a short face onto a large sloping ledge. Climb the wavy face to anchors.

65 ft, 5 bolts plus carry a set of wires and small cams to 1". Carry a mid-size cam (2-3") for the start. Fixed anchors.
FA Steve Ahlrich, 2021

4. BENEATH THE WHEEL 5.10b ★★★

At the top of The Ant Hill (north end) is a very large boulder. This bolt line is located on the right arête. Step onto the bottom of the arête with good edges. Climb through sidepulls until forced right.

40 ft, 5 bolts to anchors
FA Steve Ahlrich, Jim Barnes, 2021

5. BILL'S CRACK 5.9 ★★★

Obvious crack line that splits the lower west face. This climb is a bit ugly at first but mellows into a nice hand crack. On the first ascent Dave led off only to downclimb after finding some loose rock, Bill then took over only to pull off a large flake that scared them both. Finally, Dave managed to finish the route.

75 ft, gear to 4" to fixed anchor
FA Bill Bucher, Dave Stiller, 1974

6. JOURNEY TO THE EAST 5.9 ★★★

Located on the lower west face of Upper Rock, just right of *Bill's Crack*. Climb boulders to access the base of *Bill's Crack*. Traverse right at the obvious horizontal edge. Crank past jugs and edges. Continue on the face for fun climbing above.

65 ft, 7 bolts to anchors
FA Steve Ahlrich, Jim Barnes, 2021

THE ANT HILL CLIMBING

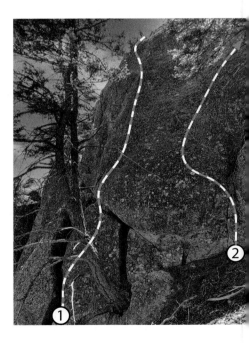

UPPER ROCK

Upper Rock's south face stands like an ancient citadel high on Sheep Mountain. This formation is the proudest formation in the area, with single pitches up to 150 ft, split down the middle by the distinct chimney system: *Stiller's Crack*. It is rich in history and adventure.

Long thought to be best approached from the main parking lot, there's also the alternative to access this area from Devils Thumb Parking by way of Irishman, Pandemic and Left Rock. Both will be described here. From Left Rock, continue right (north, east) for 350 ft gaining 125 vertical feet along the way. Cut back left for 100 ft and up the gully to The Ant Hill. From Middle Rock, hike northwest towards the summit of Sheep Mountain. Weave your way around blocks and downfall. You should come from E to W and traverse to the base of *Juniper*. As of this writing there was no distinct trail, but hopefully that improves in the near future to limit our impact. Routes described left to right.

True to the old school vibe, only a few routes on Upper Rock finish with fixed anchors. Be prepared to build your own gear anchor, permitting you've saved enough gear for the top.

Descent: Anchors for a double-rope rappel exist at the top of the routes *Bailout Variant* and *Juniper*. From there it's 55m to the ground, so bring 2 ropes. Another alternative is 2 single rope rappels—first using these anchors, then the tree in the middle of *Juniper*. Although these anchors are accessible after topping out on all routes, they can be hard to find unless you've climbed either *Bailout* or *Juniper*. A good rule of thumb, if you've climbed anything to the left of the *Bailout Variant*, do the walk off. This walk-off is an option from any route, if the anchors are not discovered. Walk-off Directions: Find your way to the shoulder between the top of *Stiller's Crack*, the true summit of Upper Rock. Scramble west, picking your way down a narrow gully where some 5th class moves and tree-hugging shimmies might be encountered. Eventually find your way around to the south face, just below *Bill's Crack* and back to the base of the other south face routes. This is always an option, and another reminder that Upper Rock yields nothing easy. More rappel anchors to come.

MAIN PARKING

UPPER ROCK

1. SUNNY SLAB 5.5
This route zigzags up the left side of the rock, taking the line of least resistance. From the base scramble up a left slanting ledge to a low-angled hand crack past a horizontal break and merge with a big corner system on the left side of wall; step left or right at the "Y".
75 ft, gear to 4"
FA Bill Bucher, Dave Stiller, 1974

2. WITCHES TIT 5.8 ★★★
Up *Stiller's* then break left on flakes and good stances. Place gear when you can then yard your way on great holds. Finish in the distinct chimney of *Stiller's*.
150 ft, gear to 4"
FA Dave Stiller, Bill Bucher, 1975

3. STILLER'S CRACK 5.6 ★★★
This chimney can be seen from the road and is the most popular route on the rock. This dude is heavy on old school adventure and may seem a bit stiff for 5.6. Use every technique to squirm past bulges then head left up the main crack. Belay off blocks and cracks on the summit.
150ft gear to 4"
FA Dave Stiller, Bill Bucher, 1974

4. NO-NAME CRACK 5.10 ★
Begin 10' left of *Sting* on lovely face crimps for 50 ft to a seam/groove system, continue to the top.
150ft, gear to 4" extra TCU's and small wires

5. STING 5.10 ★★★
Climb a low-angle ramp below a crack with a V-shaped roof. Pass the roof on the left and climb the arête past a bolt. Now's the beef—a low-angle, bottomless buttcrack that's airy and difficult to protect. This gives way to an easier broken crack system and a worthwhile face climb to finish. Enjoy this worthy adversary. Deserving of a true anchor up top someday.
165 ft, 1 bolt, gear to 4", including RPs and small wires
FA Van Alke and John Alke, 1976

6. BAILOUT VARIANT 5.8 ★★
Climb *Sting* to a small roof escape right, follow right-leaning cracks to the top. Shares anchors with *Juniper*.
165 ft, gear to 4" to fixed anchor
FA Unknown

7. JUNIPER 5.8 ★★★
This is a great intro to Upper Rock at 5.8. It also leads directly to the rappel station. Start by ramping up right on a low-angle crack system to a good stance. Next, step left out onto the face, pull a sneaky lieback move to gain a crack leading to the tree. Above the tree is a beauty of a crack starting low-angle, then bulging. Pull the bulge to the left to gain an easier face that's difficult to protect for the last 15'. Find the anchors just below the rim of a southeast face between two huge blocky formations.
100 ft, gear to 3", lots of .3-.75, fixed anchor
FA Van Alke Alke, 1976

8. JOE'S JUNIPER VARIATION 5.8- ★
Although this may not be a new route, it's recorded here for the record. At the bulge above the *Juniper*, you can also step right to gain easier ground and some thin moves to finish on *Floating Chimney* and eventually the fixed anchors of *Juniper*.
100 ft, gear to 3", lots of .3-.75, fixed anchor
FA Joe Schmechal, Bob Goodwyn 2020.

9. FLOATING CHIMNEY 5.4
Grunt up a chimney on the east side that merges with *Juniper*.
100 ft, gear to 4" fixed anchors
FA Bill Bucher, Pete Gorman, 1976

10. GLINDA THE GOOD WITCH 5.9
Climb *Floating Chimney* or *Sting* to reach this fabulous finish to the top of Upper Rock. Steep climbing on big holds lure you out on the edge.
50 ft, 4 bolts to a fixed anchors
FA Luke, Maisie, Azaria, Evans 2020

WOLF'S HEAD
This formation is up and to the right of *Floating Chimney* on Upper Rock. From the right angle, it looks like a wolf's head. Climb *Floating Chimney* and set up a trad belay to start these two spectacular short climbs. For a good time, link them with *Glinda the Good Witch* for the best view on Sheep Mountain.

11. THE WOLF 5.12b ★★
Use the stellar left edge and face climb up great golden granite holds to the fixed belay. Finish up on *Glinda the Good Witch*.
30 ft, 3 bolts to anchors
FA Luke Evans, 2019

12. WOLF HOWL 5.13 b/c Project
Radical overhanging edge in a stellar position, clip the first two bolts of *The Wolf* and lean out completely on the edge to gain the top bolt.
30 ft, bolts to anchor
Equipped Luke Evans, 2019

UPPER DECK
The highest crag at Sheep, this little zone is above Upper Rock. Again, probably found long ago, but recorded here for the first time thanks to Luke Evans. Many options exist, so we'll leave it up to the inventors. Fashion yours anchors up top with gear or trees. Walk off the backside.

1. LEFT FIELD 5.7-5.9 ★
Left of *Center Field*, there are many options.
90 ft, gear

2. CENTER FIELD 5.10 ★★
This goes straight up the middle then transitions to a crack on its left.
90 ft, gear
FA Luke Evans, 2019

3. RIGHT FIELD 5.7-5.9 ★
Same as *Left Field*, but to the right.
90 ft, gear
FA Luke Evans, 2019

WARRIOR ROCK
Lurking above Upper Deck, this piece stands as a testament to those adventuring before. It's up there.

4. THE 13TH WARRIOR 5.13a ★
Start with low hand jams and go to war. 5.12 from a high start.
40 ft, gear
FA Luke Evans, 2000s

5. WALKING POINT PROJECT V11?
To the left of *The 13th Warrior*, will take gear and has a bad landing.
40 ft, gear or highball

MIDDLE ROCK

The south and southwest faces of Middle Rock contain some high-quality crack climbs that have plenty of cool features to add to your jamming, along with some of the best settings for a crag session known to Sheep. Most routes are single pitch but many can be linked for two or three-pitch voyages. It is possible to walk off the backside but most routes have chain belay anchors from which to rap.

From the main parking area tread NW on a faint game trail switching back to avoid the boulders. Care is needed to navigate around some short cliffs, but the main climbing area is easily seen from the parking area.

MAIN PARKING

MIDDLE ROCK CLIMBING

BELOW STANDARD

Not included in early guides, this monster wide crack sits below the ledge that starts Middle Standard. Use it as an access pitch, link it to the summit for some 300′ of climbing, or walk past it wondering "Who would enjoy that?" Either way, enough times going by this guy and you'll be asking your buddy to borrow the Big Bros® to give it a go. Can you call yourself a 5.8 climber unless you can climb 5.7 off-width? I don't know…

1. LARGE AND IN CHARGE 5.7 ★★

If it's off-widthy you wanna get, here's your go. *Large and in Charge* is the obvious wide crack 65′ below *Middle Standard*. It's big.
65 ft, gear to 8″

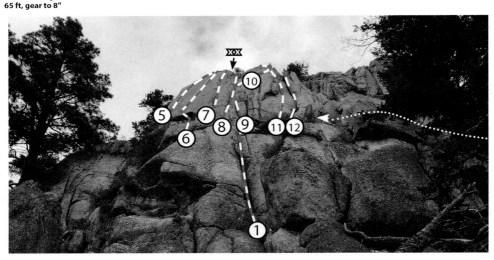

TROLL'S AREA

Found on the lower west edge of the formation, this area is characterized by a distinct left-facing corner (*Troll's Dihedral*). Routes are described left to right.

2. THE SOLOIST 5.6 ★

This route begins in a deep groove made by a boulder pushed up against the west side of Middle Rock. Up to your right will be the distinct *Troll's Dihedral*. After squirming up the groove, *The Soloist* links the left leaning thin cracks up a slab to a tree on the northwest shoulder. Potentially run-out for the uninitiated, but easy climbing.
Descent: Walk off west shoulder, or pop over the horizon to the chains of Middle Standard/Myth Slab.
100 ft, gear to 4″, tree anchor

3. TROLL'S RETURN 5.7 ★★

Face and crack climb 15′ left of a large corner system. Climb cracks to join the *Troll's Dihedral*, then pop right to the *Middle Standard* anchors, or continue up on easier terrain.
100 ft, gear to 4″, chains
FA Dave Stiller, 1976

4. TROLL'S DIHEDRAL 5.8 ★

Obvious left facing corner, just to the right of the groove marking *The Soloist*. Start in a 15-foot-high chimney to a ledge system (this is the access chimney leading to the ledge of Middle Standard/Myth Slab). Continue up a classic Sheep dihedral for about 80 ft, then step right and scamper to *Myth* anchors.
100 ft, gear to 4″, chains
FA Dave Stiller, 1976

Traditional start to the Troll's

MIDDLE STANDARD/MYTH SLAB

Packed with long, quality routes plus easy access from the main parking area, add a grand view overlooking all of Sheep, and you've got a great cragging spot. A must-do if you're looking for moderates. Most climbs are one-pitch affairs that end at chain anchors 85' up, although a few can be extended up easier ground to the summit. Often referred to as the "Standard Area," it is renamed here as Middle Standard to distinguish it from Devil's Standard. As of this writing, the author had not heard it referred to as the "Myth Slab" in years, but it might make a comeback.

Start on a comfortable ledge that can be reached by scrambling up the 5.4 access chimney on the western flank of the formation. This is the first 15' of *Troll's Dihedral*. OR, popularized in recent years, is the "Cave Approach" from the East side of the face. From the car, the approach should deposit you near the base of *Lower Your Standards* some 65ft below the Middle Standard Area. Traverse right (east) under the formation, gain 50' vertically, and look for a sneaky traverse on your left. This will take you out onto the face, back into a cave, and over to the ledge. A bit exposed, but not difficult, this can be tough to find your first time, but once you get it dialed, it's easier with packs, ropes, beverages, costumes, and whatever other crag necessities you're hauling for the day. Routes described left to right.

Descent: All routes can be adventured to the top of the formation and walked off. Or if you're in the middle of the south face, scramble to Middle Standard/Myth Slab anchors and rappel. A 60m rope will get you back to the ledge, or a 70m rope to the bottom of Troll's Area or the access chimney.

5. SOFT PARADE 5.10a ★
Begin on far west side of ledge at a thin crack under a small roof. Sketch up the crack and clip a bolt yank over the roof on the right side, and tread left up a slab and an erratic crack to chains.
85 ft, 3 bolts, gear to chains

6. THE MYTH VARIANT 5.11a ★
Start same as *Soft Parade*. Pull over a roof. Instead of going left, crank straight up for a few balancy moves. Finish same as *Soft Parade*.
85 ft, 3 bolts, gear to chains

7. DELIBERATION 5.9 ★★★
Follow a shallow left facing corner over a roof to a discontinuous hand crack past a few tricky slab moves. Finish on *Myth* anchors.
85 ft, gear to 4", TCUs, small wires

8. MIDDLE STANDARD/LEFT CRACK 5.7 ★★★
Just right of *Deliberation* a pretty crack shoots straight up. Climb this using convenient knobs to *The Myth Variant* anchors. Done more often than its neighbor to the right. Redubbe *Middle Standard* here, to eliminate confusion.
85 ft, gear to 4", chains

9. RIGHT CRACK 5.6 ★★★
Parallel to *Left Crack* and merges with it at mid-height, climb to *The Myth Variant* anchors.
85 ft, gear to 4", chains

10. TWINKLE TOES VARIANT 5.9R
Climb *Right Crack* until just after it merges with *Left Crack* then take right leaning seam and face climb (no pro!) up to ledge system that joins *Ground Out*.
Descent: Scramble left up shoulder and through cave behind tree to walk off left side of rock, or down to Middle Standard anchors and rappel.
85 ft, gear to 4"
FA Van Alke Alke, Mike Webber, 1976

11. GROUND OUT 5.9R ★
Takes the next crack/seam line just right of *Right Crack*. Boldly lead up to the crack that gets easier with the overhang, or step left from *The Mistake*. Continue up the arête (no pro!) or fade right (east) to join *The Mistake* and belay from a tree. You can scramble back to the *Middle Standard* anchors if you choose or continue up.
85 ft, gear to 4", natural/gear anchor

12. THE MISTAKE 5.7 ★
Wide squeeze chimney to off-hands seam that leads to a ledge with a tree (large cams useful). Same finish as *Ground Out*.
85 ft, gear to 4"

13. BUCKETS AWAY 5.6 ★
Right of the wide squeeze chimney are several step-like corners that zigzag up the slab to the ledge system below a squatty tree. Many variations exist, most needed cleaning at the writing of this guide, but look promising for the future. Take the line of least resistance.
90 ft, gear to 4"

SOUTHEAST FACE

This monster face is characterized by a large, low angle slab on the eastern toe of the formation offering easier starts to challenging finishes. The slab is capped by enormous roofs and the imaginative Luke Evans project *Seams Possible* and cleaved by several crack systems that angle up from right to left.

Descent: Top out and walk off the northeast side of the formation back to your packs.

14. CORNER POCKET 5.6 ★★

Can be done in 2 or 3 pitches. Scramble up to a tree on the left side of slab. Continue up a large open book on left side to a stair-step feature that breaks the left side of a book, work past the steps and around the left side of a large bulge to easier ground and the top.
145 ft, gear to 4"
FA Van Alke Alke, John Alke, 1975

15. CORNER POCKET VARIATION 5.9 ★★★

Instead of stepping left to easier terrain around the large bulge, step right and fire this steep hand crack. Easier ground ahead.
50 ft, gear to 3"
FA Van Alke Alke, John Alke, 1975

16. BLOODBERRY JAM 5.9 ★★★

This route follows the open book of the southeast face.
P1: Scramble up a crack and groove system to a ledge and gear anchor at mid-height. (5.3-5.5)
P2: Continue up a low-angle groove to a left, then right facing corner, passing an overhang with strong moves 5.9. Lightly tread past chockstones to a triangular, sloping shelf. Belay here, or it's also possible to traverse left to join the top of *Corner Pocket* or *Corner Pocket Variation*. (5.9)
150 ft, gear to 4", many runners, cams in the 1-2" range if you're going to do it in 2 pitches.
FA Dave Stiller, 1975

17. CLASSY REUNION VARIANT 5.9 ★

Step right around the corner from a sloping ledge and sketch up this left leaning beast.

18. CHOKER 5.9 ★

P1: follow *Bloodberry*; belay at midheight.
P2: From P1 head right towards the obvious overhanging off-width. Belay on a slab under the behemoth off-width.
P3: Grunt, swear and moan up physical off-width. Belay above on easier slab.
150 ft, gear to 4", extra big stuff

19. LEANING CRACK 5.10 ★

This striking line ascends distinct left leaning crack on southeast face right of overhangs. A classic sandbag of the old guidebook, this thing was previously listed at 5.6. As of 2020 it's still hard and still enticing.
100' gear to 4", natural or gear anchor

20. SEAMS POSSIBLE 5.14 Open Project

This daunting line had draws dangling off it since it was bolted in the early 2000s by the man, Luke Evans, but never climbed. It follows a slight seam in the major overhang at the top of Middle Rock. Those draws will tease you as well.
60' thin gear, bolts to 2 bolt anchor
Equipped by Luke Evans, 2000s

RIGHT ROCK

This wonderful formation is deservedly popular and well known for its easy approach, reasonable topropes and varied climbs. Check out the intricate moves on the *Stooges Slab* or monkey up the overhanging sport climb *Flame Out/Muscle Screw*. Many of the area's routes face south offering sunny climbing in early/late season conditions.

From the main parking area tread east on an ATV trail that runs across the mountain. In this first part of the trail, there is private property below you to the right. Be mindful and respectful. After 200 yards turn left up a shallow gully with a faint trail. This weaves its way up the gully, with 2 landmarks to show you're going the right way: 1) a very cool shoulder-width alley that splits a boulder in two and 2) you'll walk beneath a short exciting looking slab that offers topropes. Continue up the hill for another 10 minutes to the base of the south face. The cave formed by Multiple Screamers Block, and home to the infamous *Deliberation,* should be the first place you encounter. Routes described left to right. If anchors are not described in the route, you'll have to build one, or continue to walking off east or west. Both are fine.

MAIN PARKING

RIGHT ROCK CLIMBING

WEST FACE
These routes lie around the left/west side of another large block that guards the southwest buttress up the hill. You'll find the starts on your right.

1. MARK OF ZORRO 5.7 ★
Originally zig-zagging across the entire face, *Zorro* is now usually climbed like so: Start in a chimney formed by two large blocks leaning against the left side of the west face. Climb the chimney and step right (crux) to gain another chimney to the top of the block. Climbers usually finish here, walking off to the north and back to the belay. More adventure can be found by continuing up, or across the face.
Descend by scrambling left and downclimb a 5.2 chimney.
65 ft, gear to 4"

2. HEART STOPPER 5.10b ★★
Begin in a balancey diagonal crack that ends at a tree. Now's the business: feel your way through a steep slab to a mighty lie back. Keep cranking to easier ground. Rap from chains or walk off left.
80 ft, bolts, gear to 2", chains
FA Scott Payne, Randall Green, 1990

[The next four climbs start from the cove formed by Multiple Screamers Block that leans against the main formation. It's a great belay spot.]

3. SECOND THOUGHTS 5.11a ★★★
The route follows a blunt arête that leads to the *Heart Stopper* anchor. Start at same level as *Defoliator*. Climb a bolted face then tip toe up desperate moves along an arête, finish in an arching crack that ends at *Stopper's* anchors.
120 ft, bolts, gear to 3", chains
FA Randall Green, Aaron Lefohn, 1990

4. DEFOLIATOR 5.10a ★★★
Start on a flat sandy spot under a lone bolt. Whine up past the bolt and gain a pretty crack, jam 60' until just under a bulge with a weird flakes. Either crank straight up over the bulge or bail out right to gain a jumble of comfortable blocks under a distinct right-leaning crack, belay from blocks or a tree.
150 ft, 1 bolt, gear to 4", natural anchor
FA Sunny Stewart, Jim Scott, 1977

5. FIN-AGAIN 5.10b/c ★★★
A soaring line that tackles a slight weakness in the southwest face. This was climbed over three summer evenings after work. The first night the brothers scared themselves silly on the heady seam only to find they would need a piton for the next pitch. They returned to be thwarted by a lack of large gear for the upper pitch. Finally, the two brothers returned and finished off the entire climb. Pitch 2 of this wonder is an all-time classic steep hand-over-fist jug haul. Unfortunately, it's guarded by the tricky and difficult to protect, pitch 1. There are ways around it.
P1: Just right of *Defoliator*, is this slippery dike that heads up to a layback seam that angles up to squeeze chimney formed by the Multiple Screamers Block. Use the small seam for gear and squeeze up chimney to ledge. (5.10R)
P2: Start on the ledge, (which can be reached by climbing *The Nose* on Multiple Screamer Block) formed by large blocks. Climb up an indistinct crack and gain an arching corner with a pumpy hand crack. Excellent. Belay from chains. (5.10b)
150 ft, gear to 3", chains
FA Van Alke Alke, Chris Alke, 1976

6. AID CRACK/BOULDER PROBLEM A1/5.11R
(Not Pictured)
Farthest seam to the right in a large cave. Crank up seam under an old ¼" bolt and aid and scuffle to the top of the block; some have toproped from bolt, but this is highly discouraged and could lead to your DEATH! Safe belay not known.
1 bolt

MULTIPLE SCREAMERS BLOCK

This gargantuan block leans against the southwest face and forms a large cave. The climbs *Multiple Screamers* and *The Nose* are on the west and south faces, respectively. *Flame Out* and *Toprope Flake* are on the east. *Blood Knuckles* starts atop the block to meet up with *Rich Man's* anchors.

7. MULTIPLE SCREAMERS 5.11c ★★

For an unforgettable adventure (aptly named for the falls taken while bolting on lead) pad up this technical face climb on the s/w side of the block. Use a tree to gain the first holds, keep crankin' to the left side of the slab and follow bolts up a thinner section to chains.
75 ft, bolts to chains
FA Jim Wilson, Scott Payne, Dan Fox, 1985

8. THE NOSE 5.9R ★★

Face and crack climb up a SW ridge of block. Begin on SW crner of the huge block and climb past two bolts (be wary of falling off before clipping 2nd bolt) then pull through a crack to gain an easy slab with one more bolt then chains.
Descent: Rap from Screamers anchors
75 ft, bolts and gear (tricky placements in flaring crack), to chains
FA Scott Payne, Jim Wilson, 1985

9. FLAME OUT/MUSCLE SCREW 5.11a/AO ★★★

This steep route on the east side of Multiple Screamers Block packs a huge pump. Aid to the first bolt (stick clip foot loops, jump, or put up a ladder to reach first holds) and then bring out the big guns. Pull through positive flakes and edges past slightly runout bolts to chains.
50 ft, bolts to chains
FA Jim Wilson, Scott Payne, Dan Fox, 1985

10. TOPROPE FLAKE 5.10R or TR ★★★

A distinct flake marks this route 20' right of *Flame Out*. It is most often climbed as a TR due to the desperate and unprotectable start. To set up a TR, climb any of the routes that ascend Multiple Screamers Block and rap to chains in middle of face.
50 ft, chains

11. BLOODY KNUCKLES 5.10b ★★

Finger crack that rises from the top of the Screamers Block and joins the easy chimney of Rich Man, a nice second pitch for any routes on the Block. Added here as it is accessed similarly to *Flame Out, Toprope Flake*.
Descent: Rap to block from chains.
45 ft, gear to chains
FA Scott Payne

RICH MAN POOR MAN

To the right of Multiple Screamers lies a pretty yellow spotted face that is bisected by several crack systems. Routes described left to right.

12. RICH MAN-POOR MAN 5.8+ ★★★

Line shoots through a crazy bombay chimney on left side of the south face. Named for the considerable gear that had to be purchased for the route, some of which was then lost.

P1: Follow seams to a hand crack and the tunnel into the chimney (pro is found deep within) escape right and build a belay on a small ramp to avoid rope drag. A must do.

P2: Step left and ascend a flake system with challenging feet that gives way to a chimney on the west side. Top out on a short slab to chain anchors. A wonderful complementary pitch to its predecessor.

Descent: Rap from the anchors to the top of Screamers Block and once more to get to the ground.
140 ft, gear to 4", chains
FA Van Alke, Chris Alke, 1977

13. AERIALIST 5.10c or 5.10/A2 ★

Crack and groove system just left of *Bolts to Nowhere*. Ascend seam to the top of P1 of *Rich Man*. Climb right to a bolt and aid out the second roof to join up with *Curly/ Stooge's* anchors.

Descent: Rap from Stooges anchor and scramble/downclimb (5.4) down east side.
140 ft, gear to 4", chains
FA Van Alke, Chris Alke, 1977
FFA Luke Evans, Ron Pedraza 2016

14. BOLTS TO NOWHERE 5.11a ★★

An enticing face climb that flows through bulges on positive but sometimes small edges. Boulder up to a triangular block, then commit for one move to gain well-spaced bolts. Can be supplemented with gear in horizontal cracks.
80 ft, small to medium gear, bolts to chains
FA Dan Fox, Jim Wilson, 1986.

15. GENTLE TOUCH/PINT OF BLOOD 5.11a ★

Start just right of *Bolts'* climb past three bolts to a vertical seam (crux) follow crack to *Stooges Ledge*.
Descent: Scramble downclimb (5.4) east side of ledge.
70 ft, 3 bolts gear to 3"
FA Jim Wilson, Dan Fox, 1986

16. FEUDING EGOS 5.10 ★

To find this climb, walk right of *Rich Man* to the end of the wall where a chimney starts. Up to your left is this short face climb that leads to the base of Stooges.
Descent: Scramble/downclimb (5.4) down east side of ledge or continue up the slabs.
40 ft, 3 bolts, anchor at blocks at base of Stooges
FA Scott Payne, Jim Wilson, 1986

STOOGES SLAB

On the lower east side of Right Rock a sloping ledge angles up and left to a small bowl-shaped slab. This 75' high slab has witnessed many desperate top ropes and shaky leads. The routes may be slabby but they are full of excitement, all the climbs end on the same chain anchors. A TR can be set up by scrambling up the west gully and coming over the top or finding a less distinct chimney on the east side. Routes are described left to right.

17. LEFT STOOGE/CURLY 5.8R

Face climb on rough rock on left side; a bit runout for some 5.8 leaders.
Descent: Rap/lower from chains to ledge; scramble/downclimb (5.4) down east side of ledge.
75 ft, 4 bolts, medium gear, to chains
FA Jim Wilson, Scott Payne, Dan Fox, 1985

18. MIDDLE STOOGE/MOE 5.10a ★★

Begin on a clean, thin crack in the middle of slab. Finish on heady friction moves past bolts. Move slightly left at the last bolt to gain easier ground. Direct finish is harder.
Descent: Rap/lower from chains to ledge; scramble/downclimb (5.4) down east side of ledge. Can also be walked off.
75 ft, small cams, nuts, 3 bolts to chains
FA Jim Wilson, Scott Payne, Dan Fox, 1985

9. RIGHT STOOGE/LARRY 5.9 ★★

Thin, right leaning crack on right side of a bowl that ends in cruxy moves past bolts or continue up seams then traverse left to chains.
Descent: Rap/lower from chains to ledge; scramble/downclimb (5.4) down east side of ledge
75 ft, 3 bolts, medium gear, chains
FA Jim Wilson, Scott Payne, Dan Fox, 1985

20. CORNER CRACK 5.6 ★

Crack system up right side of a slab ends on a ramp below and right of chains.
Descent: Rap/lower from chains to ledge; scramble/downclimb (5.4) down east side of ledge.
75 ft, gear to 3.5, chains
FA Jim Wilson, Scott Payne, Dan Fox, 1985

UPPER CRACKS/SEVEN SISTERS

On the right side of Right Rock are these 7 short cracks. They can be hard to find, and many a Sheep lifer has their memory of finding them for the first time. Start by going around the right side of Right Rock, scrambling up a dirty gully with 1 head-high 5th class move. Step left around a few boulders then up into the belay area. If you see the Stooges Slab off to your left, you're doing good, keep going up. These clean lines are fun practice routes that can be lead or toproped. A chain anchor lies on top of the 3 most popular cracks. Rappel from the chains or scramble down back to the base of the routes. Routes are described left to right.

21. LEFT CRACK 5.6 ★★
Flaring crack on the far left. Hand jam up to a double-crack system and a savior ledge. Step to the left and finish on a low-angle romp as they all do here at Seven Sisters.
60 ft, gear to 4", chains
FA Scott Payne, Jim Wilson, 1985

22. MIDDLE CRACK 5.8 ★
Love another straight-in crack fest courtesy of this sweet little nook. These are the twin cracks in the middle, don't miss the bear hug with easier terrain at the top. As of 2020 there was an arm-size tree about midway up, enjoy the jug or free pro.
60 ft, gear .3- 4", doubles in 1"-2" to chains
FA Scott Payne, Jim Wilson, 1985

23. RIGHT CRACK 5.7 ★★
Left-leaning crack on the right side of a sandy ledge in the upper part of the gully. Some grass was found in 2020, but it's easily climbed over, or cleanable. Straight up crack climbing. You'll find little help from the face.
60 ft, gear to 4", chains
FA Scott Payne, Jim Wilson, 1985

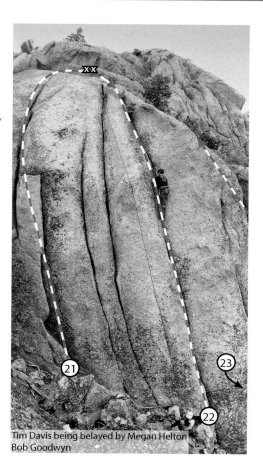

Tim Davis being belayed by Megan Helton
Bob Goodwyn

RIGHT ROCK SUMMIT BLOCK

Often overlooked, but kept in this guide for tradition, these routes can be added to extend your climbing adventure. The summit of Right Rock makes for some amazing views, and is a must do if you're hunting down all the summits of the Sheep spires. Descent: Walk north then east around Right Rock and you should be deposited somewhere below Seven Sisters, but many options exist.

24. CLAM SHELL SLAB 5.5
Above the Seven Sisters, is this low angle fissure. It will take gear, if you think you need it, make your way to the summit.
50', gear to 3", anchor unknown

25. SUMMIT DIHEDRAL
This route was lost to obscurity since the previous guide. But to inspire the true spirit of Sheep climbing, it'll be included here. Go get it.
60', gear and anchor unknown
FA Yours

Jo Straub on *School Daze 5.7*
Photo by Micheal Henderson

HAYSTACK ROCK

Haystack is a great practice area with a mixture of sport and trad routes. Better yet, it requires no hiking as you can drive right to the base. Included are a few great campsites, but in recent years, impact has been heavy. Please leave it better than you found it! This includes no new campfire rings, picking up others trash, and NOT driving off the road or beyond the pull outs.

To get here travel past the turn off to the main parking lot for Sheep Mountain Climbing. At 0.2 miles past this turn off, you'll encounter a large turn out to the right with a two-track taking off to the south. Follow this two-track for another 225 yards, and park at the base of the rock. The first area you will encounter is the Pat West Memorial side with the scramble to set up topropes right in front of you. The south and west facing routes are to the left. The North Face routes are to the right. Routes will be described as you encounter them.

Descent: If it's topropes you're after, the rock closest to the parking area can be scrambled just right above the Pat West Memorial Plaque to access the chains. This is also the best descent at the end of the day.

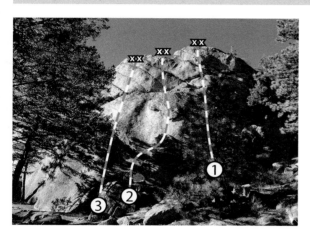

HAYSTACK

1. FINAL EXAM 5.10c ★★
This is the rightmost route and starts on the slab to the right of the memorial. Climb an increasingly blank slab through a few breaks to easier climbing and a ledge. Undercling and slap up and left, then top out on a thin slab. Technical and well bolted through the cruxes this will test your granite acumen. It is possible to reach the chains to set a TR, but they are near the edge so best to rappel or handline down to them.
55 ft, 6 bolts to chains
FA Dan Bachen, 2021

2. MEMORIAL ROUTE 5.10d ★
Start on the ledge above the memorial. Cool moves through the flakes (crowbar tested but still best to tread lightly) lead to a comfortable ledge. Step left and boulder up the steep wall until things ease up and you top out.
55 ft, 6 bolts to chains
FA Dan Bachen, 2021

3. SCHOOL DAZE 5.7 ★
Start on the southeast corner and pad up the pretty, bolted slab.
55 ft, 7 bolts to chains
FA Randall Green, 2002

4. LOOK MOM, NO HANDS 5.6–5.8 ★★
Between *School Daze* and *Broken Keg*, there are several topropes or easy trad lines available. They range in difficulty depending on how you wander, and the anchors can be reached by leading *School Daze* or scrambling to the top.
50 ft, TR or gear to 3"

5. BROKEN KEG BLUES 5.7 ★
On the southwest corner a thumb of rock leans against the face. Just to the right of this, boulder up to a ramp and clip bolts through this butt crack leading to a slabby arête.
50 ft, bolts to chains
FA Randall Green, 2002

6. BEER BARREL ARÊTE 5.7 ★
10 feet left of *Broken Keg* sits this slabby arête with cool knobs.
50 ft, bolts to chains
FA Randall Green, 2002

7. BEYOND BEER BARREL 5.8 ★★
Left of *Beer Barrel* and separated by a large dish, sits another arête climb. It can be thought provoking if you climb from the ground and stick to the arête. Bail into the dish for easier climbing.
50 ft, bolts to chains
FA Randal Green, 2002

Caleb Nylin on *Lounging Lizards 5.7*
Photo by Michael Henderson

NORTH FACE

These climbs are best approached by heading right, counterclockwise around Haystack, but they can also be approached from *Beer Barrel.*

8. JAM IT HARDER 5.6 ★

Sloping hand crack, very short, but a great first crack lead. Undeclared in the first guidebook, *Jam it Harder* is named in memory of a good friend who went out with a buddy to learn the art of crack climbing from an old timer. While he and his friends were trying it out and finding little confidence in the new techniques, the old timer kept telling them to "Jam it harder!". When my friend looked to his buddy who was ferociously stabbing his hands into a crack until they bled, he wondered if climbing would be his thing...
40 ft, gear to 3"

9. WHO PUT THOSE BOLTS THERE? 5.9 ★★

Lieback start to a 2-bolt finish. Starts in a right facing corner, right of *Jam it Harder.*
45 ft, gear to .75", 2 bolts to chains

10. GRIME TIME PRIME TIME 5.8 ★

Right of *Who Put Those Bolts,* is this grimy crack. It starts steep with solid hands to a slot. Finishes with a blocky overhang.
45 ft, gear to chains

11. LOUNGING LIZARDS 5.7 ★

Left of *Mello* and in a northeast facing corner, this dihedral pulls through some tough moves leading to your choice of cracks, pumpy and fun. Continue up the wide crack above to chains. Best sandbag on the face.
45 ft, gear to 3", chain anchor

12. MELLO YELLOW 5.10a ★★

On the north side of Haystack, a layback flake and crack system split a beautiful yellow face. Short, strenuous, and deserving of your work.
45 ft, gear to 3", chain anchor

SHINGLE BUTTE

This new crag receives nice evening sun and is a quick walk from the car making for an easy and enjoyable after-work crag with some great climbs and a variety of grades. There is currently only climbing on the Evening Rock described below, but a few more spots in the vicinity look promising.

Although the crag is named after the nearby Shingle Butte it is actually a bit northwest of the actual summit. To find the crag leave the small pullout heading west. Things quickly get confusing from here. There are a maze of social trails from hunters and hikers. The best way to navigate your way to the crag is to follow trails that go west and slightly north until you hit a barbed wire fence line for the neighboring private land. Once you arrive at this fence line the rest of the approach is relatively easy. Walk west along the fence and follow the most obvious trail which eventually leaves the fence and goes up and through a small pass with Shingle Butte on your left and a small rocky point on your right. Continue on the trail downhill and past a corner post. The trail enters an old clear cut here. Keep your eye out for some rock poking out from a high point downhill of the trail. Once you can barely see the rock, there will also be a flat spot and the trail/old two track will veer right. Do not continue on the trail and instead leave the trail where some red rocks are strewn about on the ground near a gully. Stay left of the gully and head straight toward the rock formation on the horizon. You will only be able to see a few small boulders until you start to wrap around the hill and find the large west-facing crag walls. You will arrive at the base of a striking arête and route *A Better Place*.

SHINGLE BUTTE PARKING

SHINGLE BUTTE CLIMBING

EVENING ROCK

This is the first crag encountered in the Shingle Butte area. This nugget of solid batholith granite will get you excited when you lay eyes on it. At its largest this rock is approximately 80 feet tall. Routes listed from right to left as you encounter them. Most routes can be toproped by walking around the back of the formation.

1. A BETTER PLACE 5.13b ★★
Climb the beautiful overhanging arête graced with City of Rocks style edges.
60' 7 bolts to chains
FA Hermes Lynn

2. EVENING STROLL 5.10d ★
Climb the obvious off-width crack which turns into a chimney.
60' gear and a few bolts. Bring a 5 or 6 inch piece for the start and some small gear for the chimney. The really wide stuff has a couple of bolts.
FA Hermes Lynn

3. OLD AID ROUTE
There was an anchor placed above this splitter and some fixed pitons in the crack. Will probably go free at 5.13
60' pins and small wires
FA Unknown

4. NIGHT CAP 5.11c/d ★★

Start in a right leaning crack and work out onto face holds out a bulge. Climb left and follow the bolt line to the top. There is an unmistakable hole half way up. The climb is characterized by shallow dished and edges.

75' medium gear to bolts

FA Hermes Lynn

5. FORMAL ATTIRE 5.10b ★

Climb a left-facing dihedral reaching a ledge at mid height. Step off the ledge making some committing moves protected by small wires. Climb just right of a thin crack on face holds along the arête. Reach over to place thin protection in the crack on your left.

70 ft, standard rack with extra small cams and nuts. There is a two-bolt rappel anchor.

FA Hermes Lynn, Alex Street

6. SCUTTLEBUG 5.9 TR ★★

Just left of *Formal Attire*. Climb a low-angle arête with cool holds until you reach a ledge at mid height. The upper part is a nice slab that forces you to weave your way up the rock. Crux is about halfway up the slab.

70 ft, use anchors for *Formal Attire* or build your own.

FA Hermes Lynn

Caleb Berghoff on *#11 Unknown Vision Quest Wall 5.10b*
Photo by Michael Henderson

WELCOME to Indian Creek. This canyon offers roadside sport climbing on high quality limestone. The routes are in a narrow canyon west of the Graymont Lime mine on Indian Creek Road. The unbroken portions of the cliffs often are not more than 100 ft tall and the rock is generally excellent, a compact quality abundant edges and pockets. Many cracks are surprisingly solid and suitable for natural protection. A stick clip can be helpful on numerous routes. Most of the cliffs are on public land managed by the Bureau of Land Management (BLM).

Indian Creek Road is a busy road, providing access into the Elkhorn Mountains for miners, hunters, and Sunday drivers. Watch for truck traffic and park well off the road in the parking area located about 200 yards west of the main canyon. Always use caution while climbing routes near the busy road.

Take care to stay on established trails to avoid erosion problems and general wear and tear on the fragile soils and plants. In the spring ticks can be a found here especially on the approach trails where weeds and brush have encroached. Take care to diligently search yourself, your pets and packs.

CAMPING
Primitive camping is available up the road a mile or so look for pullouts. There's also pay camping on the south side of Canyon Ferry Lake. Townsend has all the amenities including great subs and pizza at the Full Belly Deli on Highway 12.

HISTORY
Indian Creek would not be the area we enjoy today if not for the hard work of Ron Brunckhorst and his family. In the mid-1980s Ron started establishing routes here and has a real love for this place. Others came after or with Ron: Gerald Brunkhorst, Keith Brunckhorst, Debra Pratt, Bob Hicks, Randall Green, Bill Dockins, Kirsten Drumheller, Paul Travis, Jake Mergenthaler and more all contributed to the climbing here.

GETTING THERE
From Helena go southeast toward Townsend on US Highway 287 about 30 miles to Indian Creek Road. When traveling southeast from Helena, the turnoff is just before the highway bridge that crosses the Missouri River. Once on Indian Creek Road, cross the railroad tracks and take the right fork at the "Y" intersection of River Road and Indian Creek Road. At about 3 miles watch for signs designating the left turn (parking area on the left) for Indian Creek Road, which diverges left from the Graymont Lime plant road just past a transfer station. The road then winds southeastward one mile down into the canyon past old mine tailings and under two bridges used by the Graymont Lime mine. Once under the last bridges, the cliffs of the canyon become obvious ahead.

ORGANIZATION OF DESCRIPTIONS
Indian Creek areas are listed on the north side of the road first, starting at the eastern end/down creek climbs: Flume, Cowboy Wall, heading up towards Vision Quest Wall, finishing with Industrial, Peace, and Big Horn walls.
Next are the South side of the road crags starting with the eastern/down creek climbs at The Chief and Lake Scouting crags heading up towards Medicine Hole Wall, across from Vision Quest Wall.

INDIAN CREEK PARKING

Bighorn, Peace, Industrial

Parking

N

Medicine
Hole Walls

Vision Quest Wall

Bear Claw Buttress / Wall

War Wall

Sacred Grounds

Wintering Ground Walls

Upper Chief

Flaming
Arrow

The Chief

Coyote Buttress

Lake Scout Crags

Cowboy, Flume, Wind

FLUME WALL (NOT PICTURED)

The first wall you can see when entering Indian Creek canyon. And old flume is hanging from historic mining up the canyon. One old TR Route and no other climbing is on this wall.

WIND BUTTRESS

The rock is located left of Flume Wall or right of the Cowboy Wall on the north side of the road. Cross the creek at the cairn and ascend gentle ridge to the base of the wall. Or traverse around from Cowboy Wall.

1. WIND DANCER 5.10b ★★
Route follows a gray stripe on the left side of brown wall. Scramble up to a ledge at mid-height to avoid a rotten layer. Belay from the first bolt.
45 ft, 5 bolts to chains
FA Ron Brunckhorst, Bob Hicks, 1995

2. BLOOD BROTHER 5.10d ★★★
Excellent, sustained overhanging line right of *Wind Dancer*.
40 ft, 4 bolts to cold shuts
FA Randall Green, Laurent Huber, 1995

COWBOY WALL

This area has a high concentration of fun moderate routes but there's a catch; the bottom of the routes contain dubious and flakey rock (like your ex). With a little discernment you can have a ball on this sunny crag. Cowboy Wall is around the first big right-hand corner after the mine bridge, past the Flume Wall. Cross the creek and head towards the cliff about 70 yards from the road. Routes are described right to left.

1. SPACE COWBOY 5.10b ★★
Start on the far right side of the wall, climb over a tricky black bulge to finish in a tricky dihedral.
70 ft, 7 bolts to chains
FA Jake Mergenthaler, 1998

2. HANG 'EM HIGH 5.11b ★★
Start on steep broken rock with big holds and work up an irregular flake. Tackle a clean gray bulge to access better rock above.
75 ft, bolts to chains
FA Jake Mergenthaler, 1998

3. REDNECK 5.11b ★
Climb the steep brown and fragile face that surmounts a technical bulge at mid-height and ends on solid gray rock.
55 ft, 5 bolts to chains
FA Jake Mergenthaler, 1998

4. HIGH LONESOME 5.11c ★
Climb a broken pillar just right of a guano-filled cave. This climb has poor rock on the lower third but gets better up high.
70 ft, 8 bolts to chains
FA Jake Mergenthaler, 1998

5. LIMESTONE COWBOY 5.9 ★★
The left most climb on the wall. Begin on a ramp and tread left onto the fun main face. Small cave just left of the start.
75 ft, 7 bolts to chains
FA Jake Mergenthaler, 1998

6. BUCKAROO 5.10a
Variation to *Limestone Cowboy*. Climb the overhanging corner crack out of the cave to the second bolt of *Limestone Cowboy*.
75 ft, 6 bolts and small to medium gear to chains
FA Ron Brunckhorst, 1999

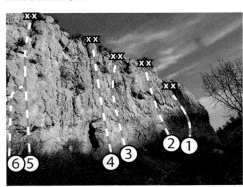

COYOTE BUTTRESS

This buttress is down from the Wintering Ground buttress and uses a similar approach. Twenty yards down from the culvert, venture into the brush and cross the creek. *Trickster* begins 20' from the creek. Good mix of steep and slab climbing.

1. TRICKSTER 5.8+ ★★

Climb on the right side up an indistinct pillar on marginal gray rock. As the name implies, the climbing is tricky to keep 5.8 but fun. Stay left to avoid a large detached block of rotten rock halfway up.
80 ft, 6 bolts to welded cold shuts
FA Randall Green, 1994

2. RABID DOG 5.10a ★

Fun route up the left side of the broken pillar. Start between trees, going up and over exciting bulges then step right to join *Trickster* (shared anchor).
80 ft, 7 bolts to shared anchor with *Trickster*.
FA Jake Mergenthaler, 2000

3. JUNGLE WARFARE 5.10 ★

Begin on a short pillar heading up steep face climbing to a fun techy slab (yes they do exist) then finish on a steeper section.
80 ft, 10 bolts to anchor
FA Jake Mergenthaler, 2000

4. HUCK FINN AND INJUN JOE 5.11c ★★

Begin on the far left side of wall, crank up small pockets on tan rock to a delicate crux and small edges. Cool slab moves keep it caffeinated to the end.
75 ft, 7 bolts to chains
FA Kevin Hutchinson and Mike Anglin, 2000

5. HOWLING DOG 5.10b ★

Climb begins on the nearly hidden southwest-facing wall left/west of main buttress. Original climb was toproped but can be lead on gear as well.
65 ft, gear to 3", chains
FA Randall Green, 1998

WINTERING GROUNDS

Down from the Bear Claw Wall and Sacred Grounds Buttress. Some of the routes are on the road. Climbs are listed from right to left.

1. INDIAN SUMMER 5.9 ★★★

Cross the creek near the culvert and head up a faint trail East along the cliff. This fine airy route is one of the best cold weather routes at Indian Creek. Scramble up a 6-foot step in a corner to a ledge with a single chain belay anchor. Traverse right past 4 bolts on a gray slab. Variation start is climbing in the corner below the first bolt using good gear for protection.

60 ft, 4 bolts to chains
FA Ron Brunckhorst, Keith Brunckhorst, Bob Hicks, 1991

2. ROAD KILL ARÊTE 5.9 R

Rare trad route immediately right of *Pale Face* on an arête. Start with a finger crack to a small roof then go left up the arête. Rumored as dirty, loose, hard to protect, and scary.

60 ft, gear to chains
FA Ron Brunckhorst, 1998

3. PALE FACE 5.9+ ★

This route is on the north side of the road just before the culvert. Start in a dull corner with a crack to a gain a blunt gray arête with a steep finish.

55 ft, 3 bolts, gear to 3", welded cold shuts.
FA Scott Payne, Randall Green, Theresa Green, 1995

4. WHISPERING WOMEN 5.11a ★★

Give this excellent steep slab left of *Pale Face* a try. I have fond memories of bolting this with two great friends in the dark using a borrowed generator, a $20 drill and a thrift store table lamp. Somehow the route ended up OK.

55 ft, 6 bolts to chains
FA Jake Mergethaler, Kim Mergenthaler, Dave Kelly, 1997

Bob Goodwyn on *Pale Face* 5.9+
Photo by Megan Helton

SACRED GROUNDS BUTTRESS
The next buttress downstream of Bear Claw Wall with two popular moderates.

1. WOUNDED KNEE 5.9+ ★
More direct start to *Twelve Nations*.
12 bolts to chains.
FA Terry Kennedy and Ron Brunkhorst, 2008/2009

2. TWELVE NATIONS 5.8 ★
Slightly easier start. Can be made slightly easier at the top by going left at a bush or finishing right on a 5.9 crux.
12 bolts to chains
FA Ron Brunkhorst, 2009

BEAR CLAW WALL
Short, low-angled face that is split with numerous grooves on the north side of the road. Bushes at the base obscure some of the cliff. A path leads around the right side of the face and up to the top to access anchors.

1. BEAR CLAW WALL LEFT 5.2-5.6 ★★
Follow low-angled grooves or narrow faces between grooves. Excellent place to introduce beginning climbers to limestone. Two top rope anchor bolts are set on a rock about 20' back from the top edge approximately in the middle of the face. Take cord or long slings for rigging an anchor system from the bolts past the top edge. Safe and easy to scramble up the gully to a ledge with the anchors.
70 ft, bolts at top for setting anchors
FA Ron Brunckhorst, Benita Brunckhorst, 1991

2. BEAR CUB 5.6 ★★
Great climb for beginning leaders. Stick clip the first bolt for the crux. A second well protected crux is encountered at the bulge near the top. 30' right of the toprope routes.
60 ft, 6 bolts

3. INCISOR 5.5 ★★
Fun short route up the gully on the last little slab. Climbing variations available on both sides of the bolts.
30 ft, 4 bolts

Will Maddock on *Bear Claw Wall*
Photo by Brad Maddock

BEAR CLAW BUTTRESS
The road side of Bear Claw Wall.

1. POCKET HUNTER 5.10b ★★★
Climb the rounded arête on slippery pockets with a
sporty slab finish. One of the most often-climbed routes
West of Bear Claw Wall.
50 ft, 4 bolts to chains
FA Ron Brunkhorst, Gerald Brunckhorst, 1990

2. MAMMA BEAR 5.10a ★★
Climb up the crack and pull through the roof. Route
eases off then gives a committing finish.
50 ft, 5 bolts to chains
FA Danielle Noonan (Mama Bear), Dan Bachen, Andrew Schrader, 2020

Andrew Schrader on *Pocket Hunter 5.10b*
Photo by Brad Maddock

ON RON BRUNKHORST
by Brad Maddock

Ron Brunckhorst was raised in the small town of White Sulphur Springs, MT, and spent much of his youth exploring the outdoors with his family. Ron, his brother, Gerald, and his dad, Keith, would take to the hills of the nearby Crazy Mountains and Castle Mountains and scramble up rugged peaks and rock formations until they ran into more technical terrain. In their early teens, Ron and his brother found a "How to Rock Climb" book at the White Sulphur Springs library, and it was then that they became inspired to take their scrambling to the next level. Equipped with a clothesline, a half dozen chocks, and the limestone cracks near town, they set out looking for their first projects and never looked back. By the time Ron was 16, he and his brother had added the Grand Teton and Granite Peak to their climbing resume.

When Ron graduated from high school, he moved to Dillon, MT to attend Western Montana College. It was there that he met his mentor and climbing partner, Craig Zaspel. Craig was a mathematics professor at the college and was well known in the early Montana climbing scene. He climbed with the likes of Jack Tackle and established many routes around the state. By the time Ron graduated college, with the partnership of Craig and many other climbers, he had many impressive first ascents around the state and was well on his way to becoming a household name in Montana climbing. A few years after graduating from college, Ron decided to try his hand at guiding and has now written and documented some of the most important books on Montana rock and ice climbing and discovered numerous climbing areas around the state.

One such climbing area is the limestone canyon of Indian Creek, near Townsend, MT. On the way home from ice climbing Crow Creek Falls in the Elkhorn Mountains, Ron decided to take a different route home instead of his usual route through Radersburg. When he first laid eyes on the virgin walls of Indian Creek he remembers thinking to himself "this is crazy! If only we could place bolts here" a reference to the fact that Ron didn't have a hammer drill at the time. During the early years of climbing in the canyon, the road and the canyon were much different than what we see today. The road was an old, narrow two-track and the creek culverts were small, causing the creek to flood the entire canyon in the winter with wall-to-wall ice between the cliff walls. After the road improvements, a few climbs were erased by road crews, and a few of the climbs near Sacred Grounds lost the first bolt of the climb due to the amount of fill brought in to improve the road in that area. Today, Indian Creek boasts over 80 climbs on generally solid gray-blue limestone, with Ron, Gerald, and Keith establishing many of the best routes.

Ron currently lives in Wilsall, MT with his wife Alana, still can climb 5.12, is developing new areas around the state, and gets out on alpine adventures regularly. We all owe Ron a debt of gratitude for his vision, hard work, and financial investment in developing climbing in Indian Creek Canyon and other areas throughout the state.

VISION QUEST WALL

The tallest continuous face on the north side of the road offers high quality roadside cragging, Routes go right to left, starting from the gully up from *Pocket Hunter*.

3. DREAM CATCHER 5.10a/b ★★
Up the gully between *Peyote* and *Pocket Hunter* on the west side; Start with steep pockets leading to fun climbing above.
50 ft, 5 bolts, sling through hueco to chains. Sling may be old or missing.
FA Ron Brunckhorst, Debra Pratt, 1993

4. MIDNIGHT RIDER 5.11a/b ★
This short line near a black water streak has some burly moves and makes you think as you flame out. I'll never forget the day I watched a heroic climber cruise it rope soloing. When asked him about the grade he said, "About .10a," I hate hard people.
45 ft, 4 bolts to chains
FA Jake Mergenthaler, Paul Travis, 1996

5. SNAKE DANCE 5.11/b ★
An airy route right of *Peyote* and on the right side of the Vision Wall. Pull up the blunt arête and into a shallow dish (crux) then cruise up the great upper section with a dirty ledge at ⅔ height.
90 ft, 10 bolts to chains
FA Ron Brunckhorst, 1999

6. WINDIGO 5.10+ ★
Must-do mixed route, can be finished into *Peyote* or done as its own pitch.
50 ft, gear protected. Tricams, medium cams helpful.
FA Olin Erickson, Ron Brunckhorst, 1996

7. PEYOTE 5.11c ★★★
One of the best routes in the area, it shares the same start as *Vision Quest*. At a ledge, the line angles up and right through sustained and pumpy underclings and lay-backs. After a no-hands rest comes the gritty part; keep your wits as you pad your way to the chains on buttery drip pockets on a smooth face.
85 ft, 11 bolts to chains
FA Ron Brunckhorst, 1994

8. VISION QUEST 5.11a ★
This classic route begins on the road under an obvious long line of bolts. A bouldery start guards easier climbing up to a ledge. Stay left for *Vision Quest* (left of *Peyote*) and tread up a cool face to a short, thin crux and continue up on a crack to chains.
100 ft, 14 bolts to chains
FA Ron Brunckhorst, 1992

9. NATIVE AMERICAN 5.11b ★★★
P1: Crack line in shallow left facing dihedral left of *Vision Quest*. (5.8, 50 ft)
P2: This wandering mixed line starts with a 15' traverse to a bolt, then up and left to more bolts. Next angle right to a gear protected dihedral, through some tricky moves that lead to the bolt-protected finish. (5.11b)
Double ropes help with rope drag if doing *Native American* as one long pitch.
80 ft, bolts and gear to chains
FA Ron Brunckhorst, 1992, 1997

10. WHITE HAWK 5.10c/d ★★
40 yards up the road from *Vision Quest*.
Start at the base of a gray slab; this is a thought-provoking fun route on cool holds and quality rock. Named after a spiraling white hawk flying above the first ascent, being belayed by Mr. Phil White Hawk.
70 ft, 8 bolts to chains
FA Ron Brunckhorst, 1995

11. UNKNOWN 5.10b ★★
20' up from *White Hawk*. Fun sporty slab climbing as *White Hawk* but on better holds. Steep and fun finish.
70 ft, bolts to chains
FA Patrick Casey

12. COUNTING COUP 5.10- ★★
50 yards up from *White Hawk*. Right bolt line that joins into *Finger Sacrifice* will keep your fingers happy. Small cam can be used before the first bolts.
4 bolts to chains
FA Ron Brunckhorst, 2012

13. FINGER SACRIFICE 5.11c ★
50 yards up from *White Hawk*. Left bolted line is a short face route that is strong and slick. Shares anchors with *Counting Coup*.
25 ft, 4 bolts to chains
FA Ron Brunckhorst, 2012

Paul Berry on *White Hawk 5.10+*
Photo by Andrew Schrader

BIG HORN WALL

This is the first clean gray wall up from the parking lot after the first corner. Take game trails north off the road up to this wall with large trees on the right side. Great south facing cold-weather wall. Anchor access for *Shape Shifter* and *Gold Digger* can be reached by scrambling up a gully left of the wall. Climbs are listed right to left.

1. **GOLD DIGGER** 5.10a ★
Start left of a golden alcove and climb through a water trough with chert.
50 ft, 5 bolts to chains. TR anchor access available.
FA Olin Erickson, Ron Brunckhorst, 2007

2. **SHAFT SHIFTER** 5.7+ ★
Great moderate route that climbs into a right facing open book. During the FA, two interested bighorn sheep walked within 50' of the belayer and scampered on to the same route to get a closer look at the "hoof" gear that enabled him to take a more direct line. Shares anchors with *Gold Digger*.
50 ft, 3 bolts, gear to chains, medium gear recommended. TR anchor access available.
FA Ron Brunckhorst, Alan Mueller-Brunckhorst, Deborah Pratt, Jerry Furtney, 2007

3. **THE SHEEPEATERS** 5.8
Quality climb to shared anchors with *The Little Bighorn*.
5 bolts to chains
FA Ron Brunckhorst, 2010

4. **THE LITTLE BIGHORN** 5.9
Blocky route with some loose rock to shared anchors of *The Sheepeaters*.
5 bolts to chains
FA Ron Brunckhorst, 2010

INDUSTRIAL WALL
Across the gully and up the creek from the Peace Wall.

1. INDUSTRIAL DISEASE 5.11a
This tall route starts left of the cave and leads to a thin upper section.
70 ft, 9 bolts to chains
FA Randall Green, Chris Alke, 2003

2. UNNAMED 5.8
Left-hand route leads to shared chains with *Industrial Disease*.
70 ft, bolts to chains
FA Randall Green, Jake Mergenthaler, 2000

PEACE WALL
A steep gully separates the Peace Wall just down from the Industrial Wall which has two route and a faded peace sign on the right side. Found ~¼ mile up from the parking lot.

1. CRAZY HORSE 5.11a ★★
A few stout moves on small crimps past the first bolt leads to moderate slab climbing to the chains. Many better routes at Indian but a good candidate for a first 5.11 if you're chasing grades.
70 ft, 9 bolts to chains
FA Ron Brunckhorst, Deborah Pratt, Jerry Furtney, 2007

2. UNKNOWN 5.10a ★
Technical climbing down low quickly eases to moderate slab climbing.
70 ft, bolts to chains

LAKE SCOUT CRAGS

These are the first crags on the left south side of the road as you're driving in. Across from the Wind Buttress approach and down from the Cowboy Wall. Walk up game trails on scree slopes to the Lake Scout Crags.

1. LAKE SCOUTING 5.9 ★★
This fun varied crack splits the left crag. Steep start eases off as the route goes.
50 ft, gear to 4", no fixed anchors
FA Kevin Hutchinson, Mike Anglin, 2000

2. BLACKFOOT WARRIOR 5.11a/b ★★
Great route with a high first bolt. **BRING A STICK CLIP OR DO THE BOULDER MOVE.**
50 ft, 5 bolts to chains
FA Ron Brunckhorst, 2009

3. LAST LIGHT 5.11 TR
This top rope route is on the right crag in the water trough.
50 ft, no fixed anchors
FA Kevin Hutchinson, Mike Anglin, 2000

4. THE GERONIMO FACTOR 5.11a
Sustained climb with a low crux. Bring a stick clip or tall climbers can clip the first bolt from the right.
65 ft, 6 bolts
FA Kevin Hutchinson, Mike Anglin, 2000

THE CHIEF EAST FACE

The Chief Wall holds a handful of cool routes generally characterized by interesting pockets on good rock. From the Vision Wall walk down the road for 150 yards and look for a steep trail that ascends a roadcut on the right. Follow this to slightly rounded gray wall 50 yards up the hill. Routes are described right to left. Trail typically leads just below *Chief Big Pockets*.

1. CHIEF PLENTY POCKETS 5.9 ★★

Farthest right of the five routes on the Chief. Scramble and stem off blocks to gain good holds on brown rock. May be useful to stick clip first bolt. Route angles up and left to join *Chief Big Pockets* anchors.
80 ft, 7 bolts to anchors
FA Scott Payne, Randall Green, 1995

2. OPEN PROJECT 5.12?

Route on overhanging white rock between *Plenty Pockets* and *Big Pockets*. Probably has been sent. Route may have poor rock.

3. CHIEF BIG POCKETS 5.10a ★★

Excellent route was the first done at Indian Creek. Climb exhilarating pockets on excellent rock. 5.10 variation start is going right of the first bolt.
60 ft, 6 bolts to chains
FA Ron Brunckhorst, Gerald Brunckhorst, 1990

4. CHIEF LITTLE POCKETS 5.11a ★★

Steep face left of *Chief Big Pockets*. Fun, sequential and pumpy.
60 ft, 6 bolts to chains
FA Randall Green, Pippen Wallace, 1994

5. CHIEF EMPTY POCKETS 5.11+ R

Bulging face left of *Chief Little Pockets*. Hard crux at first bolt leads to easier climbing, than steep bulging finish. Be wary of ledge fall potential. Some stick clip 1st and 2nd bolt.
50 ft, 4 bolts to chains
FA Hunter Coleman, Susan Zazzali, 1995

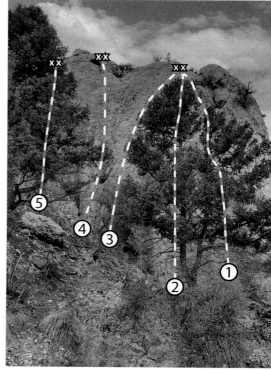

THE UPPER CHIEF
Above and east of The Chief Wall lies a short, clean cliff. Routes are described right to left.

1. DADDY LONG LEGS 5.8+
Stem a wide chimney on the right side of the wall.
45 ft, 4 bolts to chains
FA Ron Brunckhorst, Debra Pratt, 1999

2. PAINTED PONY 5.9 ★★
Steep climbing up a gray face. Perfect route for breaking into the grade.
50 ft, 5 bolts to chains
FA Ron Brunckhorst, Debra Pratt, 1999

3. WOOD GITTER 5.10a ★
Climb a tricky but fun arête on left side of the wall.
50 ft, 5 bolts to chains
FA Ron Brunckhorst, Debra Pratt, 1999

FLAMING ARROW SPIRE
Small formation above The Chief accessed from the top of The Chief climbs. Continue left to a gully, squirm through a hole behind a large chockstone and scramble to the top. Look for an arrow-shaped spire just south of the main wall.

1. FLAMING ARROW 5.8/9 ★
Short spire uphill from The Chief. Has a nice atmosphere.
30 ft, 3 bolts to chains
FA Ron Brunckhorst, Kieth Brunckhorst, 1998

2. THE SHAFT 5.7
An ugly crack on the east side of the spire.
30 ft, gear to 4", chains
FA Ron Brunckhorst, 1998

BILLBOARD WALL
Historical graffiti advertised "stables and feed" in Townsend many decades ago. An old Indian Creek classic, *Sacred Grounds* was located here but became history with widening the road. In the interest of climbers and respecting the BLM please **DO NOT BOLT, CLIMB, OR DEFACE THIS WALL.**

WAR WALL

War Wall is a continuation of the Billboard Wall. It stands across the creek from the Vision Wall and faces southwest. Access via a trail across the road from *Pocket Hunter*. Routes are listed left to right.

1. WAR PAINT 5.9 ★★
Ascend a slippery, left-leaning crack with heavy varnish and finish on a clean gray face.
60 ft, 3 bolts, med gear to chains
FA Ron Brunckhorst, 1991

2. WAR PARTY 5.11+
This route combines the start of *War Paint* and the finish of *War Path*. Double ropes are helpful for the wandering route.
70 ft, 8 bolts, med gear to chains
FA Ron Brunckhorst, 1993

3. WAR PATH 5.12a ★★★
Begin on a bouldery start get ready to crimp down through the first crux. Hold on as it gets steeper on cool pinches. After a short rest, rock on past the second crux. Don't puke. The first time I redpointed this route I puked at the anchors, my unfortunate wife was belaying me. I hope you have a better time on this wonderful climb. Most stick clip the 2nd bolt.
70 ft, 8 bolts to anchors
FA Ron Brunckhorst, 1991

4. CHIEF PLENTY COUP VISION 5.12
Shares same start as *War Path* and exits right (~5.11 traverse) to a water groove leading to the anchors. Take #5 stopper for crack between 5th and 6th bolts.
70 ft, 9 bolts (optional #5 stopper) to chains
FA Ron Brunckhorst, 1993

5. BIG HOLE BATTLEFIELD 5.12c ★★
This climb stands on the far right side of the wall as the trail beneath the cliff begins to ascend a hill. Sustained thin edges on an overhanging wall of white and gray rock.
60 ft, 5 sparse bolts to chains
FA Bill Dockins, Kristen Drumheller, 1994

6. BROWN EYED GIRL 5.10c/d ★
A narrow chimney splits The War Wall to the right. Climb just left of the chimney on marginal rock. Tread through a steeper section and keep it together to the top.
60 ft, bolts to clip-and-lower anchor
FA Jake Mergenthaler, Lance Beckert, 2001

7. TRAIL OF TEARS 5.11- ★
Route shares start with *Thunderbird* and traverses left on clean gray rock. After several bolts the line soars to the top. Route is named in remembrance of the Cherokee Nation being moved and what followed.
75 ft, 8 bolts to chains
FA Ron Brunckhorst, 1997

8. THUNDER BIRD 5.10a/b PG13 ★★
Bouldery start above the first bolt to easier terrain above. 10a start right of the bolt line which leads to an awkward reachy second clip with ground fall potential.
50 ft, 4 bolts to chains. Stick clip is recommended to avoid falling onto bolder at start.
FA Ron Brunckhorst, Bob Hicks, 1994

9. SKIN WALKER 5.10b/c R
Start right of *Thunder Bird* on the left leaning line. An indistinct crack greets you at mid-height and leads to fun climbing above. Top is runout easier fifth-class terrain.
50 ft, 4 bolts, gear to 2", chains TCUs and TriCams useful.
FA Ron Brunckhorst, Gerald Brunckhorst, 1993

10. DEFIANCE 5.11d
Next line right of *Skin Walker* on bulging gray face. The route is a 25-foot boulder problem with easy climbing above. Hard climbers can place gear in thin crack on the overhanging lower third of route or stick clip the first bolt.
45 ft, 3 bolts, small gear to chains
FA Randall Green, 1995

11. LEANING TREE 5.8 ★
Short face starts just uphill from *Defiance* under leaning dead tree (widow-maker) shares same chain anchor with *Defiance*.
45 ft, 2 bolts, small to medium cams to chains
FA Ron Brunckhorst, Bob Hicks, 1995

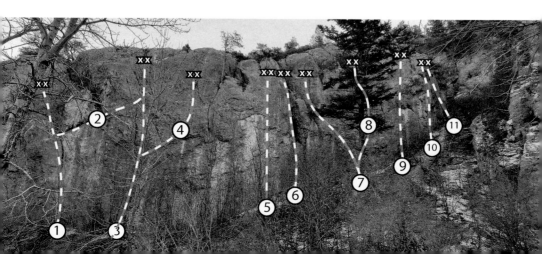

MEDICINE HOLE WALL

This wall is located directly across the road from the Vision Wall. Look for a steep path that descends from the road embankment and plunges through the brush to the base of the cliff. Routes are listed left to right.

1. LITTLE BIG MAN 5.10d ★★

This fun little climb packs a big punch. Climb a steep face with wide groove at the top. Cooler climb on a hot afternoon.

30 ft, 3 bolts to chains
FA Ron Brunckhorst, 1996

2. REDBONE 5.10d ★

Start in the *Medicine Hole* corner and stem out left up this short beautiful face on powerful sidepulls and incuts. "The first climb I ever bolted. It was named after an unfortunate encounter that I had while playing a basketball tourney on the reservation. That story is longer and better than the climb."

25 ft, 3 bolts to chains
FA Jake Mergenthaler

3. MEDICINE HOLE 5.10a ★★

Begin in an open-book corner (gear) through a 5.9+ roof and exit onto a ledge. Lower off this anchor for a short pitch or continue up past a bolt into a layback crack (gear). Ends nicely with a delicate, bolted traverse and airy move pulling to chains. Be wary of your rope getting caught on the ledge. Some recommend 2 single rope rappels.

100 ft, 6 bolts, med. gear to chains.
FA Ron Brunckhorst, Gerald Brunckhorst, 1993

4. MEDICINE MAN 5.11b ★★

Climb the lower dihedral of *Medicine Hole* to a ledge system with first set of chains (gear, 1 bolt); move right to a bolt, ascend the bulging face with dramatic and powerful moves to join upper part of *Witch Doctor*.

90 ft, 7 bolts to chains
FA Ron Brunckhorst, Todd Madson, 1995

5. WITCH DOCTOR 5.11b ★★★

This is a variation to Medicine Man that allows you to climb it in one great and continuous pitch. Start in a wooded alcove marked by a guano-filled cavity in the rock. Scream up sharp rock with crimpy clips (some stick clip to second bolt). This leads to fun stemming up a memorable feature. Finally connect with *Medicine Man*.

90 ft, bolts to chains
FA Jake Mergenthaler, Kim Mergenthaler, 2003

6. BUFFALOED 5.11a ★

This route is 75' right of *Witch Doctor* or, 20' left of the blunt arête of *Can't Roller Skate*.
Broken face route that angles up and left and finishes with runout climbing after the traverse.

80 ft, 7 bolts to chains. Shared anchors with *Can't Roller Skate*.
FA Ron Brunckhorst, 1998

7. CAN'T ROLLER SKATE IN A BUFFALO HERD 5.8 ★★★
Follows the prow of buttress left of *Cocalahishkit's* gully. Start on a steep section just right of *Buffaloed* and wander up the blunt arête. Grab a beer and enjoy the old song "Can't Roller Skate in a Buffalo Herd."
70 ft, 8 bolts to chains
FA Ron Brunckhorst, Kieth Brunckhorst, 1998

8. COCALAHISHKIT 5.8 ★★★
The indigenous name means "River of the road to the Buffalo." A good beginner delicate slab climb on right wall of gully right of *Can't Roller Skate*.
75 ft, 7 bolts Sling the tree in middle of route to chains
FA Ron Brunckhorst, Debra Pratt, 1993

9. TA-CHESLI 5.11a (Not Pictured)
Sioux for "a lot of bull." 150' up an exposed trail from *Cocalahishkit* on a gray face. Best to stay slightly right of second and third bolt to avoid bad rock on the left.
50 ft, 5 bolts to welded cold shuts
FA Randall Green, Scott Payne, 1995

10. RESERVATIONS 5.9/5.11 (Not Pictured)
Overhanging wall right of *Ta-chesli* and left of a packrat infested chimney. Belay from the low bolt and stick clip the first bolt. 5.8 if steming to the back wall.
40 ft, 4 bolts to chains
FA Randall Green, 1995

11. OPEN PROJECT 5.12? (Not Pictured)
This steep and sharp TR is waiting for suitors on the first buttress right of *Little Big Man*.

UP

UPHILL PURSUITS

SKI + CLIMB + RUN

STOP IN BEFORE YOU GO OUT

111 E. OAK ST., STE. 1E
BOZEMAN, MT 59715
(406) 404-1021

UPHILLPURSUITS.COM
@UPHILLPURSUITS

CLIMBER: @KELSEYKSATHER
PHOTO: @BLAIRSPEED

AVALANCHE GULCH

BY JAKE MERGENTHALER & TERRY COWAN

Bob Goodwyn on *Blood Stains and Bones Varient 5.10d*
Photo by Jake Hymas

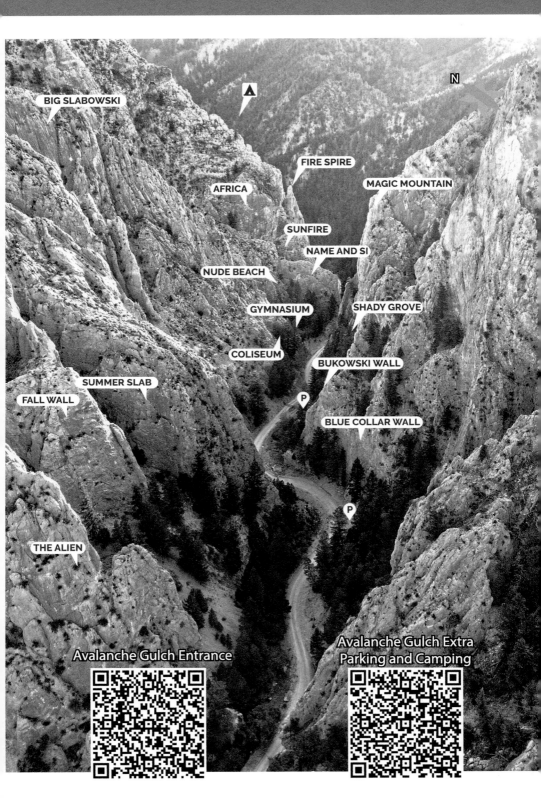

BIG SLABOWSKI

N

FIRE SPIRE

AFRICA

MAGIC MOUNTAIN

SUNFIRE

NAME AND SI

NUDE BEACH

GYMNASIUM

SHADY GROVE

COLISEUM

SUMMER SLAB

BUKOWSKI WALL

FALL WALL

P

BLUE COLLAR WALL

P

THE ALIEN

Avalanche Gulch Entrance

Avalanche Gulch Extra
Parking and Camping

WELCOME to Avalanche Gulch. This canyon lies about 25 miles east of Helena on the north side of Canyon Ferry Lake. It is the next major drainage south of Hellgate. The gulch is made up of featured limestone spires, fins, and buttresses that range in size from 40 ft to 200 ft in height and is considerably more complex than the unique fins of Hellgate. The rock is speckled with pockets and edges and sports some funky brown chert. The gulch has something for everyone with a few thought-provoking slabs, some steep jug hauls, and a plethora of enjoyable moderates. The majority of the routes are well bolted sport climbs but there are a few that can be supplemented with gear.

With walls facing north and south one could theoretically climb here year-round but the most stable weather is found in spring through fall. If you're looking for winter climbing, go to Hellgate or try the wall here called Africa. If it's sunny and 45 degrees, both of these areas can be quite comfortable.

The rock quality ranges from bulletproof to marginal so please use caution and wear a helmet. Many of the routes are a full 30 meters. Be careful when lowering off and when in doubt use a 70m cord.

HISTORY

One day, in the summer of 2001, Kim and Jake Merganthaler were rained out of nearby Hellgate Canyon. They decided to take a drive and look for new route potential. On entering Avalanche Gulch, they were blown away by the scope and beauty of the place and agreed that at least a few routes looked worthwhile. Jake called a friend to report a short clean wall next to the road that looked like it would yield a bunch of moderates—a buttress that now holds a high concentration of 5.11s and 5.12s. The next week Jake bolted one of these "moderates" on lead. It looked 5.8 but turned out to be the tricky and once dirty 5.10 he named *Love Is a Dog from Hell*. He cried his way up the slippery corner and soon the bushes he was using for holds fell out, landing on his wife, Kim. They were both covered in dirt as they drove home in silence but they were gleefully hooked.

Shortly after their first visit, Randall Green began joining Jake and Kim to develop the area. Whether improving a trail or spotting a new line, Randall's experience was invaluable. Jake and Kim are truly grateful for Randall's constructive criticism and zeal for exploring new routes.

GETTING THERE

Getting to Avalanche Gulch is much the same as Hellgate. The Avalanche Gulch Canyon access road is just north of mile marker 19 about 1.5 miles south of the Hellgate road. From Highway 284 follow Avalanche Canyon Road for 2.5 miles to a fork. Stay left. Continue another half mile to the Forest Service boundary (sign). Look for mountain goats on the sunny slopes to the left. Drive with extreme caution in this narrow winding canyon. This is a "thru-road" (to Magpie Gulch) so there may be unexpected traffic.

PARKING

You can park at the Forest Service sign but the best parking is about a quarter mile farther up in a nice pullout next to the culvert where the creek crosses the road (room for 4 to 5 cars). In the unlikely event this is fully occupied, you can park just around the corner near the cattle guard, but it is extremely limited and it is important to not block the gate. If needed, there are a variety of additional parking spots not far up the road, just past the main cliffs and nearby some nice camping.

DESCRIPTIONS

All the areas on the south side (left side in the photo) are listed in order as you move upstream from the parking area. The north-side formations and routes are described in a similar manner as they are encountered starting from the parking area at the culvert.

Ceely Heck on *Cold Water 5.9*
Photo by Bob Goodwyn

THE ALIEN SOUTH SIDE

The upper south side of The Alien is best approached by following the trails leading past The North Side and The Fall Wall. The following two areas are near the bottom righthand side of the formation and are more easily reached directly from the creek.

THE ALIEN SOUTH SIDE

This area has some new route potential but has a difficult approach. Follow the north side directions and continue up the hill to the crest, then down the other side on a faint trail. The two 5.8s are found on a cute slab and are well worth your time. Routes are listed left to right.

1. VAPOR TRAILS 5.10d

Start on the west side of relatively flat alcove in a V-shaped notch. Climb up tan rock that gets steeper as you go. The rock quality is marginal.
85 ft, bolts to chains
FA Jake Mergenthaler, Kim Mergenthaler, 2001

2. TOPROPE PROJECTS (Not Pictured)

There are several unfinished projects between *Vapor Trails* and *Solitary Smile*.

3. SOLITARY SMILE 5.8 ★

Start on the left side of a pretty slab and climb super clean rock. Great fun!
50 ft, bolts to chains
FA Jake Mergenthaler, 2001

4. GET YOUR GOAT 5.8 ★

Climb up the right side of the slab to exit on steeper blocks.
50 ft, bolts to chains
FA Jake Mergenthaler, 2001

THE MAKEOUT SPOT

Cool exposure and near perfect rock make this area a worthy choice. This shield is sunny most of the time making for a good winter crag. Although short, the approach is difficult. Cross the creek as per directions to The Danger Zone and follow a faint goat trail up the incline for 20 yards. Now comes the tricky part: look for a rocky, tree-choked gully and scramble up easy 5th class terrain for 40 feet until you reach a comfortable ledge under a clean shield. You can also reach it via an exposed ledge from the top of The Danger Zone. Routes are listed from left to right.

5. LOVER'S LANE 5.11c ★

Crank up a steep shield on drip pockets and crimpers.
90 ft, bolts to chains
FA Jake Mergenthaler, Kim Mergenthaler, 2002

6. INDECENT PROPOSAL 5.10b ★

Start right of *Lover's* on an airy ledge then pull up bulging gray rock to a dihedral. Continue on easier ground to chains.
FA Jake Mergenthaler, Kim Mergenthaler, 2002

THE DANGER ZONE

Named for the rock that rained down around the belay during early ascents. The climbs are fun and moderate, but please wear your helmets. From the culvert walk back down the road for 150 yards. When you're almost out of the canyon, cross the creek to the sunny side of the Alien formation (although it's not readily apparent). Follow the faint goat trail for 20 yards toward the roughly arrow-shaped cliff. Routes are listed left to right.

7. MUD FENCE 5.8

Begin on an ugly brown face and continue up fun but mungy flakes to a cleaner gray finish.
85 ft, bolts to chains
FA Jake Mergenthaler, 2002

8. UGLY STICK 5.8

She ain't pretty but she's fun. Start on a blunt arête treading up a left-leaning ramp.
85 ft, bolts to chains
FA Jake Mergenthaler, 2002

RED TAIL WALL

As you drive into the gulch you will notice two pretty faces of rock sitting high up on the west side of the canyon. The orange one on the right is Red Tail. To get there, continue up from the north side of The Alien on a hard-to-follow, steep trail for ten minutes. The cliff is on the right. This isn't a great for kids or dogs since the climbs start on ledges. Sunny most of the time. Routes listed right to left.

1. **WING AND A PRAYER** 5.12a
Start on a nice ledge on the right side of the cliff. Crank through a roof to easier ground.
65 ft, bolts to chains
FA Jake Mergenthaler, Kim Mergenthaler, Randall Green, 2010

2. **RED TAIL** 5.11a ★
Start on the left side of a poo-filled cave. Sustained, tall tricky climb. Rock seems friable at times.
100 ft, 15 bolts to chains
FA Randall Green, 2010

3. **DRIFTER HAWK** 5.11a
Start on the sloping ledge left of *Red Tail*. Began on ok rock covered with orange lichen. Then enjoy juggy light colored rock capped by a roof.
70 ft, bolts to chains
FA Jake Mergenthaler, Kim Mergenthaler, 2011

4. **BLUEJAY** 5.11d ★★
Start on ledge up and left of *Hawk*. Climb ok rock past one bolt to surmount a roof then amazing rock to the top. Shares anchors with *Hawk*.
70 ft, bolts to chains
FA Jake Mergenthaler, Kim Mergenthaler, 2020

5. **BIRDS OF PREY** 5.11b/c ★★
Up and left from the other climbs. Sharp. Look for a beautiful gray bulge at mid height.
100 ft, bolts to chains
FA Jake Mergenthaler, Kim Mergenthaler, 2011

6. **SCAVENGER** 5.11d ★
Just left of *Birds* on a nice flat ledge. Begin on juggy bulges to gain an orange, shallow dihedral. Sharp and sequential.
75 ft, bolts to chains

THE ALIEN NORTH SIDE

This formation sits high above the road on the left side of the gulch. It has very high quality stone and great routes in the 5.11 range. Many of these routes are two pitches but can be combined to create long pitches. The best way to get there is to go down the road from the culvert for 40 yards to where a makeshift bridge of logs and railroad ties cross the creek. After crossing, head back toward the culvert. After a steep sketchy section make a hard left and cross a few downed trees. Pass Fall Wall on your right, and continue on this steep, loose trail for a few minutes. The trail deposits you at base of *UFO*. Routes are listed left to right.

1. THE DARK SIDE 5.11b or 5.11c ★★★

P1: Start on the far-left edge of the cliff. The climb is on less-than-vertical, suspect rock to reach a fun roof on good rock then the chains. (5.10a, 70 ft)

P2: Dance out right past a few bolts to a clean corner. Supplement small gear here and then grunt up a steep hand crack to anchors. (5.11b, 50 ft)

P2 Var: Pull out left onto a steep technical bit to gain the arête. Work up the left side of the arête to gain easier ground. (5.11c, 50 ft)

Descent: Rap with an 80m or two smaller ropes.
120 ft, bolts, small to medium gear to chains
FA Jake Mergenthaler, Kim Mergenthaler, Randall Green, 2002

2. ALIEN LOVE CHILD 5.11d ★★

Start in a cave and crank up and left to gain a tricky rail. A pumpy sequence gains the gray slab above.
75 ft, bolts to chains
FA Jake Mergenthaler, Kim Mergenthaler, 2003

3. CHOSS PROJECT

4. BLOOD STAINS AND BONES 5.10d or 5.11b ★

P1: A wild adventure on marginal rock. Climb a wide, red gully. Escape left to experience a one-of-a-kind move. (5.10a, 75 ft)

P1 Var: Instead of stepping out left, continue up the steep chimney to gain better rock and the chains (5.11b, 120 ft)

P2: Continue from chains on very good rock with interesting moves. (5.10d, 45 ft)

Descent: Rap the route.
120 ft, bolts to chains
FA Jake Mergenthaler, Kim Mergenthaler, Randall Green, 2003

5. ANAL INTRUSION 5.11b ★★★

You will grunt and laugh up this fantastic climb on orange and blue rock. Look for an easy steep start in the alcove and bulge at half-height.
80 ft, bolts to chains
FA Jake Mergenthaler, Kim Mergenthaler, Randall Green, 2002

6. UNIDENTIFIED FLAILING OBJECTS 5.11b ★★★

P1: Begin at base of a left-facing easy slab. Climb this to a steep headwall with tricky sequences. (5.11b, 80 ft, bolts to chains)

P2: From the chains, climb a fun crack to top. (5.9, 40 ft)

Descent: Rap route.
120 ft, bolts, small to medium gear
FA Jake Mergenthaler, Kim Mergenthaler, Randall Green, 2002

7. SNOT ROCKET 5.11c ★

Start at the base of a tree (up and right from the other climbs). This route can feel slick as snot on a doorknob. Ends on sharp airy arête.
90 ft, bolts to chains
FA Jake Mergenthaler, Kim Mergenthaler, 2002

8. LOG DODGER 5.10a ★

Begin just right of *Rocket*. Climb a fun, blocky red face of marginal rock.

Name: Once while hiking up to bolt this route, I dislodged a huge log. It attempted to steamroll my mentor and climbing partner, Randall. He dodged it, unphased, and climbed all afternoon.
65 ft, bolts to chains
FA Jake Mergenthaler, Kim Mergenthaler, Randall Green, 2004

THE FALL WALL

This wedge-shaped buttress lies up the trail left (west) of the Summer Slab. Hike around a broken fin and continue near the top of the cliff on the right. Fall Wall is characterized by a large rust-red streak. The climbs here are fun with memorable moves, however, I was a little overzealous and they are a bit crowded. Routes are listed left to right.

1. TOO COLD TO TANGO 5.10a
Begin on the left side of a gray slab, move past the first bolt and into the crack. Then move up and right on a technical slab past a bulge.
60 ft, bolts, med gear to clip-and-lower
FA Jake Mergenthaler, 2002

2. FALL LINE 5.10a
Begin on the right side of the slab and tip-toe up the direct line. Shares anchors with *Too Cold to Tango*.
60 ft
FA Jake Mergenthaler, 2002

3. NO FALLS, NO BALLS 5.11a
The far lefthand climb near the top of the scree slope before the cliff curves. As the route begins on an ever-moving talus slope, this climb gets shorter each year. After a tricky start, pull a powerful roof. A bit mungy.
80 ft, bolts to clip-and-lower
FA Jake Mergenthaler, 2003

4. THE FALL GUY 5.11a/b ★
Follow a sloping arête with a crack on its right side. Escape the crack at the third bolt (tricky) and continue up through bulges on big holds. Way cool.
80 ft, 10 bolts to clip-and-lower
FA Jake Mergenthaler, Kim Mergenthaler, 2003

5. TANGLED UP IN GLUE 5.11a
Begin just left of the red streak and grunt through the bulges to an easier corner. The awkward, yet engaging start has moved. We recommend stick clipping the second bolt.
80 ft, bolts to clip-and-lower
FA Jake Mergenthaler, 2002

6. COLD AND HORNY 5.11a
Begin on the right of the red streak on a very sloppy arête. End on a fingery slab. The wise will stick clip.
80 ft, 9 bolts to clip-and-lower
FA Jake Mergenthaler, Kim Mergenthaler 2002

7. HEAD OVER HEELS 5.11a ★
The far right route begins under a blocky bulge. Cruise this and head up a fun slab to end on the crux shield.
80 ft, bolts to chains
FA Jake Mergenthaler, Kim Mergenthaler, 2004

SUMMER SLAB

This gorgeous crag stands 100 steep yards from the creek on the northwest side of the road. Hop across the creek where it flows around a small cliff, just downstream from the culvert. Continue up an indistinct trail that heads slightly left then switches back right. The Summer Slab is near the top where the trail starts to head left toward *The Alien*. Routes are listed left to right.

1. **ENDLESS BUMMER** 5.10d
This climb lies on the far left of this pretty, but insecure and flaky slab. Not recommended.
80 ft, bolts to chains
FA Jake Mergenthaler, 2002

2. **ENDLESS SUMMER** 5.11a/b ★
A wonderful, technical slab with some great holds. Work your way up an indistinct corner in the middle of the slab to a small but obvious roof. The slab undulates above through bulges. Highly recommended.
80 ft, bolts to clip-and-lower
FA Jake Mergenthaler, Kim Mergenthaler, 2002

3. **SUNNY SIDE UP** 5.11a ★
Start down and right a few yards from the slab. Begin behind a stunted pine tree and work past a large pocket on steep brown rock, passing a gray bulge.
80 ft, bolts to clip-and-lower
FA Jake Mergenthaler, 2003

4. **CHEAP AND EASY** 5.10c/d ★
This steep, fun climb starts behind the stunted pine. Climb up right on steep, brown rock (a little crumbly). Lunge up and right to gain a clean gray slab.
80 ft, bolts to chains
FA Jake Mergenthaler, Kim Mergenthaler, 2003

THE BIG SLABOWSKI
This large and featured slab lies high on the west flank of the gulch, directly above the cattle guard. Scramble up the steep scree and goat trails to the base of this obvious buttress (about 10 minutes from the road). Routes are listed right to left.

1. BIG SLABOWSKI 5.10a
P1: Start on a spacious ledge. Move up a fun slab onto the headwall. (5.10, 90 ft)
P2: Crank up a steeper section on wonderful holds to a slabby finish. (5.10a, 90 ft)
Descent: Rap the route.
190 ft, bolts to chains
FA Jake Mergenthaler, Kim Mergenthaler, 2001

2. LONG AND STRONG 5.10b ★★
P1: Begin on a small ledge at the base of a large dead tree (belay bolt). Work up a steep slab to a vertical head-wall with bigger holds. (5.10b, 90 ft)
P2: Continue up the jug-littered face, concluding on the slab. (5.10a, 90 ft)
Descent: Rap the route.
180 ft, bolts to chains
FA: Jake Mergenthaler, Kim Mergenthaler 2001

3. GET THE FRICTION ON 5.10b ★★
P1: Begin on a small ledge at the base of a dead tree and climb to the right of a water streak to a fun bulge, finishing at a large belay ledge. (5.10b, 90 ft)
P2: The first move off the belay may be strenuous, but the water-worn face above proves easier. (5.10b, 90 ft)
Descent: Rap the route
180 ft, bolts to chains
FA Jake Mergenthaler, Kim Mergenthaler, 2001

4. LONG DUCK DONG 5.11c ★★
P1: Begin on the south side of the alcove. One tricky move leads to an easy slab. Belay beneath huge huecos. (5.9, 90 ft)
P2: Move left through a chasm of steep huecos, scream over a strenuous bulge, and cruise up 5.10 terrain to the chains. (5.11c/d, 90 ft)
Descent: Rap the route
180 ft, bolts to chains

THE COLISEUM

This small crag sits three minutes from the road. From the cattle guard, walk up the road for 40 yards to where a steep buttress bisects the road left of Name Wall. Diagonal up and left to this semi-circle enclave. Routes are listed left to right.

1. LIONS, TIGERS, AND BEARS 5.8 ★

This is the first route on the left. Climb a pretty little face littered with brown chert.
45 ft, bolts to chains
FA Jake Mergenthaler, 2003

2. KANSAS TORNADO 5.9

There were strong winds blowing rocks from above us when Howard and I first got on this route. This climb is no gimme.
45 ft, 4 bolts to chains
FA Terry Cowan, Howard Carney, 2015

3. (BIG) DOROTHY 5.10a

Dirty, small, with loose rock down low. Pull the small roof with some wide hands and technical moves before an easier finish to the chains. Shares chains with *Kansas Tornado*.
45 ft, 3 bolts to chains
FA Terry Cowan and Carney, 2017

4. THE GLADIATOR 5.9 ★

Up the hill past a water worn depression. Climb right of this on the featured, and sometimes suspect, rock.
80 ft, bolts to chains
FA, Jake Mergenthaler, 2003

Kiersten Iwai on *Lions, Tigers and Bears 5.8*
Photo by Joe Schmechel

There are two more routes on the opposite side in an area called The Gymnasium. The left route is a 5.11d and the right one is a project.

THE LOST WORLD

From the Nude Beach Wall, continue up and left on a steep, loose trail. Continue along a tall broken slab for 20 yards. The routes are on your left around an alcove that makes an uncomfortable, sloping belay spot. Routes are listed left to right.

1. GET LOST 5.10d

Start on the root ball of fallen pine. Grunt up a steep and chossy start to gain better rock on an interesting slab.
90 ft, bolts to chains
FA Jake Mergenthaler, Kim Mergenthaler, 2012

2. DEATH BY MISADVENTURE 5.10d ★

Start on a shallow depression on reasonably flat ground. Climb up technical, flaky rock to gain a small roof, then up a clean, steep slab.
90 ft, bolts to chains

3. THE SWEDE 5.11a ★

Start in the alcove at a sloping belay spot. Climb up a bulging, pumpy seam on insecure sidepulls to reach easier, but no less technical terrain. A bit sporty.
90 ft, bolts to chains
FA Jake Mergenthaler, Kim Mergenthaler, 2003

4. CHOSS PROJECT

Marked by toprope chains.

5. PLAYING WITH YOUR INSECURITIES 5.10c

(Not Pictured)
Ten yards right of previous climbs. Start in the groove/corner on insecure but interesting moves. Heady bolting and marginal rock may play with your insecurities.
90 ft, 9 bolts to chains
FA Terry Cowan, 2020

NUDE BEACH WALL

A cool setting with fantastic routes just five minutes from the road. Like the other crags in this area, this cliff is indistinct and can't be seen from the road. Approach as for The Coliseum and continue up a game trail meandering between two cliffs and passing under a fallen tree. Hop over a few boulders, turn the corner and you're there. Routes are listed left to right.

1. DESPICABLE ME 5.4 (Not Pictured)
Angles to the right on quality rock that is a steep for the grade. Bolted for kids and first-time leaders. Shares chains with *Django*.
40 ft, 4 bolts to chains
FA Terry Cowan, 2015

2. DJANGO 5.10a ★★ (Not Pictured)
High first bolt. The intended line is to the right of the bolts. Look for an awesome sidepull.
45 ft, 4 bolts to chains
FA Terry Cowan, 2015

3. GRAVITY 5.10b ★★
When this route was established, I found two mountain goat carcasses at the bottom of the opposite cliff. This begs the question: what was the cause of their demise? Gravity or wolves?
50 ft, 4 bolts to chains
FA Terry Cowan, 2013

4. WOLF OF WALL STREET 5.10b ★
Shares anchors with *Gravity*.
50 ft, 4 bolts to chains
FA Terry Cowan, Howard Carney, 2013

5. CLIMBERS WHO STARE AT GOATS 5.10a/b ★★★
A mountain goat observed Howard and me for hours while we bolted this route. Maybe it was wondering what the rope was for. This superb line is thought-provoking, gripping, and off-balance, but once you figure it out you'll fall in love.
60 ft, 5 bolts to chains
FA Terry Cowan, Howard Carney, 2013

6. HEATHERS 5.9+ ★
Fun and powerful moves to the third bolt. Direct line to chains and shares the last bolt and anchors with *Climbers Who Stare at Goats*.
60 ft, 5 bolts to chains
FA Terry Cowan, 2020

7. NUDE BEACH 5.8 ★★
Start on a blunt arête and work up through tricky bulges.
60 ft, bolts to chains
FA Jake Mergenthaler, 2003

8. THE BEACH 5.6+
Smoke from the seasonal forest fires caused a small plane to go down in Avalanche Gulch when this route was envisioned. An undesirable 5.6 start up the slippery ramp segues to enjoyable climbing up the right side of the headwall. Shares chains with *Nude Beach*.
85 ft, 7 bolts to clip-and-lower
FA Terry Cowan, 2015

9. OVER THE SHOULDER BOULDER HOLDER 5.9 ★★
Start in a gorgeous dihedral, then work right over a crux bulge.
60 ft, bolts to chains
FA Jake Mergenthaler, 2003

SPORTS ILLUSTRATED SWIMSUIT WALL

From Nude Beach Wall, follow the wall to the right to this hidden cove. Seven routes match seven Sports Illustrated Swimsuit covergirls from years past. Routes are listed left to right.

1. MARISA MILLER 5.9+ ★
This climb requires technical footwork. Watch (or don't watch) your feet and flow to the chains. The crux is down low.
20 ft, 5 bolts to chains
FA Terry Cowan, 2014

2. BAR REFAELI 5.8
The first bolt is out to the left. She gives you two options to make it through the roof—the easier climbing is left of the bolt line. Shares chains with *Kate Upton*.
65 ft, 6 bolts to chains
FA Terry Cowan, 2016

3. KATE UPTON 5.7 ★★
The bulge in the middle of the climb make for interesting climbing. A left high-step and solid right hand make this all the more enjoyable. A family-friendly climb.
65 ft, 6 bolts to chains
FA Terry Cowan, 2014

4. ANNE VYALITSYNA 5.8+
The holds are thin but that doesn't last long. Shares chains with *Heidi Klum*.
45 ft, 3 bolts to chains
FA Terry Cowan, Howard Carney 2016

5. HEIDI KLUM 5.10a ★★
The climb is a bit awkward, but beautiful all the same. My favorite on this wall, but over way too soon. Chicken wing your right arm as you work up the lower, powerful section. Study the sequence and, you'll find this to be easy for the grade.
45 ft, 4 bolts to chains
FA Terry Cowan, 2014

6. ELSA BENITEZ 5.10a/b
Clip the first bolt of *Heidi Klum*, then toe the line by sticking to the arête. Otherwise, the climb will be too easy and nothing comes easy south of the border. Shares chains with *Tyra Banks*.
50 ft, 5 bolts to chains
FA Terry Cowan, 2019

7. TYRA BANKS 5.9 ★
Watch your head and widen those legs to get past the first two bolts. Switch gears and finish by moving left.
50 ft, 5 bolts to chains
FA Terry Cowan, 2018

THE NAME WALL

The sunny, short fin sits perpendicular to the road ,just past the turnoff to the Nude Beach gulch. A nod to the many walls unnamed walls around the world. Routes are listed left to right.

1. WILL BILLY 5.10d
Named after two childhood friends, Will and Billy. The climb is split into two distinct parts due to the risk of a ledge. Thin moves from start to finish. Shares chains with *Nikki*.
70 ft, 6 bolts to chains
FA Terry Cowan, Howard Carney, 2015

2. JAMESON 5.10b ★
It can be tricky getting to the ledge. Go for the flash if you dare. Shares anchor with *Nikki*.
70 ft, 6 bolts to chains
FA Terry Cowan, 2016

3. DARLING NIKKI 5.9 ★★★
A lovely climb. The crux at the second bolt isn't bad if you move correctly. A nice no-hands ledge breaks up the upper section. Named after the classic Prince song.
75 ft, 6 bolts to chains
FA Terry Cowan, 2015

4. DAD (RLC) 5.10a/b ★★
Stay on the main face (don't cheat and clip from *Nikki*) and find an undercling for showing off your guns.
70 ft, 6 bolts to chains
FA Terry Cowan, 2016

5. HOWARD 5.11b
Thin face climbing works left and finishes on the easier, upper headwall. Shares chains with *Dad (RLC)*. Named after the man and the myth (to some), Howard Carney.
70 ft, 7 bolts to chains
FA Carney, 2015

6. STEPHEN KING 5.9- ★
Like some of great storyteller's novels, this one can be frightening. When working up and left, use the left leg for stability to take out some of the fright. Shares chains with *Howard* and *Dad*.
70 ft, 6 bolts to chains
FA Terry Cowan, 2015

7. HEMINGWAY 5.8
Did Hemingway have a quote about mountain climbing? Unlike the author, this route is not one of the best.
70 ft, 7 bolts to chains
FA Terry Cowan, Mariah Davis, 2015

8. DIRTY DIANA 5.10c
Use the arête out left and gear up for the crux going for the chains. It looks easy from the ground, so you got this, right?
45 ft, 4 bolts to chains
FA Terry Cowan, 2016

9. KOCAINE KAROLINA 5.10d
Looks can be deceiving. The layback feature isn't all that helpful. Shares chains with *Diana*.
45 ft, 3 bolts to chains
FA Howard Carney, 2016

10. THE PARIS WIFE 5.8+ ★
True to the grade if you stay in sequence. The roof is fun for all. After pulling through the roof, work right and then up to the chains.
50 ft, 4 bolts to chains
FA Terry Cowan, 2016

11. SALMA 5.10c ★
Spicy. Use the arête or go straight up the lower face, before tackling the main headwall. The first few clips will be to your left. Kick out your left foot for a comfortable clipping stance.
65 ft, 6 bolts to chains
FA Terry Cowan, 2016

12. DAVIS 5.7
This one is OK. The start is the crux and may be harder than 5.7. Shares chains with *Salma*.
70 ft, 6 bolts to chains
FA Terry Cowan, Mariah Davis, 2016

13. DILLINGER 5.10a/b ★
Tricky to read. Use a belay bolt for security. The climbing through the first two bolts isn't difficult. Zigzag and balance your way through the upper headwall. Shares chains with *D. B. Cooper*.
65 ft, 5 bolts to chains
FA Terry Cowan, 2020

14. D. B. COOPER 5.10b ★★★
My personal favorite in Avalanche. For full value, wait for a windy day. The exposure combined with wind will make you smile (or wince). Watch out for the loose blocks at the start. The route doesn't use much, if any, of the arête out right.
100 ft, 8 bolts to chains
FA Terry Cowan, 2020

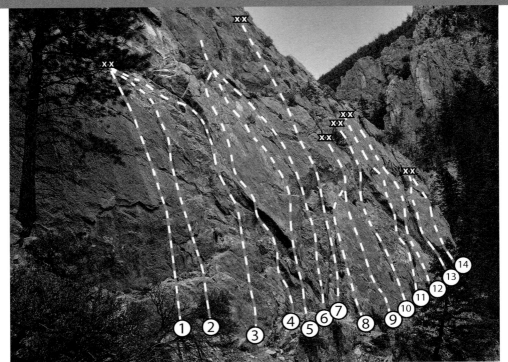

Zac Reed on *Takin' Care of Business 5.10a*
Photo by Jake Mergenthaler

BOSS WALL

Head towards Africa. The Boss Wall is across the gulch, halfway up. There are only two climbs, but it's worth a visit. Routes are listed downhill right to left.

1. **BE THE MOTHER FN' BOSS** 5.10c ★★★

You can't be timid to climb this one clean. The start and middle of the route is where all the fun is. Layback on a hold down low. In the middle, find the center digit pocket and kick out wide. Shares chains with *Legs*.

20 ft, 5 bolts to chains

FA Terry Cowan, 2017

2. **SPREAD YOUR LEGS AND TRUST THE RUBBER**
5.9+ ★

You may think twice before going for that second bolt, but it's an easy clip if you make it. Spread wide at times and trust the rubber.

55 ft, 5 bolts to chains

FA Terry Cowan, 2017

3. **BAD BOSSES** 5.11a ★

This steep climb is down from the others, fairly close to the road. Grunt up an opening boulder problem, but the climb stays tricky throughout.

55 ft, bolts to chains

FA Jake Mergenthaler, Kim Mergenthaler, 2011

FIRE SPIRE AREA

These next three areas are on the same formation but they are separated by chossy corner systems. The rock quality is stellar and the routes are vary in style. This cliff faces south, so it's sunny and warm. The area has some recognizable features: 1) **The Fire Spire** stands out like the Lost Arrow Spire—only different. 2) **Sunfire Slab** has a prominent band of red chert on its upper half. 3) **Africa** is a broad 90 ft bulletproof shield to the left.

Approach: From the cattle guard walk north 50 yards to where a steep buttress bisects the road. Follow the loose game trails to the climbs from immediately behind this fin.

THE FIRE SPIRE/SUNFIRE SLAB

This sunny and sharp crag, easily seen from road, sits on left side of road 100 yards upcanyon from the cattle guard. Look for a red band and a spire on the right. Walk up the road until under crag, then head diagonally up on a good trail that deteriorates. Routes are listed right to left.

1. THE FIRE SPIRE 5.10a ★

This is a fun and exciting climb that feels taller than it is. The trad section offers decent gear on easier ground.
P1: From the Sunfire Slab ledge, scramble right and belay on a small ledge with a belay bolt. Work up a shallow right-facing dihedral to steeper crack and face moves. Use gear to supplement bolts. Ends on a nice ledge. (5.10a, 85 ft)
P2: From the ledge, work up and left to gain a steeper headwall split by an irregular crack. Place gear near the top. (5.10a, 75 ft)
Descent: Rap the route.
160 ft, bolts, medium gear to chains
FA Jake Mergenthaler, Randall Green, 2002

2. SON OF A BOLT GUN 5.10a ★★★

Start on the right side of the slab then move up and right. The climb steepens on red rock, eventually merging with *Orange*.
75 ft, bolts to chains
FA Jake Mergenthaler, Randall Green, Ted Sims, 2001

3. ORANGE CRUSH 5.10c ★★

Move up the middle of a pretty slab to surmount a pumpy roof. Continue on sharp red stone. Shares anchor with *Son*.
75 ft, bolts to chains
FA Jake Mergenthaler, Randall Green, Ted Sims, 2001

4. DIRTY OLD MEN 5.10c ★

Begin on the left side of the large ledge. Start up on the gray, ever-steepening slab.
75 ft, bolts to chains
FA Jake Mergenthaler, Randall Green, Ted Sims, 2001

AFRICA

Separated from Sunfire by a mungy corner, Africa is characterized by its uniform gray color and consistent height. Continue up the gully from Sunfire on a steep loose trail. Routes are listed right to left.

5. BLASPHEME 5.11c

Cry up the left side of an arête and wonder why you climbed this choss pile.
90 ft, bolts to chains
FA Jake Mergenthaler, Randall Green, 2001

6. MODERN ART 5.11c ★★

Start among small junipers near a striking 7-foot-high slab. Work up a broken corner on marginal rock, then surmount a well-bolted bulge. Finish in a very featured corner on great rock. Save some juice.
95 ft, bolts to chains
FA Jake Mergenthaler, Kim Mergenthaler, 2003

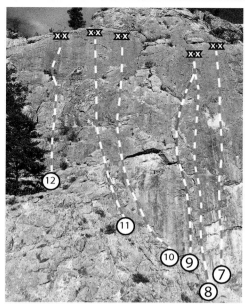

7. VOICES IN MY HEAD 5.12a/b ★★

Start 20 feet right of a large steep boulder. Work up the corner system to a beautiful but blank shield (crux). Wander up a tricky slab.
95 ft, bolts to chains
FA Jake Mergenthaler, Kim Mergenthaler, 2003

8. NOBODY'S FOOL 5.11b/c ★★★

Start from a large ledge on top of the steep boulder. Move across a small ledge to begin this strenuous, techy journey.
80 ft, bolts to chains
FA Jake Mergenthaler, Randall Green, 2003

9. STURDY GURDY 5.10b

Begin on the triangular block just left of *Nobody's Fool*. Climb the awkward, difficult seam before the roof. Plug in some gear on easy terrain and end on *Nobody's Fool*.
80 ft, bolts, medium gear to chains
FA Jake Mergenthaler, Randall Green, 2003

10. SUPER BOWL 5.8 ★★

Start on a pretty slab on the middle of the platform. Crank through a roof (watch for loose rock out left), then continue up a delicate slab.
90' bolts to chains
FA Jake Mergenthaler, Micah Hecht, 2003

11. RUMBLE IN THE JUNGLE 5.8 ★★

Start on the left side of the platform. Grunt up the short flake that leads to easier, fun climbing. Name: On the FA I dislodged a cooler-size block that rumbled down and ended up in the creek across the road.
90 ft, bolts to chains
FA Jake Mergenthaler, 2002

12. BRICE JESSEN 5.9

Start up and left in a steep gully. Terry says: "I miss you, yet don't fault you." The climb is like the guy—tougher than you think.
85 ft, 9 bolts to chains
FA Terry Cowan, 2012

BLUE COLLAR

This crag sits just above the road before the culvert. There are nice steps leading up to it. It's shady until mid afternoon. Routes listed from left to right.

1. TRUCKER'S SPEED 5.11c
The furthest left route in wooded area above the road. Fun if you like choss. I do!
80 ft, bolts to chains
FA Jake Mergenthaler, Kim Mergenthaler, 2017

2. DRIVE BY 5.12a/b ★
Start in a nice wooded area above the road. Pull up a chossy flake. Power up sandy slopers (5.11b/c). The thin crux hits you at mid-height for two bolts. Fun 5.10 to chains. Not for rock snobs. Name: While cleaning the route I pulled a large block off. It exploded on the slab below ricocheting onto our car where my wife was reading. The shrapnel disintegrated one plastic hubcap, badly dented our car, and scared the crud out of my wife.
90 ft, bolts to chains
FA Jake Mergenthaler, Kim Mergenthaler, 2017

3. CHOSS PROJECT

4. MINIMUM WAGE 5.11d ★
It's hard to grade this climb because it has a very bouldery start. Start in a wooded area above the road. After stick clipping to the first bolt, power through the opening crux on slopers. The remainder is fun and thought-provoking (5.11b/c).
80 ft, bolts to chains
FA Jake Mergenthaler, Kim Mergenthaler, 2016

5. ROUGH NECK 5.11a
Begin on easy rock until you gain a hard shield.
60 ft, bolts to chains
FA Jake Mergenthaler, Kim Mergenthaler

6. K-MART CARHART 5.10a
Start left of a large boulder and pull over a small roof. Pad your way to the top.
60 ft, bolts to chains
FA Jake Mergenthaler, 2007

7. BLUE COLLAR 5.10a ★★ (Not Pictured)
Just right of a boulder. Climb up a brown dihedral.
70 ft, bolts to chains
FA Jake Mergenthaler, 2003

8. TAKIN' CARE OF BUSINESS 5.10a ★★★
Start at the top of the steps on a gray face. After a steep start, gain an arête and finish on cool jugs.
70 ft, bolts to chains
FA Jake Mergenthaler, 2003

9. LUMBERJACK 5.10d ★
Start in a small alcove with loose, steep rock up and right. Crank out left on good rock. Pull over a small bulge and hold on til the top.
70 ft, bolts to chains
FA Jake Mergenthaler, Brad Maddock, 2017

10. BEER FIGHT 5.10b ★
Start in the same alcove as *Lumberjack*. Head up right on a slab to gain steeper ground. Cool moves over the bulge lead to better rock above. The rock quality isn't great.
70 ft, bolts to chains
FA Brandon Alke, Randall Green, 2006

11. DIRTY BIRD 5.8 ★★
Start right on the road. Climb up some slabby pillars and flakes. The rock is better than it looks. Name: There was a dead crow in a huge hueco on this route during the first ascent.
70 ft, bolts to chains
FA Jake Mergenthaler, 2003

12. BELLY FULL OF BEER 5.9 ★
Starts just right of *Dirty Bird*. Wander through several bulges to reach better rock towards top. Shares anchors with *Dirty Bird*.
75 ft, bolts to chains
FA Brandan Alke, Randall Green, 2006

13. PBR AND CLAMATO JUICE 5.10d
Start up the slope on the roots of a large pine tree. The bouldery start flows into intricate climbing, then into steep jugs. As of 2017 there's some loose rock to the right and left, stay on the bolt line. Name: A local climber and adventurer started this climb before his untimely and sad death. I finished it years later. His drink of choice was red beer.
80 ft, bolts to chains
FA Jake Mergenthaler, 2017

BUKOWSKI WALL

This popular wall sits 40 feet from the road and has fun but mostly short routes on good stone. Rock can fall from up high with no warning. Wear a helmet! Park at the cattle guard, climb the fence that crosses the creek and go straight up the trail. Routes listed left to right.

1. SHORT, FAT, LOOSE 5.10a
Just left of the cattle fence. OK climb.
45 ft, bolts to chains
FA Jake Mergenthaler, 2009

2. SERENITY NOW 5.10a ★
Just right of the cattle fence. Follow the left-leaning weakness, then over a bulge to the chains.
45 ft, bolts to chains
FA Jake Mergenthaler, Kim Mergenthaler, 2004

3. TALL BOY 5.9 ★
Start where a large pine nearly touches the wall. Climb up slippery cracks to gain a fun face.
80 ft, bolts to chains
FA Jake Mergenthaler, Kim Mergenthaler, 2004

4. BURNING IN WATER 5.10b ★★★
Three routes go up the pretty slab. This one is on the left.
60 ft, bolts to chains
FA Jake Mergenthaler, Kim Mergenthaler, 2001

5. DROWNING IN FLAME 5.11a ★★★
The middle route on the cliff face. Climb a dramatic, technical slab.
60 ft, bolts to chains
FA Jake Mergenthaler, Kim Mergenthaler, 2001

6. LOVE IS A DOG FROM HELL 5.10c ★★★
This is my first climb at avalanche. Done on lead, I dumped a lot of dirt and rocks on my belayer (Sorry, Kim). Climb up an intricate, left-facing corner.
60 ft, bolts to chains
FA Jake Mergenthaler, Kim Mergenthaler

7. WAR ALL THE TIME 5.12b ★
Start where a pine tree nearly touches the bulging rock. Very tricky in the top section.
50 ft, bolts to chains
FA Jake Mergenthaler, Kim Mergenthaler, 2004

8. ORDINARY MADNESS 5.11d ★★
Start just left of a small, broken pillar. A thought provoking start leads to steep incut holds before a hard finish.
50 ft, bolts to chains
FA Jake Mergenthaler, Kim Mergenthaler, 2004

9. I'D RATHER BE READING BUKOWSKI 5.11d ★★★
Start right of a small pillar. The real business begins in the short dihedral with a nasty clip. The crux is climbing over the bulge before a slippery crack awaits.
50 ft, bolts to chains
FA Jake Mergenthaler, Kim Mergenthaler, 2003

10. PLAY THE PIANO DRUNK 5.12a ★★
A steep and exciting climb characterized by a blank shield at ⅓ height with Gymnastic moves toward the top.
50 ft, bolts to chains
FA Jake Mergenthaler, Kim Mergenthaler, 2004

11. BARFLY 5.11b ★★
A must-do up steep flakes in an indistinct dihedral.
50 ft, bolts to chains
FA Jake Mergenthaler, Kim Mergenthaler, 2003

12. TRICKY DICK 5.10d
Start on big holds for a few bolts. Look out right for good sidepulls. Clipping the chains may be the crux.
45 ft, bolts to chains
FA Jake Mergenthaler, Kim Mergenthaler, 2009

13. BANG FOR BUCK 5.10b
Start on a bulging arête where the wall mellows off to the right. Shares anchors with *Tricky Dick*.
45 ft, bolts to chains
FA Jake Mergenthaler, Travis Jensen, 2004

14. BEER BELLY 5.8
Fun slab climbing. I gave it zero stars because the holds keep filling up with leaves from above. Bring a leafblower and you'll be fine.
65 ft, bolts to chains
FA Jake Mergenthaler, 2012

15. REACH FOR THE SUN 5.11b (Not Pictured)
Beautiful, short climb on the far right.
35 ft, bolts to chains
FA Brad Maddock, Jake Mergenthaler, 2017

Rocky Mountain National Park
&
Mount Evans
BOULDERING

By Jamie Emerson

COMING 2022

SHADY GROVE
From the fence just left of Bukowski walk up a faint trail that gets very steep towards the top. Routes are in a rough semi-circle, listed right to left.

1. DON'T DIE ON A 5.9 5.9 (Not Pictured)
This route sits on the trail about 20 yards from the fence. It begins at the base of a fallen tree. Not recommended because of bad bolting and very poor rock quality.
85 ft, bolts to chains
FA Jake Mergenthaler, 2005

2. BOYS DON'T CRY 5.10b ★
This arching flake is the first climb on the right of the steep slab. Good, but a bit awkward.
70 ft, bolts to chains
FA Jake Mergenthaler, Kim Mergenthaler, 2002

3. VEGETABLE OR VISIONARY 5.11b
The middle route on the slab, shares the anchors with *Boys Don't Cry*.
70 ft, bolts to chains
FA Jake Mergenthaler, Randall Green, 2004

4. SLIM SHADY 5.10c ★★
A good, long climb on the left of the slab just right of a choss corner. There's an abandoned bolt to nowhere out left for reference.
85 ft, bolts to chains
FA Jake Mergenthaler, 2009

5. AIN'T EASY BEING SLEAZY 5.11a
Start left of the choss corner. Shimmy up a groove under a large roof just left of an indistinct dihedral. The rock quality isn't great.
85 ft, bolts to chains
FA Jake Mergenthaler, Kim Mergenthaler, 2003

6. SAPPER CRAPPER 5.11c ★
This baby is steep and exciting. Start just left of *Ain't Easy Being Sleazy* under a tan bulge. Grunt through this on marginal rock to gain a crisp slab and intense roof. Watch out, the tree at the base is loaded with sticky sap.
Bolts to chains
FA Jake Mergenthaler, Kim Mergenthaler, 2002

7. TWO LEFT FEET 5.11a ★★
This is worth the walk. Stick clip high for the first bolts. Cruise up the bulge on suspect rock before tackling the tricky, well-bolted, slab crux. Shares anchors with *Sapper Crapper*.
85 ft, bolts to chains
FA Jake Mergenthaler, Kim Mergenthaler, 2002

8. RUSSIAN BIKINI WAX 5.11a ★ (Not Pictured)
Begin just left of *Two Left Feet* on an intricate slab. Stick clip high for the first bolt. Surmount a bulge using a mantle from hell and continue up to nice, steep rock.
75 ft, bolts to chains

ON JAKE MERGENTHALER
by Randall Green

Jason "Jake" Merganthaler is an artist, choreographer, blue-collar craftsman and visionary. Ever since I met Jake in the early 1990s I've marveled at his creative ideas and projects. He has the ability to visualize and create a work of art that can be inspiring, interactive and provocative, the perfect mix for someone who likes to put up new climbing routes. His wife, Kim, is his inseparable climbing partner and his muse, a climbing force in her own right but who often is the source of Jake's inspiration for creating new climbs.

Jake immediately saw the potential of more routes on the unclimbed stone of Indian Creek Canyon, Hellgate, and Avalanche gulches, and eventually Blackleaf Canyon. Once the idea took hold of Jake, his blue-collar craftsman side came to light. He borrowed a generator, a 100 feet of extension cord and an electric hammer drill to install his first bolts on a short slab of rock at Indian Creek. Unabashed by having to flag down a couple red-neck miners to restart the stalled generator while he hung on a fixed line, Jake installed his first bolts and created a good climb in the process.

When I loaned him a battery powered hammer drill, the crags became his new art medium: choreography on a vertical stage. And then every weekend became an exploration of his new routes.

One of my fondest climbing memories is when Jake and I installed the first multi-pitch route at Blackleaf: *It's Only Money*. Once we figured out the line and had the final two pitches bolted we retired to basecamp and sat around the campfire telling embellished climbing stories. Our bellies full of beer and butterflies, neither one of us got any sleep the night before the first continuous ascent. I know Jake was as nervous as I was, but neither of us would admit to it. Then when Jake redpointed the crux pitch you could hear us hoot and holler clear to Bynum.

Climbing with Jake and Kim and sharing their friendship has been a great honor and a cherished experience for me. In my mind, Jake and Kim share the elite company of the great pioneers of Montana climbing. Jake told me he thought putting up a new route was his ultimate expression of an art form. To climb Jake's and Kim's routes is an interactive experience with a work of art.

MAGIC MOUNTAIN

This huge chunk of stone lies on the east side of the gulch on the same side as Bukowski. It's roughly 40 yards from the cattle guard on the right. As of 2021, there's only one route on this formation. It starts on the opposite side of the creek from the road, just before you would head up to the Nude Beach area.

1. **COLD WATER** 5.9 ★★

P1: Belay from the creek bank or just above. An easy slab leads to more difficult face climbing before easing off once you sink your hands in the corner crack. (75 ft)

P2: There is a large space to belay the second pitch. It starts with some exposure stepping out left and working up through a fun sequence. Traverse in the middle then follow the easy arête to the top for a fantastic view of the canyon. (75 ft)

150 ft, bolts to chains

FA Terry Cowan, 2015

Leslie Gains-Germain on
Girl with the Dockins Tattoo 5.12a
Photo by Brad Maddock

HELLGATE GULCH

BY JAKE MERGENTHALER

WELCOME to Hellgate Gulch, located only 25 miles southeast of Helena. The steep limestone fins that bisect this peaceful canyon provide easy access to some of the best sport climbs in Montana. With more than 90 pitches of mostly bolted routes, Hellgate beckons climbers to the tightly stacked, vertical walls of this unique area.

Tucked away in a lonely gulch that drains the west side of the Big Belt Mountains on the east side of Canyon Ferry Reservoir, Hellgate is a quiet and serene retreat. It's not uncommon to hear the clatter of rocks dislodged by mountain goats scrambling up a gully or to see swallows and hawks swooping and soaring among the rocks. Climbers are not the only human visitors to the area, which is also popular with ATV and 4-wheel-drive enthusiasts and hunters. But even on a busy weekend, it is unusual to see more than a handful of people.

Most of the rock is the color of concrete. Browns and reds enrich the palette. The rocks texture ranges from polished to prickly. The climbing is as varied as the color and texture. Most routes are vertical, with a few roofs and bulges to test your anti-gravity skills. Your fingers will happily find a few perfectly shaped pockets, but positive edges—albeit sometimes small and sharp—are generally the rule. Erosive forces have textured the southern faces to such an extreme that holds seem invisible, lost in a sea of spines and shallow drip pockets. Meanwhile the north sides are often slick and polished.

Some of the routes at Hellgate can be described as heady and committing. While the climbs are protected well from ground or ledge falls, few are over-bolted. The bolt spacing on some of the earlier routes was more a function of the ethic at the time. In that era, bolts were used sparingly (and if hand drilled, even more sparingly) and were not placed if there were cracks or other reasonably-protectable features. Most early route developers were influenced by the climbs at Smith Rock and the traditional climbs of Gallatin Canyon. With permission from Bill Dockins we have tried to adjust the grades of the older routes to make them more modern and reasonable for us soft climbers. Usually we added two letter grades. Our hopes are with the tweaked gradings more people will come to enjoy this amazing canyon. That being said, it might be smart to try a few routes below your limit to get the feel of the rock and the ratings.

Hellgate Gulch could be called a "5.11 heaven" as the majority of the best older routes are 5.11 or harder. It was only after Randall Green's vision to bolt under the big roof that the area began to see more moderate routes. But beware, although extremely fun, most routes in that area are on less than perfect rock. Please wear your helmet, even while hanging out at the base of the cliff.

GEAR
Although bolts are plentiful, Hellgate cracks often provide good natural gear placements. *Purgatory* is one of the best 5.10 cracks around. In addition to a dozen quickdraws, take a selection of wired stoppers and small to medium TCUs, Friends, and TriCams. Most anchors are chained but you will find a few modern "clip-and-lower" anchors.

SEASON
The climbing season typically is best from March through October. The road turns to gumbo in the spring or after periods of rain, but the rock is generally dry and can usually be climbed during warm days in the middle of winter—given it's above freezing, sunny, and the winds are calm.

HELLGATE CLIMBING HISTORY
People reportedly scrambled to the top of some of the fins before the first technical climbing routes were established in the mid-1980s by Bozmanites Bill Dockins and Kristen Drumheller. Tom Kalakay, Brian Hagerty, and others accompanied Bill and Kristen on their first-ascent forays. Bill and Kristen set the standards by establishing the first 5.11s and 5.12s. Bill's testpiece, *Inferno*, modestly rated 5.12+, has seen three free ascents in over 30 years. Although Bill and Kristen continue to add quality lines, Helena local Randall Green and others (Scott Payne, Aaron Lefohn, Jaime Johnson, to name a few) have contributed to the growing list of popular routes from the 80s through mid-2000s My wife and I have had the pleasure of contributing to the new route list since 1996. Another testpiece, *Devil's Highway Roof* at 5.13a, was free-climbed by Luke Evans during the summer of 2003. In 2019-2020 Jeff Ho, Henry Shlosthauser, Whit Magro, Kyle Omeara, and Taylor Fragomeni have added some beautiful but very hard climbs to the canyon.

IMPORTANT ROCK CLOSURE AT PICTOGRAPH WALL!
No climbing is allowed anywhere on the entire fin that lies across the creek from East Gate Wall. This includes not only the south side which holds significant Native American rock art but the road side and northeast face as well. Our continued access to this premier climbing venue is predicated on our stewardship of these priceless artifacts and climbers' abilities to restrain from any encroachment on this feature—regardless of how careful you think you might be.

TRAIL EROSION

Trail erosion on the steep banks of the gullies between the fins and at the base of West Gate Wall can be a problem. If we do not stay on established trails we will soon have no spots from which to belay. DO NOT CUT SWITCHBACKS.

GETTING THERE FROM HELENA

Option I: Go east on Custer Ave past the airport to Canyon Ferry Road #430. Once at the dam, stay on the main road past the visitor center (beware of speed traps). Continue about eight miles on Route 284 to the Hellgate Gulch access (to the east) and the Hellgate Recreation Area (toward the reservoir). Turn left and follow the winding dirt road 2.5 miles to the national forest boundary.

Option 2: Go south on U.S. Highway 12/287 toward Townsend. About 7 miles south of the smelter in East Helena, turn left on Spokane Creek Road, marked "Canyon Ferry Recreation Area." Follow a very winding road for 9.5 miles to the Canyon Ferry Dam. From here follow the same directions for Option 1.

GETTING THERE FROM BOZEMAN

Go west on Interstate-90 to Exit 274 (Wheat, MT) and take US Highway 287 north for 32 miles to Townsend. At the 4-way stop (Broadway St) go right (east) on U.S. Highway 12 toward White Sulphur Springs for 2.5 miles and turn left on Route 284 (north) following signs for Canyon Ferry State Recreation Area. The road to Avalanche Gulch is just north of mile marker 19. The Hellgate Gulch Road is another 1.5 miles north of Avalanche. Turn right (east) and go 2.5 miles to the national forest boundary near the mouth of the canyon.

PARKING

It is recommended to park in the large area next to the Forest Service sign. There are limited pullouts in the canyon and the easy I0-minute walk is a nice warm-up.

**HELLGATE GULCH
ENTRANCE**

**EXTRA PARKING AND
MARGINAL CAMPING**

Kim Mergenthaler on *Thin Fine Line 5.12a*
Photo by Jake Mergenthaler

HELLGATE GULCH ORGANIZATION OF DESCRIPTIONS

Hellgate's unique fins are roadside but their double-sided parallel nature poses a dilemma on how to best organize the route descriptions. This chapter is broken into separate sections, each representing a different aspect of each fin. The formations on the north side of the creek are listed first—starting at the mouth of the gulch with the prominent West Gate Wall. Following the final fin on the north side, the East Gate Wall, the description order returns to the mouth of the gulch and begins with Baker's Rock and continues with the formations along the south side of the creek ending at Wasp Wall. Each section begins with the routes nearest the road, since they are the easiest routes to identify. If the fin has climbs on the sunnier southwest-facing wall, the order travels around the fin on that side. Afterward, it returns to the road then follows any climbs up the northeast or backside of the feature. In general, all routes are described in the order they are encountered.

WEST GATE WALL

This is the stunning wall you first see as you drive up the road and cross the creek. It is gray and brown and about 200 feet tall. Routes are listed right to left.

1. THE CONTRARY 5.12a ★★★

On the far-right side of the wall, just off the road, lies this stunning and steep slab climb. It is thin, techy, and exciting—very nice rock. Name: There once was a pictograph thought to be a picture of a Contrary Warrior on a boulder at the base, but road crews demolished it.
80 ft, 7 bolts to chains
FA Bill Dockins, Kristen Drumheller, 1991

2. QUEEN BEE 5.11d ★★

Behind some bushes just off the road lies this sequential, fun climb. A bouldery start leads to improbable holds and then a well-bolted crux. Name: In the fall, large but docile bees rule this wall, but on the FA, Kim was the queen.
80 ft, 8 bolts to chains
FA Jake Mergenthaler, Kim Mergenthaler, 2004

3. SEDIMENTAL JOURNEY 5.11c

On the right side of the wall lies an intimidating bulge. Climb marginal rock to the roof, then start the journey. The rock is good after the roof, and the gear section isn't the crux.
85 ft, 5 bolts and gear to chains
FA Bill Dockins, Kristen Drumheller, 1988

4. LOOSE ATTRACTION 5.11a ★★

This exciting climb starts just after a rock staircase at a flat spot. Climb up the slick white rock to gain a bulge, grunt over this, then continue up into a seam. The seam is 5.10 with delicate holds. The crux is after the seam and bolt protected.
85 ft, bolts and small gear to chains
FA Bill Dockins, Kristen Drumheller, 1993

5. BURNING IN HELLGATE 5.11a ★★

Climb the face using big guns and big commitment. Start on the light rock under a significant overlap. Pull a bulge (hard but not the crux) to gain delicate face climbing. At ⅓ height, there is a committing move while your feet are near the last bolt. On one of my early attempts of this route, I stalled out at the top on a 20 ft runout to the chains. Randall growled, "It's only 5.9 up there." I pawed the razor-sharp holds like a teenager on lover's lane, but my feet kept blowing off the snot-slick nubbins. I shamefully lowered to the ground. Kim was belaying me (we were just friends, not even dating). A few months before, I had taken her climbing for the first time. After a few minutes of listening to my excuses, she asked if she could take a spin on it. Soon she was at the bolt where I had bailed. "I think I'll just go a bit farther," she said. I looked at my friend and whispered, "If she makes this, I'm gonna marry her," She made it.

85 ft, bolts to chains
FA Randall Green, Chris Coveny, Laurent Huber, 1996

6. PROJECT 5.13?

Second pitch of *Burning.*
135 ft, bolts to chains
Equipped by Jeff Ho, 2018

7. HOT, HOT, HOT! 5.12a/b ★★★

P1: Start on the flat spot by the stump of a small tree. Pad up the technical slab to a bulge with a prominent undercling below it. Pull over the bulge on screamer crimps. 5.10 climbing leads to chains. (5.10d, 85 ft, bolts)
P2: This pitch is seldom climbed. It's a bit sharp, but the rock quality is fantastic. (5.12a/b)
80 ft, bolts and TCUs and 1.5, 2.0 Friends
Descent 165' to ground.
FA Dwight Bishop, Randall Green, Bill Dockins

8. GIRL WITH THE DOCKINS TATTOO 5.12a ★

P1: Start on the flat spot below a faint right-trending corner. Climb easy rock to the edge of the arête, pull up and left on tricky ground. Gain good holds and jug haul until ¾ height. Thin climbing for several clips leads to the chains. Bill doesn't like this name. Sorry but it's perfect. (5.10d, 85 ft)
P2: Done in one long pitch from the ground. Continue after the chains on super-techy ground. (5.12a/b, 40 ft)
120 ft
P1. FA Jake Mergenthaler, Ted Simms, 2013
P2. Equipped by Jake Mergenthaler, Kim Mergenthaler; FA Leslie Gains-Germain 2020

9. BENEVOLENCE 5.11c ★★

P1: A classic climb that starts between two Mountain Mahogany trees. Do the bouldery start or use the tree. The crux comes at ⅓ height on small holds. This climb can be like a patient mother: sometimes it comforts you, and other times it can give you a spankin'. Be good and love your mother. (5.10b, 85 ft, 7 bolts)
P2: Pull hard off the chains and navigate several bulges on bolts. At ⅔ height, reach friendly ground and plug in your 1.5 Friend. (5.11c, 80 ft)
Descent: 170 ft to ground
165 ft, 9 bolts and gear to chains
FA Randall Green, Theresa Green, Martin McBirney, 1996

10. HELL OR HIGH WATER 5.13c PG13 ★★★

Meant to be climbed as one long pitch but with chains in the middle. Climbing to the chains is 5.12c and techy. After the chains, move into a 30-foot-long crack then through a cruxy boulder problem. There's a no-hands rest up there, but above that, more hard climbing.
170 ft, 18+ bolts and small-med gear to chains
FA Jeff Ho, Henry Schlotzhauer, 2019

11. POMEGRANATE 5.11c ★★

This can be found up the hill from *Benevolence* on a sloping rocky trail. The climbing is very engaging. It has a sharp crux, but the rock is impeccable. This is highly recommended if you're tough enough, but it's hard for 5.11c.
100 ft, 13 bolts, shares chains with *Chewed*
FA Meg Hall, Rand Swanson, 2003

12. CHEWED BY RATS 5.11b/c

Start right of *Thin Fine Line* from a small belay spot. Follow a right-leaning dihedral (5.10) supplementing bolts with #1.5 and #2.0 Friends. The crux is on a bulletproof shield. A stopper may be placed above the last bolt. This is a somewhat serious climb with the chance of a ledge fall.
90 ft, bolts and gear to 2 inch, chains
FA Bill Dockins, Kristen Drumheller, 1997

13. THIN FINE LINE BETWEEN PLEASURE AND PAIN 5.12a ★★

P1: On the far-left side of the wall lies this sequential climb on white and gray rock. Climb the bolt line to an airy arête that finishes on a ledge. (5.12a, 80 ft, bolts)
P2: Best to belay from the hangers rather than the small rusty chain. Slap up the clean arête. The crux comes low. Finish on the steep slab—not a gimmie. There's a chossy project that heads left from the ledge. Don't be confused, stay right. (5.11d, 80 ft)
Descent 185 ft to ground
160 ft, bolts to chains
P1. FA Randall Green, Aaron LeFohn, Martin McBirney, 1995
P2. FA Kim Mergenthaler, Randall Green, 2004

14. SNAKE EYES 5.10d

Start right of a guano-filled cave. Cry up the tricky slab to bigger holds and an easier finish. Not the best climb.
60 ft, 7 bolts to chains
FA Jake Mergenthaler, 2004

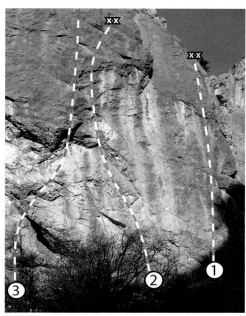

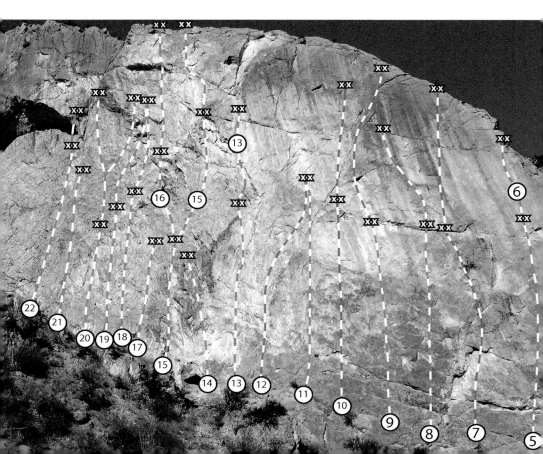

WINTER WALL

This area is an extention of the West Gate Wall. This is the steep and orangish-brown area that includes the routes under the huge roof and all routes west of *Thin Fine Line*.
Routes are listed right to left.

15. FATAL ATTRACTION 5.11b ★★

P1: Begin on a dirt ledge. Step right onto the route, pull through tricky and airy first moves, then cruise up a corner to a comfortable ledge. (5.9, 60 ft)
P2: Crank up steep brown rock onto steeper gargoyle-like flakes. These have been tested, but climb at your own risk. Pumpy, fun, gymnastic moves. Not for rock snobs. (5.11b, 85 ft)
P3: Start on sharp but bomber rock, gain a left-leaning traverse (crux), and finish on incut holds. Excellent rock quality. (5.11b, 70 ft)
Descent: 200 ft rappel from top chains or three shorter raps.
215 ft, bolts to chains
FA Jake Mergenthaler, Kim Mergenthaler, 2003

16. TSUNAMI 5.12a ★

P1: Same as *Fatal*. (5.9, 60 ft, 6 bolts)
P2: From the comfortable ledge, head up left on tricky ground to gain a slightly loose, but juggy, section. Finish on a more technical bulge to a semi-hanging stance. Not great, but it gets you to the money pitch. (5.11a, 75 ft)
P3: Steep heady climb up wave-like feature save some juice for the top. (5.12a 85 ft, bolts)
Descent: 200 ft rap from top or three shorter raps.
220 ft, bolts to chains
FA Jake Mergenthaler, Kim Mergenthaler, 2003

17. AKs AND BAD BELAYS 5.8

Start uphill from *Fatal* just right of a stinky corner. Crank up the steep start to gain better rock on the right side of the arête. Resist the temptation to stay in the corner because of the pooey choss. Name: I put this route up one day by myself (bad belay) with bullet-heads shooting semi-automatics in the meadow below.
60 ft, bolts to chains
FA Jake Mergenthaler, 2017

18. NEUROTIC VULTURE 5.12a ★★

This is one of the more approachable of the second pitch 5.12s due to its short crux.
P1: Begin 10 feet left of the chossy corner on brown rock that looks much better than it is. It ends at a stance shared with some creature who uses it as a bathroom. (5.10b, 65 ft, bolts)
P2: Start up a fun corner then cranks right onto wave-like gray rock. Pull the obvious bulge on slopers (crux). Finish on pumpy, brown, fragile jugs and hidden pockets. Can be led as one pitch and TR'd on a 70m rope. (5.12a, 65 ft)
Name: A song by the Pixies.
Descent: A 120 ft rap or two shorter ones.
130 ft, bolts to chains
FA Jake Mergenthaler, Kim Mergenthaler, P1. 2002, P2. 2015

19. FIFTY SHADES OF CHOSS (AKA ROPE SNATCHER) 5.12a ★★

P1: Start on a sloping stance, climb up a nondescript gray face to reach steeper brown terrain. Fun and thought-provoking. (5.10b, 65 ft)
P2: Move off the ledge to featured brown rock. Get slapped in the face by the lower crux, keep it together, then charge over the roof on positive holds. No rock snobs, but not super loose. A laugh a minute. Can be led in one pitch and TR'd with a 70m rope. (5.12a, 65 ft)
Name: Tie me up and slap me, but I'll still love the choss.
Descent: A 120 ft rap or two shorter ones.
130 ft, bolts to chains
FA Jake Mergenthaler, Kim Mergenthaler, 2003, 2016

20. CALIFORNIA DREAMIN' 5.12b/c ★★

P1: Start at the beginning of the stairs. Move from gray rock into brown jugs, then crimp up a gray shield on good, sharp rock. (5.10b, 55 ft)
P2: *California Screamin'*
From the sloping ledge, crank up through fragile jugs. At the second bolt, head right to avoid a loose flake (5.10 jugs). Continue up a steepening technical face following right-trending bolts to an exciting steep scoop. Head out right on good holds. Fun and pumpy. (5.12b, 75 ft)
P2: *Hollywood Variation* ★★★
Start on the same sloping ledge, head up the fragile jugs through techy terrain, then follow bolts up to the left on a slopey rail. Cruise up a thin but superb face. Finish on 11a jugs. Very steep and well bolted. Powerful. CAUTION: Can be led in one pitch and TR'd with a 70m rope, but you must walk up the hill and perform various shenanigans. (5.12c, 75 ft)
Descent: Very carefully rap with one 70m rope or 2 shorter raps.
130 ft, bolts to chains
P1. FA Randall Green, Brandon Alke, 2002
P2. FA Jake Mergenthaler, Kim Mergenthaler, 2017

21. SEA OF CHEESE 5.10d ★★

Commence on a flat area 6 feet right of steep steps. Scream up the super thin start on good rock, then crawl thru the obligatory choss band. Prepare to smile once reaching the great orange rock with long pulls between good holds. Pumpy fun. Can continue past the chains to reach *Sea of Choss's* anchors.
Name: Primus album, plus it looks like cheddar.
85 ft, bolts to chains
FA Jake Mergenthaler, 2006

22. SEA OF CHOSS 5.12b ★

P1: Start on steep steps. Climb up easy gray rock with dark hangers. Navigate a bit of gravel on orange steep rock to gain more jugs. Fight the pump to the chains. Positive holds, long pulls, and a bit sequential. (5.11a 90 ft)
P2: Up and left on dirty jugs then up a very thin dihedral. Finish with a powerful move below the chains. It's not great, but the corner is memorable. There's a choss project that heads right from P2 and shares the same chains. Needs some cleaning as it's thin and friable. Can be led from trhe ground and TR'd with one 70m rope. (5.12b, 35 ft)
125 ft, bolts to chains
FA Jake Mergenthaler, Kim Mergenthaler, 2016

23. UNCOMFORTABLY NUMB 5.12b ★★
P1: Starts on a flat section above the steep stairs on a short sharp slab, then becomes steep and pumpy on gym-like holds. Next comes a thin crux followed by many jugs to a small ledge. (5.10a, 90 ft)
P2: Head up a blocky roof (a little guano never hurt nobody) then crank over it on small holds. There's more adventure waiting above as another hard section hits you at mid-height. Good rock throughout. (5.12b, 85 ft)
Name: You guessed it, put it up in January...brrrr.
Descent: Bring two ropes and rap to the ground. If fixed draws are there it is possible to rap twice with one 70m rope making sure to clip these draws (or you will be hanging in space). Not as convenient or good as some of the other 2-pitch 5.12s.
175 ft, bolts to chains
FA Jake Mergenthaler, Kim Mergenthaler, 2002

24. HELL ON WHEELS 5.10a ★★
This line is full of memorable holds. Start on *Weird* and after the second bolt move out right and begin your tour of cool moves on great holds.
90 ft, bolts to chains
FA Jake Mergenthaler, Kim Mergenthaler, 2012

25. WEIRD SCIENCE 5.10a ★★
A great route on super featured rock. Start on a platform near an 8'x 10' flat boulder. The climb leans left after the tricky start and is steep right away with a technical crux at mid-height. Name: 80s movie. Resist the urge to put a brassier on your head and take a shower?
90 ft, bolts to chains
FA Randall Green, Paul Travis, 1999

26. IRRATIONAL EXUBERANCE 5.10b ★★
More sustained and technical than most routes under the roof. Use *Weird* as a reference and move 8 feet left. Start on big holds and a cool undercling to gain steep technical terrain. When the hands run out there's always good feet. Name: My zeal for bolting has made me squeeze a few routes in this area.
90 ft, bolts to chains
FA Randall Green, Kim Mergenthaler, Jake Mergenthaler, 2004

27. DEVIL'S HIGHWAY 5.13 ★★
This is the climb that started it all. Randall had the vision to bolt this, though I thought it would be too chossy. We started from the ground with hooks and gear, making it about halfway the first day, then he and John finished it up. Mark Pelletier and Jack Childress equipped the second pitch. With the obvious second pitch, this climb can be used as a reference for other climbs.
P1: Start on a flat belay ledge directly under the huge roof with fixed draws. Crank through the opening moves on big holds. Follow a left-leaning crack system that ends with a 10-foot runout on positive holds. At ⅔ height, a tricky crux hits you. Finish on big scary jugs. Classic route. (5.10b, 90 ft)
P2: From the chains head up nondescript 5.11 climbing on somewhat fragile rock. At a roof, start grunting on good holds. Near the top of roof, the holds get smaller. Turning the roof is the crux. (5.13, 60 ft)
Descent: Rap with one 70m or two shorter ropes.
150 ft, bolts to chains
P1. FA Randall Green, John Burbich, Jake Mergenthaler, 1998
P2. FA Mark Pelletier, Jack Childress, 1998
FFA Luke Evans, 2003

28. MELT DOWN 5.11a ★★
Start uphill from *Highway* on a small flat spot. Move through a fragile start to z-shaped jugs. Head up a steep slopey section. When the bolt is to the left, make one more move to a jug at the crux, then reach left to clip. Continue up on fun sustained rock.
90 ft, bolts to chains
FA Jake Mergenthaler, Kim Mergenthaler, 2004

29. SPONTANEOUS COMBUSTION 5.11a ★★
This climb will make your forearms feel like they are on fire. Two climbs left of *Highway*, commence on thin holds to gain bomber rock on a light brown face. Hold on and be rewarded by sustained and fun climbing to the top.
90 ft, bolts to chains
FA Randall Green, Chris Alke, and Van Alke, 1998

30. THE LAST UNICORN 5.11a ★★
Start on the right side of a vaguely arrow-shaped feature (15 feet tall). A tricky and painfully thin start leads to jugs, and a small roof pulls through the roof on the right, then continues up for a tricky move or two. Head for the chains on good, but pumpy, holds.
Name: A tongue-in-cheek homage to a goat horn found at the foot of the route.
90 ft, bolts to chains
FA Jake Mergenthaler, Kim Mergenthaler, 2014

31. HORIZONTAL MAMBO 5.11a
Start on the left of the vaguely arrow-shaped feature. Move through choss to an insecure face on bolts that are 7 feet apart.
65 ft, bolts to chains
FA Jake Mergenthaler, 2000

32. GUN SHOW 5.11d ★★
This was once a terrible and chossy single-pitch route called *Dirt Nap*. I added a steep second pitch and reworked the first one. Both pitches turned out pretty cool. I recommend climbing this as one pitch, as it would be very awkward starting the second pitch while your partner belayed from chains.
P1: Move up a blocky start on fragile rock. Pull through a small roof onto a brown face. Fun sequential climbing leads to more fragile holds that trend left into the crack before a short pumpy lieback to the chains. (5.10c, 65 ft)
P2: We just don't get many steep jug hauls here in Helena, so take the stars with a grain of salt. Move past chains on tricky underclings and liebacking. Once you gain the roof, it's a matter of hanging onto steep jugs. A tricky and challenging section awaits just beneath the chains. (5.11d, 60 ft)
Descent: Can be rapped or TR'd with one 70m rope.
125 ft, bolts to chains
FA Jake Mergethaler, Kim Mergenthaler, 2016

33. FIGHT CLUB 5.12a ★★
A great climb that starts on large flakes to gain a handrail to a ledge. Power up a steep crack on the brown rock with dark-colored bolts. The crux is at the end of the crack. Sport climbers are not allowed to jam!
75 ft, bolts to chains

34. BASS CRAZY 5.11c/d ★★
Start on the far-right side of the roof on a flat spot. Begin on a toothy boulder, follow a seam to a no-hands rest, step back left onto arête, then charge up the white overlaps. The top is lower quality 5.10 climbing. So good without having perfecr stone! Name: It was a cool trucker hat, and also there's a long story about me being a terrible fisherman.
75 ft, bolts to chains
FA Jake Mergenthaler, Kim Mergenthaler, 2006

35. KIMMY AND THE BANSHEES 5.11d
(Not Pictured)
Same start as *Bass*. After a no-hands rest, traverse left on white rock. Pull through bulges and finish on the friable rock. Not great. Name: On an early attempt, I was close to the top and flaming, so I got suckered out left on some gnarly blocks. They blew, I flew. I screamed so loud that Bill came up from the Wasp Wall to check on us. Kim does not like getting hit by rocks.
85 ft, bolts to chains
FA Jake Mergenthaler, Kim Mergenthaler, 2010

36. SLEEPER 5.11b (Not Pictured)
Up the hill from *Bass* there's a chossy climb (that looks like a 5.8) with a chain link for first bolt. It's a slopey boulder start to an ok-climbing kind of thing.
65 ft, bolts to chains
FA Jake Mergenthaler, 2012

Eric Christianson on *Hell or High Water 5.13c PG13*

THE ATRIUM

Found at the upper end of West Gate Wall's southwest face, this area is neither tall nor wide, but it does have superb views and is the sunniest wall in the area. The routes are short and sharp, yet have a cool quality due to their supreme position. The stone is high quality, and the protection is solid and fairly spaced. The routes are popular in late fall to early spring.

Approach

Continue along the base of the Winter Wall until it ends beyond a huge roof at a shattered dihedral. Work up the scree slope on a goat trail until almost at the top of the formation, then head back east on a narrow trail to an exposed ledge. The routes are described left to right as you encounter them across the ledge.

1. **CLASSIC NEW JERSEY** 5.11b/c
This pumpy climb is no joke. Powerful moves on steep rock. It is the farthest left of the five routes on this wall.
45 ft, 5 bolts to *Sundance* chains
FA Randall Green, Neil Sexton, 1998

2. **SUNDANCE** 5.11a ★
The second route from the left.
45 ft, 5 bolts gear (optional #1.5 Friend) to chains
FA Randall Green, Theresa Green, Gordon King, 1993

3. **EL CHORRO GRANDE** 5.10a ★
Fun face climb to a heady seam. Keep it together and gun for the chains.
45 ft, 3 bolts, gear (wired nuts & #2 friends) to chains
FA Mark Pearson, Jamie Johnson, 1990

4. **HEAVY WITH YOUNG** 5.10b
The climb ascends sharp, cheese-grater-like holds on brown rock right of *El Choro* to an obvious hole and seam above bolts.
45 ft, 4 bolts, gear (#3.5 and #1.5 friend) to El Chorro chains
FA Mark Pearson, Jamie Johnson, 1990

5. **RAZOR EDGES** 5.10c ★
Farthest right at The Atrium. Clip first bolt by standing on top of the crumbling block at the right side of the ledge. The first 20 feet is thin and sustained on sharp holds.
45 ft, 6 bolts to chains
FA Randall Green, Brian Knaff, 1993

Anju on *Thin Fine Line 5.12a*
Photo by Jake Mergenthaler

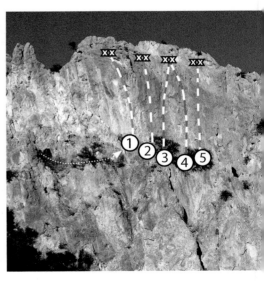

Kim Mergenthaler on *Fight Club 5.12a*
Photo by Jake Mergenthaler

ON KRISTEN DRUMHELLER AND BILL DOCKINS
By Jake Mergenthaler

As a partnership, Kristen and Bill have left their mark on Montana climbing since the late 70s. Not only have they put up many first ascents, but together they authored and designed three Montana guidebooks. Bill began climbing in 1974 and soon thereafter began establishing routes in Gallatin Canyon. In 1985 he and Kristen took a yearlong climbing road trip. They witnessed the birth of American sport climbing at Smith Rock, Joshua Tree, and elsewhere. With this newfound perspective they returned home to Montana looking for possibilities.

They began exploring limestone outcrops in the Big Belt and Little Belt mountain ranges, driving and hiking up many of the major canyons and minor drainages. One canyon, Hellgate Gulch, drew them back again and again to climb. In 1987 they cleaned and put two bolts on the testpiece *Inferno*, which Bill climbed the next year. Also in 1987, Tom Kalakay and Bill started working on the Wasp Wall, bolting three routes by hand. Tom and Bill hand drilled many granite routes before, but the chalky nature of Hellgate limestone made drill bits bind and break, frustrating development of the awaiting lines. In 1988, fully armed with a power drill, Bill and Kristen set about to establish many of the area's classics.

In talking with Bill, two things stand out: his respect and admiration for Kristen, his wife of nearly 40 years, and his sense of stewardship for Hellgate. The pair worked together to find, clean, and bolt the lines and were often surprised that the blank-looking walls were actually laden with hidden drip pockets and other features that allowed passage. The movement that these technical climbs demanded, coupled with the often-exquisite rock, led them to put up new routes for decades.

Bill Dockins and Kristen Drumheller

Their love and respect for the rock led them to endeavor to keep the area as pristine as possible and minimize both damage to the rock and the visual impact of climbing. This, combined with the ethic of placing gear in cracks and pockets—placing a bolt only when necessary—led to some heady, if not bold, leads. They once proposed adding a bolt to *The Flying Popoffskis* only to have a fellow pioneer of Montana climbing respond, "If we did that it would cheat all the climbers who climbed it before." After all, those earlier climbers mustered up the courage to make those final, insecure moves with their feet smeared well above the last bolt. That seems as reasonable an argument as any to leave these testpieces as they are. And truly most are heady, but seldom dangerous.

Kristen and Bill both have a gift for envisioning aesthetic lines on sheer, seemingly blank faces. They are also able to keep their heads about them and climb these classics. Climbing in Hellgate and Montana would not be the same without their contributions.

NORTHEAST FACE

Basically the backside of the huge Westgate Wall. There are three climbs directly on the road, and the rest are up the steep bushy hill to the west. Walking up the trail, these climbs are on the left. Routes described left to right.

1. ALTERED STATES 5.10 ★

Find this climb directly on the road. *Altered* is the left-most route and shares anchors with *Fatman*. Better than it looks.

40 ft, bolts to chains
FA Randall Green, Aaron Lafohn, 1995

2. FATMAN/CHOSSMAN AND ROBIN 5.10 ★★

Very popular despite poor rock quality. Fun and reachy, climbing up a pocketed vertical face.

40 ft, bolts to chains
FA Randall Green, Aaron Lafohn, 1995

3. A DESPERATE MEASURE 5.10b

Start 15 feet uphill.

45 ft, bolts to chains
FA Jake Mergenthaler, 2003

4. FOREIGN POLICY 5.12

One of a few projects on the immaculate but hold-deficient wall located up the steep trail between West Gate Fin and Circus Wall. These routes tend to be slippery and challenging.

65 ft, bolts to chains
Equipped by Martin McBirney, 1996

5. NEVER MIND 5.10+

Near the top of the steep trail, look left, and you will see the flat belay spot of *Unforgiven*. Down and left of that fine route is this lost, lonely and homely line.

65 ft, bolts to chains
FA Jake Mergenthaler

6. UNFORGIVEN 5.11b/c ★★

Near the top of the steep trail between fins of Westgate and Circus walls, look left to find the stellar belay spot with a bench under this great, steep, gray line. Begin on easy suspect rock through two bulges. Head up overlaps on wonderful rock.

80 ft, 10 bolts to chains
FA Jake Mergenthaler, Kim Mergenthaler, 2002

7. DIRTY WORK 5.12c ★★

Just right of *Unforgiven* lies this crazy amazing climb. Bouldery start leads to an improbable roof to slab move. Stay right past the next bolts, then head up thin gorgeous rock. My claim to fame is Frank Dusel said it was Hard. Name: I bolted this climb for my wife. You could say, I was doing all the "dirty work" for her.

85 ft, bolts to chains
FA Jake Mergenthaler, Kim Mergenthaler, 2008

8. BOOMERANG 5.12b ★★

Start on a nice belay ledge up and right from *Dirty*. Climb up striking arête that ends in a triangle roof. Continue slightly easier but sporty climbing. Great rock, heady climb.

90 ft, 10 bolts to chains
FA Bill Dockins, Kirsten Drumheller, 1990

9. SEASONAL WEASEL 5.12a ★★

Start on an indistinct blocky seam on the upper end of the wall. Smear carefully past miserly bolt placements. Runout on juggy ground near top. Sporty. 70m needed for TR.

120 ft, 11 bolts to chains
FA Bill Dockins, Kirsten Drumheller, Brian Haggerty 1990

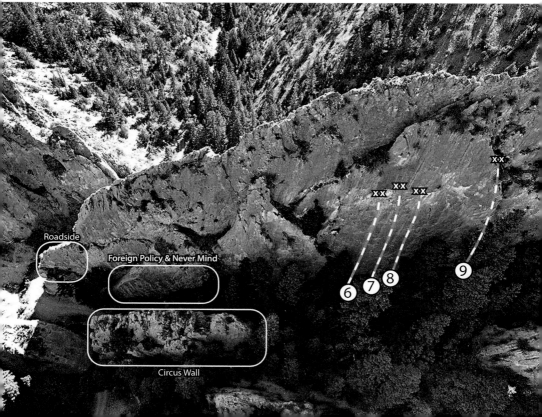

CIRCUS WALL

This featured tan and gray fin is the next one behind the West Gate Wall on the north side of the creek. Routes described uphill from right to left.

1. CRASH 5.10b ★★
Begin from the road. Climb an insecure gray bulge, gain an easy corner, and move left on a beautiful shield.
65 ft, bolts to chains
FA Jake, Kim Mergenthaler

2. FOUR WHEELER 5.10b ★★
Begin on the road down from other climbs. A couple of doable bulges mark this route.
65 ft, bolts to chains
FA Randall Green, Brandon Alke

3. ROAD SHOW 5.10a/b ★★
The road side arête on the end of the buttress. Technical moves past several bulges make this an exciting and sporty climb for the grade.
100 ft, 11 bolts to chains
FA Randall Green, Theresa Green, Tom Lund, Hunter Coleman, 1993

4. LEARNING TO FLY 5.12a/b ★★★
This climb leads the pack of quality 5.12s in the area; it offers cool moves on memorable features. Follows con-cave weakness on extreme right side of the Main Circus Wall. Merges with *Road Show* at the top and shares one bolt on the upper ramp.
90 ft, 10 bolts to chains
FA Randall Green, Theresa Green. Martin McBirney, 1993

5. ALL NEW EPISODE 5.12a ★
The word cerebral describes this half-moon-shaped climb on steep brown rock. Start on sharp brown stone to a slight dish; head left on fun ground to a desperate crux. Keep your wits about you as you surge to finish.
85 ft, 9 bolts to chains
FA Kristen Drumheller, Bill Dokins, 1991

6. CRAZY ZONE 5.12a ★
A right-slanting bolt line on brown rock that turns to gray at top. Excellent sustained climbing through a crowd of pockets leads to an elegant, yet devious, finish.
75 ft, 8 bolts to chains
FA Kristen Drumheller, Bill Dokins, 1993

7. POOPY BANDALOOPY 5.11b ★
When we were working on this climb, the wind twirled us like manic trapeze artists while we hung from our rope. Also, the Banclaloup Dance Troupe was in the area, so we honored them with this crass name. Steep/pumpy, laybacking up a plumb line on marginal to good rock.
80 ft, bolts to chains
FA Jake, Kim Mergenthaler, 2002

8. HUMAN CANNONBALL 5.11c ★
This route climbs vertical rock through bulges and has some interesting moves. It stands just left of *Bandaloopy*. climbing near some bad rock, but the line is good.
80 ft, some small/medium stoppers and TCU's to protect be-tween bolts, chains.
FA Kristen Drumheller, Bill Dokins, 1993

9. THE FLYING POPOFFSKIS 5.11c ★★★
Steep and fun pulling leads to a pumpy crack with good rests. A devious crux then rears its ugly head; get ready to run it out to the chains on great rock.
75 ft, 5 bolts, small-med gear to chains
FA Kristen Drumheller, Bill Dokins, Briand Hagerty, 1988

10. BROWN EYED GIRL 5.11a ★
Begin on sloping belay just after the trail turns back towards the wall. The start is a bit loose. Climb through the "eye" feature to gain better climbing.
Bolts to shared chains with *Flying Popoffskis*
FA Jake Mergenthaler, Kim Mergenthaler 2010

11. TIGER TEETH 5.11b ★★
I think this baby's a bit of a sandbag! I hope it is since I've never climbed it clean. The route is good but expect some difficult moves. Climb up the sporty bit through cool pockets and edges to a desperate lay-back crux and then easier to the top.
65 ft, 7 bolts to chains
FA Kristen Drumheller, Bill Dokins, 1991

12. SIDE SHOW 5.11b
Climb steep pockets to a horizontal break before taking the bolt line on the left to the ridge crest.
65 ft, 6 bolts, tricams for finger pockets to chains
FA Kristen Drumheller, Bill Dokins, 1990

13. BEARDED LADY 5.10a
This short and steep climb is the farthest left on the wall and is an OK warmup. It starts on a precarious belay spot and climbs marginal rock to a cool lay-back with some fun moves on good rock.
45 ft, bolts to chains. Stick clip 1st bolt.
FA Jake Mergenthaler, Kim Mergenthaler, 2002

JURASSIC ROCK

Twenty feet up the road from the Circus Wall are two fins that converge on the road. The one on the left is Jurassic. Routes described left to right.

1. HIDING FROM RAPTORS 5.11a ★

Begin on the left side of the rock. Climb up fragile underclings to pumpy, blocky terrain. It ends on easier, better rock. Fun and physical. Wear a helmet.
50 ft, bolts to chains
FA Randall Green, Paul Travis, Laurent Huber, 1998

2. EXTINCTION 5.11c

Intense climb up the middle of the tan face. A bit fragile. Rose bushes often cause swearing at the base.
50 ft, bolts to chains
FA Randall Green, Paul Travis, Laurent Huber, 1998

3. JURASSIC PARK 5.10a

Forgettable climb that starts on road. Climb up the arête on suspect rock. Wear a helmet—about same difficulty as *Steg* but better bolted.
55 ft, bolts to chains
FA Jake Mergenthaler, 2017

4. STEGOSAURUS 5.9+

This fun climb starts on the road. Easy start leads to a crux roof on fragile chert. Leading the route is heady, so be comfortable on 5.10.
65 ft, bolts to chains
FA Scott Payne, Randall Green, Brian Knaff, 1993

STEPCHILD WALL
(EAST FACE OF JURRASIC ROCK)
Continue up the road around the corner for another 20 yards. Wall is on left. Shady most of the time. Described left to right.

1. RAZOR DANCE 5.10b
Start on the road. Work up a fragile (but easy) death flake to gain a sharp and intense one-move-wonder crux. Easier climbing follows.
50 ft, bolts to chains
FA Jake Mergenthaler, Kim Mergenthaler, 2001

2. ANCIENT GRAFFITI 5.11c ★
Commence on very techy terrain that gains a bulge. Hug the rounded arête using seams out right.
45 ft, bolts to chains
FA Jake Mergenthaler, Kim Mergenthaler, 2011

3. RED-HEADED STEPCHILD 5.10c ★★
A memorable climb that starts on slippery gray rock and continues up tricky ground to a cool flake. Finishes on portable chert.
Name: The first climb I bolted at Hellgate. It was done with a generator and pawnshop drill. I was definitely the unwanted child.
70 ft, bolts to chains
FA Jake Mergenthaler, Kim Mergenthaler, 1998

4. HERSHEY CHERTS 5.10b ★★★
Fun and popular. Start up on the dirt hillside. Easy ledges lead to a thin, fun flake, then more thought-provoking climbing on good rock.
75 ft, bolts to chains
FA Jake Mergenthaler, Kim Mergenthaler, 2000

EAST GATE WALL ROADSIDE
This wall sits on the north end of the canyon directly on the road and across from the wall with the Pictographs.

1. LEA'S 5.6 ★★★
A fun climb up a clean face on the left edge of the fin. Look for the name "Lea" inscribed near the base of the climb (climbers did not do this, please do not write on the rock). This is one of the only beginner routes in the canyon.
70 ft, bolts to welded chains
FA Randall Green and Darrin Schreder, 1993

2. BESSIE 5.10
Right of *Lea's* on the end of the fin. Graffiti inscription near ground level marks the base of the climb. Bouldery starts past two bolts leads to easy face climbing above.
70 ft, 6 bolts to *Lea's* anchor
FA Jim Semmelroth, Randall Green, 1993

3. NIGHTMARE ON BUMBLY STREET 5.8
This climb ascends the right shoulder on the end of East Gate, facing the road.
45 ft, 4 bolts to chains
FA Randall Green, Nate McCormick

Kyle Perkins on *Red-Headed Step Child 5.10c*
Photo by Brad Maddock

EAST GATE WALL NE FACE

This steep and beautiful wall is on the far north end of the canyon. There is good parking just upstream from here. Since it is in the shade, this area holds some fine warm-weather climbing. From the base of *Lea's*, hike around the cliff to the right and up a steep trail along the base of the towering wall. Routes are described left to right ascending the hill. The last two require an alternate approach method.

1. AIN'T NO SUNSHINE 5.11a ★★★
The first short face climbs uphill from *Bumbly*. Sharp but fun!
40 ft, 5 bolts to chains
FA Bill Dockins, Kristen Drumheller, 1999

2. WORM HOLE 5.12a ★★★
An excellent undulating route. Sequential and gripping cruxes. Sporty!
90 ft, 10 bolts to chains
FA Bill Dokins, Kristen Drumheller, 1997

3. DEATH POPCORN 5.12a ★★
Begin on a nice belay platform. Work right into underclings then straight up minding the limestone "popcorn" under feet. Sharp and sequential.
75", bolts to chains
FA Jake Mergenthaler, Kim Mergenthaler

4. CANYON FAIRY 5.11b ★★★
You must try this quintessential Hellgate route: powerful, heady, and very rewarding! Climb immaculate stone through bulges just left of *Cold Day*.
80 ft, 8 bolts to chains
FA Bill Dokins, Kristen Drumheller, 1995

5. COLD DAY IN HELLGATE 5.10d/11a ★★
This route begins with layback moves up a flake then face climbing past 3 bolts (crux). Move left to a diagonal crack. Crack may be full of grass.
100 ft, 8 bolts, medium gear to chains
FA Kristen Drumheller, Bill Dockins, 1992

6. DYNAMITE 5.11c
Short on good rock.
40 ft, bolts to chains
FA Jake, Kim Mergenthaler

7. GREAT FULL DEAD 5.10d ★★
Start on steep featured rock to gain a corner and easier ground.
85 ft, bolts to chains
FA Jake, Kim Mergenthaler

8. SWITCHBLADE 5.11d
Start just right of *Great Full Dead*. Insecure moves reaches a pumpy flake, easier climbing above.
85 ft, bolts to chains
FA Jake Mergenthaler, Kim Mergenthaler

[Next routes are a few hundred yards up]

9. POP TART 5.11d/12a (Not Pictured)
It is easier to approach this and *Sweet Tart* by walking farther up the road and angling up the hillside along a faint game trail. Lefthand of two routes near the top of the fin.
40 ft, 5 bolts to cold shuts
FA Meg Hall, Rand Swanson, 1998

10. SWEET TART 5.12a (Not Pictured)
Right of *Pop Tart*.
40 ft, bolts to cold shuts
FA Meg Hall, Rand Swanson, Bill Dockins, 1995

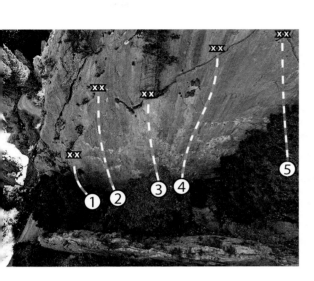

Maiza Lima on *Death Popcorn 5.12a*
Photo by Drew Smith

DANTE'S WALL

A beautiful northeast-facing wave of gray rock. Traverse in from the Wasp Wall or directly across the creek across the road from the Westgate Wall. Either way you will be navigating an unstable scree slope until you reach the base of the cliff.

1. INFERNO 5.12+ ★★★
This is a thin crack line in the middle of the wall. Crux is a thin barn-door lieback below the bulge. This route has not seen many redpoint ascents.
120 ft, 2 bolts, small wires and gear to 2" to chains
FA Bill Dockins, Kristen Drumheller, 1988

2. SEVENTH CIRCLE 5.13b ★★★
The first ascensionist described it as quite a wild pitch, with five distinct crux sections (4th one being the most difficult) that each test a different set of technical skills. Starts right of *Inferno* and left of *Purgatory*.
115 ft, 16 bolts to chains
FA Kyle O'Meara, Taylor Fragomeni, 2020

3. PURGATORY 5.10a ★★★
A superb limestone crack with a tree growing out of the base on the east side of the wall.
70 ft, gear to 4" to chains
FA Bill Dockins, Kristen Drumheller, 1992

4. BETWEEN HEAVEN AND HELL 5.13b ★★★
Said to be an excellent well-bolted route that is very "projectable" with fun moves and a few tricky boulder problems. Follow the obvious arête to the anchor.
85 ft, bolts to chains

BAKER'S ROCK

First wall on the right when you enter the canyon. Steep dark gray slab directly across from the West Gate Wall that holds two slabby routes. To approach choose the path of least resistance across the creek and to the base of the wall.

5. GOOD CLEAN FUN 5.9 ★★
Fun bolted slab climbing to chains.
90 ft, bolts to chains
FA Bill Dockins, 2019

6. CARVED IN STONE 5.11a
Face climb up an ever-steepening slab left of a carved monogram by B.F. Baker.
80 ft, 8 bolts to chains
FA Bill Dockins, Kristen Drumheller, 1999

SETBACK BUTTRESS

Between Dante's Wall and Wasp Wall is a buttress set back above the creek. The routes are on northeast side of the fin and are described left to right. Hike to the buttress following a faint brushy "trail" from Wasp Wall.

1. LAME DUCK 5.10d ★

An exciting climb on featured rock on the far left side of the wall. Begin on a blunt arête and gain a steep water-worn slab. Keep your wits about you as you conquer the fun but sporty terrain above.

65 ft, 7 bolts to chains
FA Bill Dokins, Randall Green, 1995

2. SOMETIMES YOU FEEL LIKE A NUT 5.11a ★

Right of *Lame Duck*. Climb up steep rock, past bolts, to a stunning, yet dicey, crack (these gear placements are not for freshman) and finish on a broken face.

90 ft, 4 bolts, gear to 3", chains
FA Bill Dokins, Randall Green, 1995

3. SOMETIMES YOU DON'T 5.11d

This ain't no gimmie! Slither up steep and slick rock to a technical crux, pad up steep stone to chains.

60 ft, bolts to chains
FA Kristen Drumheller, Bill Dokins, 2001

Maiza Lima on *Between Heaven and Hell 5.13b*
Photo by Drew Smith

WASP WALL

The Wasp is the stunning wall around the first bend as you enter the canyon (past West Gate Wall). This area is easily recognized by steep, nearly perfect stone sparsely accented by huecos and marked with water streaks. On a hot summer evening this is the place to be with your toes in the creek and a beer in the laughing eddies. Routes go left to right.

1. SLIPPERY NIPPLE 5.10c/d (Not Pictured)

Begin on the arête that rises from the creek just left of *Round*. A bouldery and reachy start gives way to fun juggy climbing. Watch out for sharp edged roofs; take longer draws to avoid rope damage.

80 ft, bolts to chains
FA Jake Mergenthaler, Kim Mergenthaler, 2001

2. ROUND THE BEND 5.12c ★★

On the left side of the Wasp Wall, this gently curving line waits to make you cry uncle. Boulder up to a left-leaning crack, throw some gear in and reach the business. The crux comes in the middle with sequential micro-moves but the climb doesn't ease up until you finish a committing traverse to the chains. Shares chains with *Shadowplay*.

80 ft, 7 bolts, gear (med cams) to chains
FA Kristen Drumheller, Bill Dokins, 1989

3. SHADOWPLAY 5.12a ★★

This fine line ascends a brown streak to the right side of a roof. It's slightly overhanging and sustained.

80 ft, 7 bolts gear (2"-3" cams) to chains
FA Kristen Drumheller, Bill Dokins, 1988

4. RIGHT DYNAMIC 5.12c ★★★

One of the proudest lines in the book. This beauty begins on an off-vertical face, gains a short left-leaning seam (gear useful) and then shoots up through insecure and powerful bulges to a 6" diameter hole. Move right at hole and continue straight up to chain anchors.

85 ft, 6 bolts small gear to chains
FA Kristen Drumheller, Bill Dokins, 1988

5. STINGER 5.9 R

The wide, grungy crack to the same chain anchor as *Dynamic*; seldom climbed

80 ft, gear to 4", chains
FA Kristen Drumheller, Bill Dokins, 1988

6. STREET IN A STRANGE WORLD 5.11c ★★★

One of the first climbs in the canyon this was bolted with a hand drill; this climb will make you want to buy Bill and Tom a beer or curse them after getting sandbagged. Bill originally called this route a 10b. Start just left of a large tree and climb past a distinct hueco (15" diameter) and wander through a sustained face, finally gaining an easier crack. After fiddling in some great gear, launch into an unprotected 5.7 section for 30 feet.

105 ft, 7 bolts gear to 2", chains
FA Tom Kalakay, Bill Dokins, 1987 (bolts updated in 2020)

7. LIMBO 5.12c ★ (Not Pictured)

Deserving of a start if you are not faint of heart. This sequential climb on bulletproof stone has a well-protected crux but sporty bolt placements otherwise. Starts right of a tree and parallels *Street*.

105 ft, 6 bolts, small gear to chains (shares chains with *Street*)
FA Kristen Drumheller, Bill Dokins, 1988

8. PINCUSHION 5.10c ★

This fun thin crack and face climb is protected with gear but is a tad runout off the ground. Go right at a ledge to chain anchor directly above *Coral Seize*. A good toprope line exists between *Pincushion* and *Coral Seize* (goes at 5.12 something) but too close to aforementioned routes to bolt.

65 ft, gear to 4", chains
FA Tom Kalakay, Bill Dokins, 1987

9. CORAL SEIZE 5.12a R

Start right of *Pincushion*. Move left at 1st bolt and climb to a bulge. Protection above the bulge is difficult.

65 ft, bolts (once hand drilled, updated in 2020), small gear (small nuts, tricams and TCU's very useful) to chains
FA Kristen Drumheller and Bill Dokins, 1988

10. STYX AND STONES 5.11a

Starts the same as *Coral* and shares its first bolt (sequence is a bouldery 5.11). Move up right on a leaning stairstep-like feature to vertical crack. From ledge near top go straight up on easier terrain to chains.

65 ft, 4 bolts, gear (up to 3", small tricams, #2 Rock, #2 Friend and TCUs useful) chains
FA Kristen Drumheller and Bill Dokins, 1988

11. BARTO TAKES A WING-WING 5.10a

Start at a triangular hole (5.11 boulder move). Work up beautiful stone to a ledge. Travers left at ledge to share anchors with *Styx*.

65 ft, 1 bolt, small gear (TCU's, friends to #1.5 and a few wires) to chains
FA Tom Kalakay, Bill Dokins, and Bart Cannon, 1988

12. TOPROPE 5.12 (Not Pictured)

To the right of *Barto* and a chimney/crack system on shield-shaped buttress. Fixed nuts for anchor.

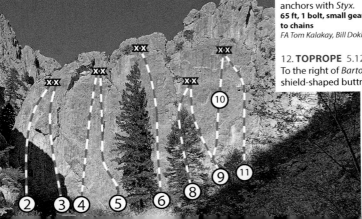

Drew Smith on *Shadowplay 5.12a*
Photo by Dylan Gordon

WASP WALL ROADSIDE/BACKSIDE
This section of fin lies next to the road across the creek from Jurassic Wall. Routes go right to left.

1. SHOT HOLE 5.11a X
This is a pretty piece of gray rock on the end of the fin. You can virtually reach over the creek from the road to the overhanging start. Move past a drilled hole (from the road crew) to crack. The line has been preserved as-is out of respect for the bold FA.
80 ft, no bolts, no gear, no anchors
FA Alex Lowe solo,1989

2. RAINBOW CONNECTION 5.11a/b
Ascends a blunt arête left of *Shot Hole*. Start next to the creek and pull up an arête to a toothy overhang; rip up this onto more delicate climbing above.
50 ft, bolts to a clip-and-lower
FA Jake Mergenthaler, Kim Mergenthaler, 2001

3. PIECES OF EIGHT 5.11b
This climb stands on the dark, slick northeast side of the Wasp Wall. The rock is clean and the line proud but some feel frustrated on the snot-slick smears. If you are insecure about your footwork, this one will take you to school. Named for the date it was done (8/8/88) and for the number of protection points (including anchor).
70 ft, 7 bolts to chains
FA Kristen Drumheller, Bill Dokins,1988

NO CLIMBING ON THE PICTOGRAPH WALL

This is the wall across the road from East Gate Wall and the last prominent fin on the right side of the road on your way in.

No climbing is allowed anywhere on the Pictograph Wall. This includes not only the south side which holds significant Native American rock art but the road side and northeast face as well. Our continued access to this premier climbing venue is predicated on our stewardship of these priceless artifacts and climber's ability to restrain from any encroachment on this feature—regardless of how careful you think you might be.

HELLGATE SCHOOL OF ROCKS: THE QUARTZITE FINS

Another 1.5 miles farther up Hellgate past the main limestone area is a great little area on short quartzite cliffs—a type of rock otherwise uncommon to this region. The tallest of the fins (red-black) in appearance on the northwest side of the road have permanent toprope and rappel anchors installed for a few different climbs (5.5 to 5.8+). There is likely room for a few more topropes and possibly a few harder lead climbs.

Getting There

Drive about 1.5 miles past East Gate Wall to a series of reddish and blackened quartzite outcrops bisecting the road. Park at a wide pullout on the left just before a rough but short hill.

Danielle Noonan on the *Unknown 5.10a at Trail Side Crag*
Photo by Dan Bachen

WELCOME to Trout Creek Canyon. The upper reaches of the canyon are among the most scenic areas near Helena. Large limestone cliffs tower above forested hillsides forming an impressive and rugged canyon. An old road grade, now closed to vehicles, follows the canyon bottom for three easy miles through the most rugged portion of the drainage. Any climber hiking this trail will be awed by the quantity of stone and amazed that there aren't hundreds of routes ascending the walls. The scenic and accessible nature of this trail makes it popular with hikers, bikers, and equestrians. The climbing isn't bad either.

To date, the bulk of developed routes are found along a three-mile-long canyon accessed by hiking an old forest road upstream from the Vigilante Campground at the end of York Road, or by making the long circuitous drive from Beaver Creek to the upper canyon and hiking back down toward the campground. In general the rock quality improves with elevation and most routes are found within a mile of the upper trailhead. If this area had road access similar to that of Hellgate, Avalanche, or even Beaver Creek there would likely be many more routes.

The climbing is almost exclusively bolt-protected sport climbing. Some single-pitch crags have been developed, and there are also several moderate multi-pitch routes as well. With the exception of a handful of pitches, all climbs are 5.10 or harder. Several developers are actively chipping away at the near limitless potential, so encountering routes not listed within this guide should be expected.

GETTING THERE
There are a few ways to access Trout Creek Canyon. From Helena navigate to York Road which heads northeast from town and drive this to York. Alternatively, you can also reach York from the Canyon Ferry area using Jimtown Road which heads north from the east side of the town of Canyon Ferry. Once at the York Bar, the turn to Nelson and Beaver Creek is used to access the upper canyon trailhead. To access the lower canyon trailhead, stay straight on York Road.

Lower canyon access is straightforward and accessible year-round as the road is plowed to the trailhead in winter. From the York Bar, continue on York Road 6.5 miles to the end of the road. Park at the trailhead located at the entrance to the Vigilante Campground.

Access to the upper canyon is a long drive on backroads, thus the 45 miles from Helena can take over an hour and a half. The roads can get muddy during wet weather and large snow drifts can linger well into May or even June making the road impassable. It may be a good idea to bring a separate map or navigation aid such as a GPS as the route can be confusing the first time. From the York Bar head north (left if coming from Helena or Canyon Ferry) to Nelson in the Beaver Creek drainage. At the Nelson junction turn right, as you would to reach Refrigerator Canyon. Follow the Beaver Creek Road past Refrigerator Canyon and other climbing areas. At the head of the canyon you may see a sign about entering private property—continue past this. A short while later, the road begins to climb to the divide with Trout Creek. Keep right at the first junction as for Indian Flats Cabin and Hogback Mountain. Continue on the main road ignoring any small spur roads until the road forks below Hogback. If you start to switchback or end up on top of a mountain with a communications tower, you missed the turn. Head left (south) as for the cabin. Bear right just before the cabin and then stay on the main road past the hair-pin turn at My Private Montana and you should reach the end of the road and trailhead approximately 4.5 miles later.

SEASON
York road is plowed to Vigilante Campground during the winter and the trail does not seem to accumulate much snow, so it is possible to access the climbs at any time of the year from the bottom trailhead. Access from Beaver Creek is best left until after Memorial Day through early/mid fall, as the forest roads can be impassable during the winter and spring. Typically the best conditions for climbing will be found from late spring through fall. Unfortunately during the summer the creek seldom runs above ground above the second bridge, so bringing extra water may be a good idea.

ACCESS ISSUES
While climbing here it is unlikely that you will encounter other climbers, but that does not mean you will have the canyon to yourself. The trail used to access the climbs is very popular with hikers, mountain bikers, and equestrians. As some of the climbs are close to or directly above the trail, please keep a low profile. Leash your dogs, stash your gear off the trail and yield to other users. Livestock graze in the upper canyon so keep you dogs under control to avoid conflicts with the local ranchers. Access depends on maintaining good relationships with other user groups and the Forest Service who manages the land. Please make sure to do your part!

CAMPING
Camping is readily available at both the upper and lower trailheads. Vigilante campground, a US Forest Service managed fee site is adjacent to the lower trailhead and has restrooms and a nice creek to enjoy on a hot day. Dispersed camping sites are limited along York Road, but camping is not prohibited and it may be possible to tuck in somewhere if need be. There is abundant dispersed (free) camping along the access route to the upper trailhead. Sites can be found throughout Beaver Creek and on public lands along the Beaver/Trout Creek divide and near the upper trailhead. Indian Flats Cabin is a USFS rental cabin that sits on the divide between upper Beaver and Trout creeks 4.5 miles from the upper trailhead along the access road.

HISTORY
Trout Creek has seen a trickle of development over the years both documented and undocumented. The first recorded climbs were established in the early 1990s by Bill Dockins and Kristen Drumheller. A little later Randall Green
developed another small area called My Private Montana, a few miles up the road from the upper trailhead. Kevin
Hutchinson was inspired by Bill's reports to explore the Grayling Wall and enlisted Ron Brunkhorst to establish two
routes. Additional development has been undertaken by Frank Dusl, Jake and Kim Mergenthaler and Paul Travis. More
recent development has undoubtedly occurred, but details regarding many of the lines of bolts scattered across the
canyon are sparse. The amount of stone in this drainage is truly staggering. For the intrepid developer willing to hike,
Trout Creek provides a vast canvas and new route development will undoubtedly continue.

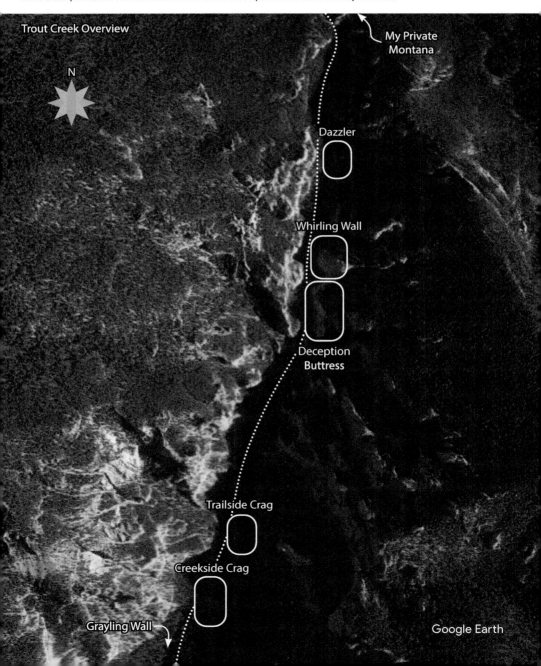

Trout Creek Overview

N

My Private
Montana

Dazzler

Whirling Wall

Deception
Buttress

Trailside Crag

Creekside Crag

Grayling Wall

Google Earth

GRAYLING WALL

This is the first crag encountered when hiking from the lower trailhead. Despite the abundance of rock in the lower canyon, it's hard to miss this shield of bomber gray stone in the sea of choss. Three routes can be found on the prominent slab, and it is possible to scope some of the bolt and belay locations from the trail due to the zinc staining below the bolts. The wall is accessed by a bushwhack from the main trail.

1. KEEP EM AND EAT 'EM 5.10c ★

This line shares the first crux pitch of *Grayling* but wanders climber's left before ascending the gray slab above.
P1: Start left of the chossy corner. Climb past two bolts and traverse left then straight up to the belay. (5.10c, 110 ft)
P2: Traverse significantly left off the belay before heading up through the crux bulge. (5.9, 60 ft)
P3: Ascend the slab past a low crux to the anchors above. (5.9, 80 ft)
Descent: Due to the traversing nature of the climb double rope rappels are recommended. From the top anchors make a 130' rap to a rappel anchor left of the climb. From these anchors make a second rap 120' to the ground.
250 ft, bolts to chains

2. THE GRAYLING 5.10c ★

Fun climbing on good gray stone that eases once you pass the first crux pitch which is shared with *Keep 'Em*. This is the center of the three lines established on the face.
P1: (5.10c, 110 ft)
P2: (5.8, 80 ft)
P3: (5.8, 50 ft)
Descent: Rap the route with a 70m.
240 ft, 8 bolts to chains

3. SMEARS FOR TEARS 5.9+ ★

Located 50 ft right of the previous routes.
P1: Begin by climbing right of a right facing corner on marginal rock. (5.7, 60 ft)
P2: Climb through a bulge than up a brown face to a ledge. (5.9+, 90 ft)
P3: From the belay make your way up the immaculate slab to a sloping ledge with a tree and belay. (5.8+, 70 ft)
Descent: Rap the route with a 60m.
220 ft, bolts to chains

CREEKSIDE CRAG

Creekside Crag encompasses several short cliffs next to and near the trail. If hiking up from the campground, this crag is a quarter mile beyond the point where the old road bed has washed out and the trail climbs more steeply away from the creek to bypass this section.

1. WILLOW 5.12c ★★

Located immediately off the trail at the upstream edge of the cliff band. Steep and sustained climbing with long reaches. Said to be one of the better 12s in the area.
60 ft, bolts to massive bolt and hanger
FA Frank Dusl, 2002

2. THE TOOTH 5.11- (Not Pictured)

Apparently harder than it looks and harder to find than the previous route. Right of *Willow*.
FA Bret Justin, 2002

TRAIL SIDE CRAG

This short and accessible wall is about two miles from the lower trailhead and one mile from the upper. Although short in stature, the rock quality is excellent and the routes fun. If you choose to climb here, it is likely to be a social experience. Belays are just off the main trail, so climbers should expect plenty of interaction with mountain bikers, hikers, and horseback riders. Fortunately the nearby dry creek bed provides a good staging area to keep most of your gear off the trail.

1. UNKNOWN 5.10a ★★

Starts just outside of a left-facing dihedral above some bushes. May be easier to traverse the ledge from the left to the first bolt. Sustained and fun climbing on good holds.

45 ft, 5 bolts to chains

2. I'D RATHER BE FISHING 5.10b ★★

This is the steepest route on the wall. Climb textured budges up a gray streak.

45 ft, bolts to chains

FA Kim Mergenthaler, Jake Mergenthaler, and Paul Travis, 2000

3. WOOLLY BOOGER 5.10b ★★

Steep slab up good gray rock. Holds are not as good as they appear from down low. Shares a final bolt and anchor with *Live Bait*.

45 ft, 5 bolts to chains

FA Kim Mergenthaler, Jake Mergenthaler, and Paul Travis, 2000

4. LIVE BAIT 5.10b ★★

Slab with deceptively positive-looking holds. Shares a final bolt and anchor with *Woolly Booger*.

45 ft, 5 bolts to chains

F.A. Kim MErgenthaler, Jake Mergenthaler, and Paul Travis, 2000

5. BAIT FISHING IS NEITHER 5.10 X

Currently the leftmost route on the wall. Two bolts low-down lead to a significant runout to the chains.

45 ft, 2 bolts to chains

FA Kim Mergenthaler, Jake Mergenthaler, and Paul Travis, 2000

DECEPTION BUTTRESS

The Deception Buttress is a wide expanse of slabby gray stone facing the creek, across from the trail. Although it seems like tens of routes should be found here, only two have been established. With all the rock next to the trail, locating this wall can be a little challenging. The established climbs are approximately a half mile upstream from the Trailside Crag. These two routes are located across the creek from the trail on the leftmost (upstream) margin of the wall. As there is quite a bit of rock in the area that looks similar, it is helpful to first locate the Whirling Wall with it's distinct roof and the east margin of the buttress which is a large cave facing the Whirling Wall routes.

1. **CATCH AND RELEASE** 5.12a
Lefthand bolt line. Long pitch of hard climbing.
160 ft, 14 bolts to chains
FA Bill Dockins, Kristen Drumheller, 1993

2. **THE MOZART EFFECT** 5.12
Righthand line. Climb the steep slab through a low crux to the chains.
80 ft, bolts to chains
FA Kristen Drumheller, Bill Dockins, 1994

WHIRLING WALL

This towering cliff is located just upstream of the Deception Buttress. It can be easily identified by the prominent roof. To date one multi-pitch outing exists on the west face.

1. **THE WHIRLING WALL** 5.10d/5.11a R ★★★
A fine adventure that ascends the wall in four pitches. Although this route is predominately protected with bolts, do not expect a modern sport experience; bringing a light rack of nuts, tricams, and/or a few cams is a good idea. There are two starts. The original start to the left has some space between bolts and a little loose rock. The right variation is much more friendly both in grade, rock quality, and protection.
P1: Start on a slab and aim toward the right side of the prominent arching roof. Halfway up, the rock quality deteriorates with limited options for protection. Some runout climbing across hollow rock is encountered. After passing the lower difficulties traverse right to the anchor. (5.10R, 150 ft, 9 bolts and a light rack, chain anchor)
P1 Alt: This pitch avoids the hollow rock on the original start. Start to the right of the original pitch, climb the slab over compact gray rock to the chains. (5.8, 140 ft, 13 bolts to a chain anchor)
P2: Follow the bolts up the slab to a ledge on climber's left. (5.10a/b, 100 ft, bolts to chains)
P3: Climb to a pod, exit left from this feature, then angle up right on steep rock. (5.10d/11a, 140 ft, bolts to chains)
P4: Climb past a few bolts then head toward a notch on the ridge using natural protection. (5.7, 70 ft, bolts and a light rack to chains)
Descent: Rappel the route with two ropes.
450 ft, bolts and a light rack, chains.
FA Bill Dockins, Kristen Drumheller, 1995

THE DAZZLER
The Dazzler is a smaller cliff of good limestone located about 300 yards upstream of the Whirling Wall across the creek from the trail. Currently four routes have been established. The wall is easy to miss as it is hidden in the trees. A large rusting culvert beside the trail serves as a good landmark.

1. HOLLY'S MISAVENTURE 5.11a
Technical slab climbing, reported to be a bit of a sand-bag. This route is the farthest right.
75 ft, bolts to chains
FA Bill Dockins, Kristen Drumheller, 1994

2. BACKCAST 5.12a
This climb is located to the right of a prominent cave. As-cend an orange streak up the steep right-facing corner, tackle a roof crack (wires useful), then exit left and climb the face to the roof. Cast for the jug at the lip, finishing up the easier ground above.
80 ft, bolts and light rack of small-medium wires/cams
FA Bill Dockins, Kristen Drumheller, 1994

3. DAZZLER 5.12c ★★★ (Not Pictured)
An area testpiece, thin and sustained. Located between the cave and *No Trout*.
75 ft, bolts to chains
FA Bill Dockins, Kristen Drumheller, 1993

4. NO TROUT ABOUT IT 5.12a (Not Pictured)
Thin and sequential through the roof. This is the farthest left (upstream) route.
70 ft, 6 bolts and light rack of small-medium wires/cams to chains
FA Bill Dockins, Kristen Drumheller, 1993

MY PRIVATE MONTANA

This smaller crag is tucked away in the mountains high above the main Trout Creek drainage. Several outcroppings of compact gray stone are found below a hairpin in the road leading from Beaver Creek to the Upper Trout trailhead. In the mid-1990s Randall Green authored three lines on Snaggleface, the cliff directly below the road and on The Fin which sits across the drainage. This area epitomizes much of the potential and development in the Big Belts. These lines are on high-quality stone and more could certainly be established in the area, but the drive to these cliffs passes many developed routes (and areas that have yet to see a bolt or climber). The crag is in close proximity to both the Upper Trout Creek trailhead and Indian Flats Cabin, so if you are in the area it may be worth a visit. Chances are you will have the routes all to yourself!

GETTING THERE

Although it would be possible to hike the Trout Creek trail then continue on the road above, the best way to reach these cliffs is to drive through Beaver Creek and continue over the divide as per the Upper Trout trailhead. Once you drop off the ridge and start descending into the Trout Creek drainage, you will pass Indian Flats Cabin, an old USFS guard station. The crag is 1.5 miles farther on this road. Look for a tight hairpin turn/ switchback and park.

THE FIN

As the name suggests, this crag is a fin of rock located across the drainage from the hairpin. Both of the established routes are found on the east face. To reach these you can either rappel to the ground using the anchors on *Private Montana* or skirt the cliffs uphill from the parking spot and make your way into the drainage.

1. RUMORS OF GLORY 5.11b ★★
Righthand route first encountered when approaching The Fin. Climb cracks and grooves through chossy rock to reach a gray headwall. Crank through this to the anchors.
95 ft, 13 bolts to shunts
FA Randall, Theresa Green, 1995

2. BALANCE OF POWERS 5.11c/d ★★
Left of *Rumors*, this climb ascends the fin from a ledge. Climb through the soft rock to a bulge and bomber gray rock beyond.
70 ft, bolts to shunts
FA Randall Green, Gordon King, 1995

MY PRIAVATE MONTANA PARKING

SNAGGLEFACE (NO PHOTOS)

This cliff is located directly below the road and the single established route requires a rappel to reach the semi-hanging stance. From the parking spot begin walking down the road, but quickly descend the embankment and angle back right. A dead tree hanging over the cliff marks a set of cold shunts and the top of the route.

1. MY PRIVATE MONTANA 5.11 b/c ★★
This route is not accessible from the base, so rappel to the lower two-bolt anchor from the shuts. These are located below the cliffline at the apex of the trunk. Climb back up the steep and sustained face.
65 ft, 7 bolts to cold shuts
FA Randall Green, 1995

2. SUPRA DUPRA PROJECT
5.11ish project below the parking spot. Established by Kevin Hutchinson and named in honor of his 82 Toyota Supra which slid off the road while scoping routes. **The top anchor seems to have been chopped.**

BEAVER CREEK BY DAN BACHEN

Henry Scholtzhauer on *Perfectly Ripe 5.12d*
Photo by Jared Pickens

WELCOME to Beaver Creek. This area winds through a magnificent canyon about 40 miles northeast of Helena in the Big Belt Mountains. The semi-remote location and stunning vistas give this area an adventurous and rare flair. Routes range from short single-pitch outings, to longer multi-pitch adventures over 500 ft in length. Climbs vary from thought-provoking slabs to steep, pumpy routes ascending overhangs. Like most of the Big Belts, the limestone is mostly compact and gray and sometimes chossy, but areas of steep blue and orange rock—reminiscent of the great european sport crags—can be found in and around Refrigerator Canyon. Pockets exist on some routes, but most climbs ascend crimps, edges, and slopers. The diversity of rock across Beaver Creek gives the climber unique sectors and a range of aspects, movement, and angles. Many routes are close to 30 meters and some of the newer ones are closer to 40, so use caution when lowering. Most climbs are equipped as sport climbs with bolts placed at reasonable intervals, but a few routes are more adventurous and require a single rack to supplement bolts. There are even a few cracks that have been maintained as traditional climbs. The steep nature of most routes does not favor the lower grades. Although there are enough climbs rated 5.10 and under to keep a climber busy for a few days, the area shines for those who are climbing 5.11 and above.

The highest concentration of routes are in the vicinity of the Refrigerator Canyon trailhead. Many worthwhile routes have been established on both of the side canyons. Across the creek, the towering Eye on the Needle formation (which stands 500' tall, just south of the road) holds a number of worthy multi-pitch climbs from 5.8 to 5.13, as well as a few classic single-pitch lines. The climbing on the Needle is mostly technical and vertical on beautiful, good quality limestone. The west face holds steeper, blue-streaked pitches that are sure to challenge even the most adventurous climbers. Across the canyon, a short walk up the Refrigerator Canyon Trail leads to the Mustard Wall and the Gatorade Wall—family-friendly zones with short approaches, sure to satisfy climbers looking for routes in the 5.10-5.12 range. The Squeeze Sector of Refrigerator Canyon is incomparable to any other area in the state. Slick rock from ancient waters sculpted the towering walls of this slot canyon, and an almost constant breeze blows through these narrows. Ideal for hot summer days, temperatures can be 20-30 degrees cooler than the surrounding area making it an ideal summer crag. Two huge caves can be found on opposite sides of the trail that hold a handful of steep testpieces and are sure to produce more hard climbs in the years to come. The majority of development has occured on walls with approaches under 15 minutes. As one ventures farther off trail and up Sheep Mountain (different than the climbing area near Clancy), a handful of single- and multi-pitch routes are encountered, but the potential for future development is vast. In addition to the crags in and near Refrigerator Canyon, crags have been developed both up and downstream. Pike Creek has a handful of moderate routes in a unique and quiet setting that is perfect for a relaxing afternoon, and Shangri La is very kid friendly.

Beaver Creek is easily accessed with a two-wheel-drive vehicle and camping is found all along the creek. The ease of access, diversity and quality of the climbing makes the area an enjoyable spot for a weekend stay. The creek itself provides welcome comfort on the hot days of summer when it slows to provide easy crossing. Spring can make access difficult for routes on the Eye formation as well as those in the Pike Creek area.

All crags are on the Helena-Lewis and Clark National Forest and access has not yet been an issue. To ensure this relationship please treat the place and everyone you meet there with respect, including the slow drivers on the way in, and hopefully we can climb here forever.

A WORD ABOUT HORSES
As encounters with equestrians are likely when climbing in the Narrows, the Mustard Wall, Gatorade Wall, and Minifridge. When encountering horses:
- Move off the trail (downhill if possible) but remain visible. If you look like you are trying to hide it will make the animals nervous.
- Don't make sudden movements.
- Talk to the riders in a calm voice. This will help the animals understand that you are a person, not a threat and help everyone come up with a plan for getting past each other.
- Leash and control your dogs. The canyon is narrow, if your critter does not immediately come when called, stay quiet and calm around stock, and stay next to you and off the trail please tie them up.

ACCESS

Not only is the climbing in Beaver Creek unique, unfortunately the access issues are as well. Refrigerator Canyon is one of the only areas covered within this guide where climbs have been established next to or off of an official USFS trail. Not only that, this trail is very popular with hikers and equestrians. Although blocked trails and uncontrolled dogs can be a nuisance at any crag, these behaviors present a serious injury risk to riders and their stock. It is absolutely critical that climbers maintain control of their dogs (use a leash!) and avoid blocking the trail with themselves and their gear when climbing routes on the Gatorade Wall, Mustard Wall, the Beach and in the narrows. Please consider climbing on the more secluded walls during holidays, weekends, or other busy times or if the parking lot is full. Please also be considerate of other users and minimize use of project draws on walls visible from the trail. Remember, most folks come here to enjoy the natural beauty of this area which may or may not include you and your gear. While climbers certainly have as much right to do their thing as other groups, we are a relatively new user group and being good stewards of the area now will undoubtedly pay dividends in the future should any issues arise.

HISTORY

Climbers no doubt have been scrambling around these formations for decades, but the summer of 1994 was the first time any bolted sport routes appeared. Scott Payne and Randall Green came here equipped with Scott's well-used (worn out!) drill and bolted Batteries Not Included and Bassackwards. These climbs have become must-do adventures. Although they are not over-bolted due to issues with the drill battery, all the hard parts are well protected and the intrepid climber is rewarded by wonderful exposure and a sport climbing experience more reminiscent of areas like Idaho's City of Rocks.

Randall, Bill Dockins and Kirsten Drumheller teamed up for a zealous endeavor when they set their sights on the west face of the Eye of the Needle formation. After much hard work they completed This Ain' Nothin'. With 3 pitches of in-your-face climbing this baby aint' for Mama's boys or girls and has seen very few redpoints.

In the mid-90s the local youngster Aaron Lefohn put up a unique crack climb on the east side called Walk on the Ocean and a cool sport climb by the creek with the great name of Dancing with Roofs.

Randall added the choice line Forearm Flambe along with Gimpy on the west side of the formation and started exploring the rock on the north side of the road. He established several lines there (Powerline, Willy Wire Hands to name a few) before enticing Jake and Kim Mergenthaler along with Ted Simms to add some fun and sunny climbing there. Don't miss Parts Is Parts and Sticker both rope stretchers with memorable climbing.

During the early and mid-2000s the canyon began to fade into obscurity as other areas like Hellgate, Avalanche and Blackleaf began to take off. While folks still climbed the routes, few if any were added. This began to change in the latter 2000s when Luke Evans began exploration of Refrigerator Canyon and surrounding cliffs, opening some hard sport climbing on superb rock as well as several long adventure routes. After this initial round of development, this resurgence was joined in the mid-2010's by a dedicated group of climbers, mostly living in Bozeman. Henry Schlotzhauer, Kyle O'Meara, Jackson Wetherall and many others have molded this canyon into one of the premiere hard sport climbing areas in Montana. This began with Henry opening "Whipstitch" on the Eye of the Needle and other hard lines like Best Before in the caves of Refrigerator canyon. O'Meara spent the summer of 2020 helping establish lines alongside Henry as well as opening 'Room of Requirement' and other classic test pieces. Not to be left out, Jake and Kim revived their interest and have authored many fine lines, often at the more "approachable" 5.11 grades. Dan Bachen and Danielle Noonan began exploring the outlying outcrops around this time as well and established several smaller crags at the upper and lower extremes of the drainage. Given the vast potential of the area, development will undoubtedly continue across the area into the future and provide an ever-expanding resource for local and visiting climbers.

CAMPING

No formal USFS managed campgrounds exist in the canyon, but dispersed options are plentiful on public lands both upstream and downstream from Nelson. Please be aware that not all lands are public and avoid trespassing on posted private property. There are established dispersed campsites near the Lower Beaver Creek wall, midway between Nelson and Refrigerator Canyon trailhead, about half a mile past the trailhead and at wide spots along the road before and at Pike Creek. Dispersed camping also exists farther along the road after the private ranch on your way to the upper Trout Creek trailhead. The closest established (fee) campground, Vigilante Campground is at the lower Trout Creek trailhead (see description in that section for details). Additionally, the USFS maintains a rental cabin, Indian Flats Cabin, that sits on the divide between Beaver and Trout Creeks. Reservations are necessary and can be made online. Contact the US Forest Service, Helena Office for farther details.

Currently the nearest pubic toilets are about 40 minutes away at the lower Trout Creek trailhead and the nearest trash cans are back towards Helena. Given this, use your best Leave No Trace techniques. Bury your waste at least 6-8 inches deep and 200 feet from water sources, or even better given the narrow nature of the canyons, use a wag bag and dispose of your waste when you get back to town. Pack out all trash. If you have a fire, make sure it's out when you leave camp.

GETTING THERE

To reach the canyon head northeast from Helena on York Road for about 16 miles to the small town of York. At the York Bar turn left (north) on a gravel road and travel 7 miles to the tiny 'burb of Nelson, the self-proclaimed cribbage capital of the world. To reach most of the climbing, turn right at Nelson and follow a narrow gravel road up Beaver Creek for 4.4 miles. The Eye of the Needle comes into view just after passing the well posted and popular Refrigerator Canyon Trailhead. Pike Creek is located farther up the canyon approximately 1.8 miles past the Refrigerator Canyon Trailhead. To reach the Lower Beaver Creek Wall, at Nelson take a left and follow the main road 3.7 miles. Depending on traffic the drive to the crags takes about 45minutes to an hour from town and is only about 5 miles farther than Hellgate or Avalanche.

Individual crags are dispersed along the main road. Lower Beaver Creek Wall is located near the confluence of the Missouri River about 8 miles downstream from the other crags. The Refrigerator Canyon area, located about 4 miles upstream of Nelson holds the highest concentration of climbs. Pike Creek is located a few miles farther upstream. Crags are described from the mouth of the canyon on the Missouri River upstream to where the road traverses to Trout Creek, and specific directions are found in each description.

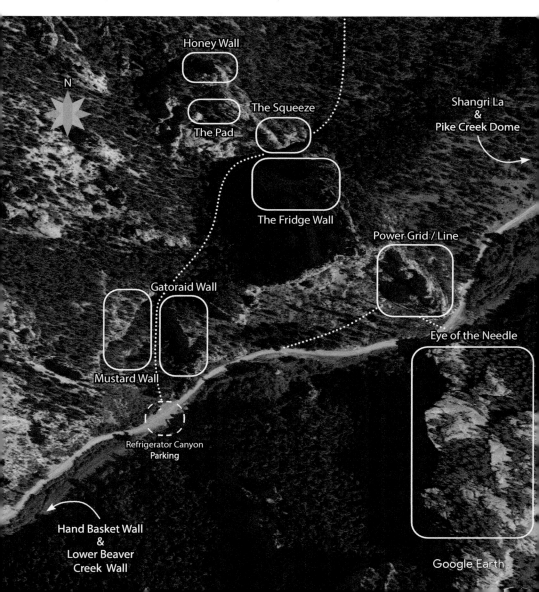

Henry Schlotzhauer on Best Before 5.14a
Photo by Ben Herndon

LOWER BEAVER CREEK WALL

This small crag home to a handful of high-quality sport routes. While this will never be a popular destination due to the limited number of routes and distance from the other developed areas. If you are in the area, these routes are worth checking off your list. In particular Beaver Fever is as fine as any route near Helena. The area is also close to several nice campsites, pleasant hiking trails, and the Missouri River.

Getting There

At Nelson turn left (downstream) toward American Bar and the Missouri River. The road gets smaller and rougher but can still be done with a low clearance vehicle if care is taken. Continue on the road past the Hunters Gulch trailhead and a private inholding. After a few miles, the valley pinches to a narrow canyon. After the road ascends away from then descends back to the creek you are almost there. The crag is at the westernmost toe of the southern cliff band. Look for a stream gauge shed and power pole and park here. Alternatively, the campsite immediately down the road can provide a better parking spot if unoccupied and stones may be placed in the creek allowing you to cross without getting your feet wet. The natural arch on the opposite side of the road is a good landmark.

LOWER BEAVER CREEK WALL

1. **RODENTS OF UNUSUAL SIZE** 5.10a ★★
Farthest climb to the right. Start up large pockets through delicate moves right of the first bolt. Stick clip can be useful.
60ft, 6 bolts to rings
FA Dan Bachen, Danielle Noonan, 2018

2. **BEAVER FEVER** 5.11c ★★★
Bolt line left of RoUS. Slopers, pockets, flared crack, and thin slab, this climb has a little bit of everything and it's all good! Start below the obvious line of large huecos. Crank through the lower boulder problem then dig in your fingernails and pull the delicate moves above.
65 ft, 7 bolts to rings
FA Dan Bachen, 2018

3. **TR PROJECT**
Using the anchors for *Rex* and a directional bolt, climb the blank arête to the right. May get bolted for lead in the future.

4. **REX THE TEXAN** 5.11+ (Not Pictured)
Located upstream around the corner from the previous routes. A short step with a bolt leads to contrived climbing on a short face (stay out of the corner!) and a desperate move transitioning to the slab below the chains Not really recommended but worth a spin if you're in the area.
35 ft, bolts to ring anchors
FA Dan Bachen, 2018

HANDBASKET WALL AND EAGLES WING

Both routes are found on opposite sides of the road on the first really good looking gray limestone after the turn from Nelson. This striking uplifted band extends across the canyon on both sides of the road. The Handbasket Wall is perched well above the valley bottom to the north. Currently one route is found at its highest point. When viewed from the road it is surprising that the other obvious lines have not been established, however after crossing the creek, fighting through the jungle down low and scree up high the paucity of routes begins to make sense. The Eagles Wing formation is the large slab on the opposite side of the canyon from the Handbasket Wall. It currently is home to a single adventure route that takes the striking line up the middle of the formation. To reach this route, bushwhack from the road near the parking for the Handbasket Wall.

Getting There

Turn right at Nelson and drive about 4 miles up Beaver Canyon. Look for *Handbasket* on your left and *Eagles Wing* on your right and park where convenient. If you reach the Refrigerator Canyon trailhead you have gone about 0.5 miles too far.

1. HELENA HANDBASKET 5.11b
Crimpy and sharp route up a slab.
7 bolts to chains
FA Kevin Hutchingson, 1999

2. EAGLES WING 5.8 ★★
A fine adventure that soars through the center of the formation in about three pitches. Start in the left facing dihedral and climb to the obvious ledge, clipping bolts and placing gear as needed. Move the belay up the low angle ramp until you are below the prominent "S" shaped crack that ends between the "ears". Climb this crux pitch to the top on a mix of bolts and gear.
Descent: Double rope rappel down the route, or scramble and rappel off the back. You will probably need to provide your own tat for this. This route was put up on lead and has seen few ascents, so be prepared for anything including loose rock and runout climbing!
Single rack of stoppers and small- hand sized cams, quick draws/ alpine draws, extra slings and a few rap rings if you're feeling generous.
FA Luke Evans, Liza Cabizares, 2000s

REFRIGERATOR CANYON

Refrigerator Canyon is quickly becoming one of the finest sport climbing crags within the Helena area and is among the best in the state.

Routes are primarily single pitch clip-ups on steep, bullet hard limestone. Some multi pitch and trad routes have also been established for those seeking to get a little higher on the larger formations. This canyon has some of the best quality limestone in Montana and the setting is spectacular. Although there are a handful of moderate routes here, the area really shines at and above 5.11 with several routes breaking the 5.14 barrier and projects that promise to be at least as hard if not closer to 5.15. The canyon stays cool throughout the summer and is climbable on even the warmest days. Like most areas in Montana the season really depends on the cold weather tolerance of the climber, but conditions are generally best from May through October.

Of all crags in the Helena area, Refrigerator Canyon has the highest potential for interaction with other user groups as some of the routes are belayed on the trail and most are in full view of other users. On a busy weekend you can expect to interact with hikers, horseback riders, their dogs, and their children. Please be respectful of other users, keep your gear tidy and out of the trail, dogs under control, and strive to minimize your impact. If you establish routes, please use camouflaged hangers and consider if location of the route, climber, and belayer will create farther impacts on other user's experiences. Our access to these routes is largely dependent on your behavior.

Getting There

Park at the Refrigerator Canyon trailhead. Follow the trail to reach the climbs. Once on the trail, the Gatorade wall is immediately visible across the creek. The Mustard wall is above the first switchback a few minutes from the trailhead. The slot canyon including the Fridge and Honeysuckle Slab are encountered a few minutes beyond where the walls meet the trail.

REFRIGERATOR CANYON PARKING

Honey Wall

The Pad

Platform 9 ¾

The Cooler / Squeeze

The Beach

Powerline

Call of The Wild

Mustard Wall

Gatorade Wall

MINI-FRIDGE

The small wall/ large boulder located to the left of the trail when first entering the canyon. Home to two short enjoyable routes.

1. **MOUSSE AU CHOCOLAT** 5.10b ★★
Climb the corner full of blue flowstone
5 bolts to anchors
FA Miriam Schlotzhauer, 2020

2. **OLIVE JUICE** 5.12d
To the right of *Mousse Chocolate*. Short and stout. Stick clip the second bolt.
3 bolts to chains
FA Kyle Redberg, 2020

Kyle Redberg on *Olive Juice 5.12d*
Photo by Ben Herndon

GATORADE WALL

The Gatorade wall is found immediately across the creek at the start of the trail. Routes are listed as encountered (downstream to upstream).

1. HYDRATE OR DIE 5.11d ★★★

First route on the wall. Cross the creek and belay on a flat spot. Bouldery start to techy pulling over bulges on small holds. Do your best to lengthen draws for reduced rope drag. Superbe line!

An 80m rope is needed to lower or toprope.
130ft, bolts to chains
FA Henry Schlotzhauer, Luke Evans, 2019

Ian on *Labat Blue 5.12c*
Photo by Ben Herndon

2. VANILLA ICE 5.12a ★★

Just left of *Hydrate* is this overhanging climb on tan rock. Very engaging crux but a little hollow feeling above the crux.
55 ft, bolts to chains
FA Jake Mergenthaler, Kim Mergenthaler, 2020

3. EASY SQUEEZIE 5.11c ★★

Cross the creek and belay on a raft made of tree limbs. This may not be there in the spring. Clip high for bouldery technical start on perfect gray rock. Climb through steep tan slab to gain a flakey roof and easier finish.
85 ft, bolts to chains
FA Jake Mergenthaler, KimMergenthaler, 2020

4. LABAT BLUE AKA THE GATORADE OF BEERS 5.12c ★★

Climb technical slab of superb quality to a rest before climbing the steep panel with a bouldery crux.
95 ft, 11 bolts to chains
FA Ian Whorral, 2020

5. MOORE CREEK 5.13b

This climb starts on the left margin of then ascends a semi-free-standing pillar.
50ft, 6 bolts to chains
FA H. Schlotzhauer, 2020

6. FREEZER BURN 5.12d/5.13a ★★★

Last route before starting the switch back. Climb through an aesthetic overhang than up a steep headwall.
85 ft, bolts to chains
FA Luke Evans, Zac Bushilla, 2008

MUSTARD WALL

This wall is located above the trail at the first switchback just after the end of and opposite the Gatorade Wall. Home to a number of quality routes in the hard 5.10 through mid 5.11 range, this area is perfect for pushing your climbing into the 5.11s or warming up for the harder routes on the surrounding walls.

1. THE FLYING RANERI 5.10b

Farthest climb to the right, belayed from the trail. Easier climbing on blocky edges leads to a reachy crux. The belayer will block the trail so please do not climb this route on the weekends and during other busy times. Horses will not be able to pass you so be prepared to lower the climber quickly or have them go in direct and off-belay if you see equestrians! If you choose to climb this route, remember this is your opportunity to be a good steward of the sport and ambassador to other user groups!
45 ft, 5 bolts to ring anchors
FA Hermes Lynn, 2017

2. SPICY MUSTARD 5.12a ★

Second line from the right and directly above the trail on the switchback. Boulder up a seam before the angle eases to the chains First bolt is a little wonky so consider stick-clipping the second if you're not into the spice. The belayer will block the trail so please avoid this route on the weekends and during other busy times. Horses will not be able to pass you so be prepared to lower the climber quickly or have them go in direct and off-belay if you see equestrians!
45 ft, bolts to chain anchor
FA Luke Evans and Ron Pedraza

3. HONEY DIJON 5.10d ★★

Just left of the trail. Start on a small ledge and move up and right through drip pockets and edges and finish on a steep prow. A stick clip can be nice for this one and a few bolts require committing moves to reach.
70' bolts to chains
FA Luke Evans (lower section), Jake Mergenthaler and Kim Mergenthaler (upper finish) 2020

4. DOWNTON SLABBY 5.11b ★★★

Starts on the same ledge left of the previous climb. Elegant climbing up bulletproof stone.
60ft, bolts to chains
FA Jake Mergenthaler, Kim Mergenthaler, 2020

5. SARACHA 5.11c ★★

Easier climbing leads to a crux boulder problem on immaculate stone.
55 ft, 6 bolts to chains
FA Jake Mergenthaler, Kim Mergenthaler, 2020

6. SCHNIPPO 5.11b ★★★

Follow jugs up a blue streak to a short and stout crux corner.
55 ft, bolts to chains
FA Jake Mergenthaler, Kim Mergenthaler, 2020

7. BURNT TOAST 5.11a ★

Start on the right edge of the fire pit cave, climb through steep flakes
55 ft, bolts to chains
FA Jake Mergenthaler, Kim Mergenthaler, 2020

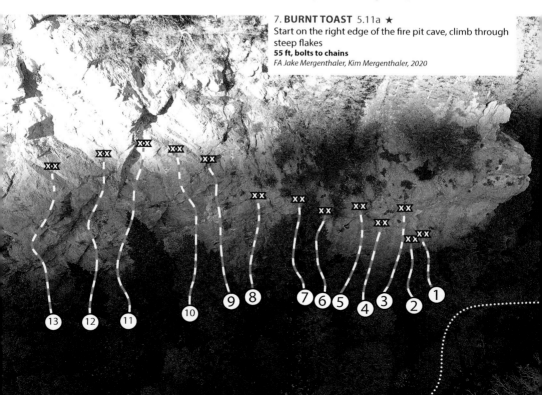

8. EASY CHEESY 5.11b ★★

First line left of the small cave. Powerful moves up a flake leads to a high first bolt and large hueco. Tricky to the chains.

60ft, bolts and chains

FA Jake Mergenthaler, Kim Mergenthaler, 2020

9. MIRACLE WHIP 5.10d ★★

Bouldery start gains easier ground than fun steep climbing. Best to stick-clip the first bolt or traverse in from the left.

70ft, bolts to chains

FA Jake Mergenthaler, Kim Mergenthaler, 2020

10. SHINY BOLT PROJECT

Open project bolted by Luke Evans. Starts by the prominent blue streak. Bolting is a little funky and it may need some cleaning so if you jump on this before it gets a rework use caution, can be toproped from Lost Cause so consider a TR lap if you really want to try leading. Included mostly for reference.

11. LOST CAUSE 5.11b ★★

Fun flake start to ugly corner below the roof leads to beautiful rock and memorable moves. Shares anchor with *Shiny*.

65 ft, bolts to chains

FA Jake and Kim Mergenthaler, 2020

12. STEEP AND SPICY 5.11c ★

Climb the features slab to a bulge. Belay pad is formed by three large rocks.

55 ft, bolts to chains

FA Jake Mergenthaler, Kim Mergenthaler, 2020

13. GRAY POOP ON 5.11a ★

Climb through a tricky bulge at last bolt move up and right then reach over to clip chains.

55 ft, bolts to chains

FA Jake Mergenthaler, Kim Mergenthaler, 2020

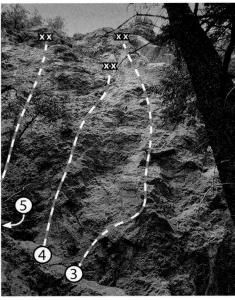

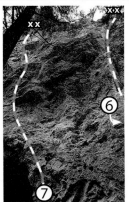

Mariam Schlotzhauer on *Lost Cause 5.11b*
Photo by Jake Mergenthaler

UPPER MUSTARD WALL
Short east facing wall above the main wall. Visible from the trail just after the switchback. Bushwhack along the upstream side of the buttress to reach.

14. ALEXANDRIA 5.11b
Climb an arête with a prominent crack to a short upper headwall. Be mindful of loose rock.
35 ft, 4 bolts to two hangers. Walk off to descend
FA Luke Evans

15. SHARMAGEDDON 5.10c
Interesting edges up a slightly overhanging wall.
Descent: Walk off
30ft, 4 bolts to a DIY anchor.
FA Chester Carlson

THE FRIDGE

The Fridge is a large alcove perched above the trail just before the narrows to the south (right). The routes found in this area are diverse, ranging from lengthy nails-hard sport routes tackling the overhanging walls to techy slabs and even a few traditionally protected cracks! Several of the lines require an 80m rope to lower or TR, so bring a long cord and plenty of draws. To find the climbs, follow the trail for a few minutes past the Mustard wall to just before the slot canyon/narrows and look right for a faint trail heading up the slope. Routes are listed from the south (downstream) wall to the north.

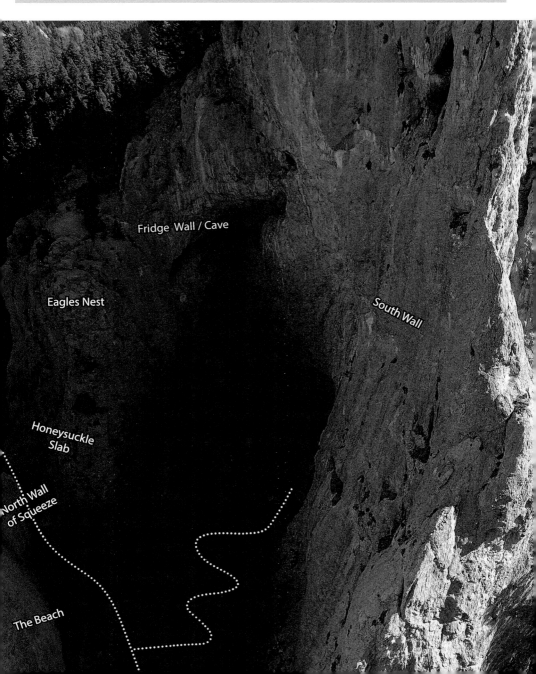

Fridge Wall / Cave

Eagles Nest

South Wall

Honeysuckle Slab

North Wall of Squeeze

The Beach

SOUTH WALL

1. EVAPORATIVE COOLING 5.12a ★
Two pitch mixed sport and trad line. This route starts on the first line of bolts up the slabs on the south wall downhill from the other routes. Follow bolts for a bit and make a belay where convenient (single bolt). Continue up to the hand crack (gear). Walk off past the summit and scramble down the backside following the path of least resistance, expect some 4th and low fifth class downclimbing.
250ft, quickdraws and gear from nuts to fist sized cams.
FA Luke Evans

2. MAPLE SYRUP 5.11a ★★
Uphill from *Evaporative* and second from the right. Start on the low-angle slab, pull through the bulge and journey to the chains
100ft, 10 bolts to chains
FA H. Schlotzhauer, 2020

3. PANCAKES 5.11c/d ★★★
Uphill from *Maple Syrup*. Climb through large holes, over a cruxy bulge and into water runnels and a technical finish.
100ft, 9 Bolts to chains
FA H. Schlotzhauer, 2020

4. FLAPJACKSON 5.12c
Link of *Pancakes* into *Appendicitis*.
135 ft, 17 Bolts, an 80m rope is needed to lower!
FA Henry Schlotzhauer, 2020

5. PANCAKES FOR DINNER 5.13a
Link of *Pancakes* into *Afternoon Delight*.
135 ft, 18 bolts, an 80 Meter rope needed!

6. TURKEY SANDWICH 5.11c
The intro pitch to the Fridge's upper shelf. Climb a few bolts to a bouldery crux and finish on easier technical slab
85 ft, 9 bolts to chains
FA H. Schlotzhauer, 2018

7. MOOSE TRACKS 5.13b/c ★★★
Climb left out of the cave into a steep roof. Access this climb via *Turkey Sandwich*.
70ft, 11 bolts to chains
FA Whit Magro, 2020

8. AFTERNOON DELIGHT 5.13a ★★★
The left of the two pillar lines. Steep, big moves lead to a great lip encounter. Access this climb via *Turkey Sandwich*.
70ft, 7 bolts to chains
FA Jackson Wetherill, 2020

9. APPENDICITIS 5.12b ★★
The right of the two pillar lines. A crux down low on the route leads to a pumpy steep finish on amazing rock. Shares an anchor with *Afternoon Delight*. Access this climb via *Turkey Sandwich*.
70ft, 7 bolts to chains
FA Jackson Wetherill, 2020

Henry Schlotzhauer on *Best Before 5.14a*
Photo by Ben Herndon

THE FRIDGE WALL/CAVE

These routes begin with the intimidating cave up and right of the trail, and are found down and left on the north wall of The Squeeze. Routes are listed right to left.

10. THE BIG FREEZE PROJECT

Open project following the line of draws out of the belly of the cave.
Equipped by Luke Evans and Henry Schlotzhauer

11. HALF PINT 5.12d

Right most route on the ledge. Look for a large pocket / hueco half way up.
40ft, 4 Bolts to anchor
FA Whit Magro, 2019

12. BEER FOAM OPEN PROJECT

Bolted by Sam Magros and shares anchor with *Half Pint*.

13. BEST BEFORE 5.14a ★★★

Three cruxes of different styles with amazing pockets, tufas and beautiful rock. One of the hardest pitches in the state!
100ft, 11 bolts to anchor
FA H. Schlotzhauer, 2020

14. EXPIRED OPEN PROJECT 5.14 a/b?

Take the blue streak out right after the first two cruxes of *Best Before*.
Equipped by Henry Schlotzhauer

15. POPSICLE 5.12c

Down and left of *Best Before* is this stunning line characterized by a small roof down low to beauty slab above. Stick high.
75 ft, bolts to chains
FA Luke Evans, Jake Mergenthaler, Henry Schlotzhauer, 2020

16. COOL HANDS 5.10

Obvious crack climb splitting the wall to the left of *Popsicle*. No anchor so you will need to build a belay and walk off or traverse to a set of anchors at the start of Box of Rain and rappel. To walk off work back toward the upstream side of the buttress. Scramble up a small step work climbers left and begin to descend down exposed steps and slabs.
80ft, Rack of stoppers and cams, doubles in the thin hands to fists. Build your own anchor.
FA Luke Evans, 2000s

17. BOX OF RAIN 5.10

To approach this climb go through the narrows and scramble up the backside of the formation to the ridge overlooking The Fridge or climb *Cool Hands* or *Popsicle*. Find a bolted belay on the eastern margin of the broad ledge where these climbs end. From this belay head right then up to a finger crack, climb this to the top. Shares a start with Ice Box, and it's possible to clip the first bolt on this climb to take some sting out of the runout to the crack.
40ft, Single rack of nuts and cams with extra in the finger/ hand sizes. Single chains.
FA Luke Evans, 2000s

18. ICE BOX 5.13c

Start as per Box of Rain but traverse out to the bolt line onto the steep headwall and finish on *Best Before*.
40ft, 4 bolts to chains
FA Luke Evans, 2000s

19. FRENCH DIP 5.11a ★

Downhill from the obvious crack route *Cool Hands*. Start uphill from prime. Boulery start (look for crimp to clip second bolt). Techy climbing above.
70ft, bolts to chains
FA Jake Mergenthaler, Kim Mergenthaler, 2021

20. PRIME RIB 5.11a ★

Boulder start in a broken corner to easier fun climbing.
70ft, bolts to chains
FA Jake and Kim Mergenthaler, 2021

21. MIDNIGHT SNACK 5.11d ★★★

Start at the right side of the squeeze. Pumpy, bouldery fun.
35 ft, bolts to chains
FA Jackson Wetherill

22. PARADOXICAL UNDRESSING 5.12+ ★★★

Basically a v7/8 boulder. Short and on excellent rock
30ft, bolts to chains
FA Jackson Wetherill

THE COOLER / SQUEEZE

This is the defining feature of Refrigerator Canyon, where the towering walls pinch down to a narrow slot. The shade, shallow stream, and near-constant wind create a chilling effect that can cool even the warmest summer day. This serene and peaceful setting belies the hard climbs found on the polished slab and steep overhangs found on the towering walls above.

When climbing these routes, please consider the narrow nature of the corridor and other users' needs. Belay close to the climbs, keep your gear contained, restrain your dogs, and generally seek to minimize your impacts. In particular it is difficult for horses to pass due to the narrow nature of this area. It is a good idea to be prepared for the climber to lower quickly or go in direct and off-belay to allow the belayer to move out of the way. Farthermore, please refrain from creating belay platforms from the rocks in the narrows. These are there for hikers to keep their feet dry and making folks wade the stream around you is poor form! Given these potential user conflicts, please consider that there are better places to climb during busy times such as weekends and holidays. Remember, continued access is contingent on your behavior!

HONEYSUCKLE SLAB
Within the cooler look for a shield of polished rock that extends out from the south wall.
Routes described right to left.

23. ICE CREAM SUNDAY 5.11a ★★★
Short Fun Climb. Bouldery start.
30ft, bolts to chains
FA Jackson Wetherill, Brandon Brown

24. DEATH BY BROCCOLI 5.10d ★★★
Start on slab to reach juggy terrain then a harder finish.
30ft, bolts to chains
FA Jake Mergenthaler, Kim Mergenthaler, 2021

25. NOWHERE TO RUN 5.11b ★★★
Start on easy slab on far right side of wall. Climb heady 11a terrain to a ledge high on route where a boulder problem crux awaits. Potential access issues, see text in description for belay etiquette.
90ft, bolts to chains
FA Jake Mergenthaler, KimMergenthaler, 2020

26. SUGAR MAGNOLIA 5.12a ★★★
Some access this masterpiece by traversing in on under clings from left. It's intense and fun through scoops on techy holds. Stay right when routes merge down low. Potential access issues, see text in description for belay etiquette.
90ft, 9 bolts to anchor.
FA Luke Evans. K. O'meara, H. Schlotzhauer, 2020

27. HONEYSUCKLE ROSE 5.12a ★★★
Same start as *Sugar* but stay left at the 4th bolt. Improbable climbing on amazing stone leads to a bouldery crux guarding the Eagle's nest. Potential access issues, see text in description for belay etiquette.
90ft, 7 bolts to chains
FA Luke Evans, H. Schlotzhauer

28. WILDFLOWERS 5.9 ★★★ (Not Pictured)
This route is on the far side of the narrows across from *Frigid Aire*. Start by a tree uphill from the memorial. Climb the face eventually merging with *Grapevine*. A great way to access the top ledge to set topropes on routes in the Eagles Nest or the north wall of the Fridge.
70ft, 8 bolts to chains
FA Luke Evans, Maisie Lima, Azaria Evans, 2015

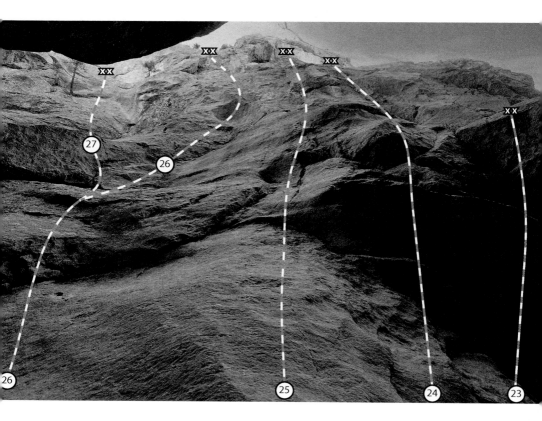

EAGLES NEST

The Eagles Nest is a hidden alcove high above the Honeysuckle slab. Fortunately, no nesting raptors have discovered this alcove but some wonderful lines await those who can access this perch.

To access these climbs, climb Honeysuckle Rose.

29. GRAPEVINE 5.10b ★★★

Take a hard left off of the anchors and cruise up moderate ground around the corner.

60ft, 7 bolts to chains

FA Luke Evans, Chester Carlson, 2015

31. PERFECTLY RIPE 5.12d ★★

Step right then climb straight up through overhanging rock. Tricky palming and tech crux.

70ft, 6 bolts to chain and hanger anchor

FA Kyle O'Meara, Henry Schlotzhauer, 2020

30. HAND FULL OF BERRIES 5.13a ★★★

From the Eagles Nest chains, climb left up a steep crack then transfer onto the face with a small hold. Amazing stone. Outstanding location

65 ft, 6 bolts to chains

FA Henry Schlotzhauer, Kyle O'Meara, 2020

Kyle O'Meara on *Meneghini 5.14b*
Photo by Jules Jimreivat

THE SOLUTIONAL CAVE

This cave looms over the canyon just uphill of The Beach and can be reached by following the left wall just before the narrows. Currently there is a single proud line that punches through the center of the feature and can be seen from the main trail.

1. CLASSICAL ANTIQUITY 5.13d ★★★

Follow bolts to the wildly overhanging crack through the roof of the cave. Turn the lip (crux) and punch it through spaced bolts to the chains physical, pumpy and steep!
115 ft, 13 bolts to chains
FA Henry Schlotzhauer, 2020

THE BEACH
The Beach refers to the wall to the left of the narrows. Routes are right to left.

2. REEF RASH 5.11d
Begin on small belay spot. Clip high and out. Slopey choss to a sharp and easy finish.
75 ft, bolts to chains
FA Jake Mergenthaler, Kim Mergenthaler, 2021

3. BLOOD IN THE WATER 5.12a ★
Start in a techy corner, move out left on crazy pinches then up a thin shield.
65 ft, bolts to chains
FA Jake Mergenthaler, Kim Mergenthaler, 2021

4. SHARK BAIT OPEN PROJECT 5.12+
Start in a techy corner then up on insecure holds to overhanging folds.
65 ft, bolts to chains
Equipped by Jake Mergenthaler, Kim Mergenthaler, 2021

5. SURFER ROSA OPEN PROJECT 5.12+
Stick clip high first bolt off of a large boulder. Climb up clean rock to reach the roof, then less than perfect rock to the chains.
75 ft, bolts to chains
Equipped by Jake Mergenthaler, Kim Mergenthaler, 2021

6. BOARD SHORTS OPEN PROJECT 5.12+
Start on flat "beach" continue up well bolted difficult terrain. Eases at half height.
75 ft, bolts to chains
Equipped by Luke Evans, Jake Mergenthaler, Kim Mergenthaler, 2021

7. WAVES OF MOTION 5.12d ★★★
A slippery crux down low to a rest. Then a pumy redpoint crux up high guards the last two bolts of climbing.
110ft, 12 Bolts to Chains
FA Kyle O'Meara, 2020

8. SILICA 5.13a ★★★
Start around the corner from the pine tree. Tech crux on flowstone that leads to sustained climbing on immaculate stone.
110ft, 11 Bolts to chains
FA Henry Schlotzhauer, 2020

9. TRANS ATLANTIC 5.12d ★★★
Climb the first three bolts of Ripple then move left to clip a bolt that allows you to climb into *Silica* and finish on *Waves of Motion*. Amazing rock and movement.
115 ft, 12 bolts to chains
FA Henry Schlotzhauer, 2020

Henry Scholtzhauer on *Classical Antiquity 5.13d*
Photo by Ben Herndon

LEFT WALL
These routes are found on the wall opposite the Honeysuckle Slab in the Cooler. Cool and shady, little sun reaches these climbs. Routes are listed left to right.

10. **RIPPLE** 5.12c/d ★
Start in the gray corner just left of the tree and scream through the first five bolts, climbing eases in difficulty to the lower anchor. Extension: the extension to the upper anchor and the following pitch are open projects. Please be aware of other users and do not block the trail.
60′ 8 bolts to chains
FA Luke Evans, Whit Magro, 2020

11. **COCONUT WATER** 5.11d ★
Take your pick of starting points. Left start begins at the pine tree, right is on just left of *Splash Down*. Both meet after 3-4 bolts. Difficult start leads to easier romp to chains A second pitch is currently under development. Potential access issues, see text in description for belay etiquette.
90ft, bolts to chains
FA Luke Evans, Jake Mergenthaler, Kim Mergenthaler, H. Schlotzhauer, 2020

12. **SPLASH DOWN** 5.11a ★★
Located on the slab right of the tree and left of the overhangs in the gut of the narrows. Climb through a scoop to a small ledge. Follow the weakness up to a steep section. Stick clip the second bolt. Potential access issues, see text in description for belay etiquette.
90′ bolts to chains
FA Jake Mergenthaler, Kim Mergenthaler, 2020

13. **BRAIN FREEZE** 5.12a ★★
Climb the immaculate gray slab out of the depths pf the squeeze.
100ft, 9 bolts to chains
FA Miriam Schlotzhauer, 2021

14. **PROJECT** (NOT PICTURED)
Bolt line between *Black Ice* and *Splash Down*. Potential access issues, see text in description for belay etiquette.
Equipped by Henry Schlotzhauer

15. **BLACK ICE** 5.12d ★★★ (NOT PICTURED)
First line of bolts downstream from the previous three routes. Fun climbing up steep, slippery rock. Potential access issues, see text in description for belay etiquette.
45 ft, 5 bolts to chains
FA Henry Schlotzhauer, 2019

16. **MENEGHINI** 5.14b ★★★
Downstream side of *Dometic*. Slippery grips, toe hooks, knee scums, delicate and powerful. A mini masterpiece! Please be cognizant of others and do not block the trail.
45 ft, 5 bolts to chains
FA K. O'Meara, 2020

17. **DOMETIC** 5.13b ★★
Left of *Frigid Aire* climb the overhanging prow to a spicy topout. Helmet suggested as fall above the last bolt can be awkward. Please be cognizant of other users and do not block the trail.
45 ft, 5 bolts to chains
FA H. Schlotzhauer, 2020

18. **FRIGID AIRE** 5.12b ★★
Start on the wall just left of the corner just after the trail exits the narrows. sustained climbing. Please be cognizant of other users and do not block the trail.
35 ft, bolts to chains
FA H. Schlotzhauer, 2019

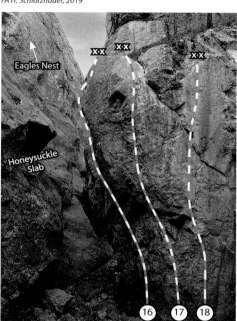

HONEY WALL

This steep wall is located uphill from the trail above the upstream side of the narrows. Unsurprisingly, it holds hard climbing on immaculate stone although several more moderate routes have been recently established on the right side. According to Luke Evans, one of his best routes and first in the canyon, Huckleberry Honey is found on this wall. To reach the Honey Wall and the Pad hike through the narrows then bushwack uphill following the margin of the North wall (left). The walking is easiest if you start in the small valley just beyond the wall and follow game trails for most of the ascent. Your goal is to reach a saddle that is the upper margin of the cliff band where you can cross to the southwest/ downstream side which faces the parking lot. This is not nearly as bad as it looks and should take about 10 minutes. The Honey Wall is located on the northeast face just before this saddle and can be seen for most of the hike, providing a good reference for when to traverse back to the wall.

1. PROJECT

Line of bolts up the slab to a steep finish. Far left arette downhill from *Huckleberry* and associated routes.
Equipped by Jackson Wethrill

2. YOGO SAPPHIRE 5.13a ★★★

A jewel of a route. Begin climbing on *Huckleberry* (using the newer start bolted by Kyle O'Meara is best). Hang a long draw on the 5th bolt then climb left into a steep but thankfully short crux. Finish on immaculate holds. Climbing is a bit runout to the anchor, but the holds are big and views are amazing so you may not even notice. Shares an anchor with *Huckleberry*.
100' bolts to chains
FA Luke Evans, 2020

3. HUCKLEBERRY HONEY 5.13b ★★★

Start up a lieback flake then ascend the increasingly steep wall on amazing holds. A stick clip for the high first bolt is strongly recommended. A left start variation into this line has been bolted but has not yet been sent.
100ft, bolts to chains
FA Luke Evans, Klemen Mali

4. PROJECT

Start on, then climb the arête right of *Huckleberry*.
Equipped by Luke Evans

5. HONEYCOMB 5.11d ★★

This route is located a little uphill from the previous routes near the saddle. Ascend the face using the honeycomb esk features and crack. Stemming the back wall takes some of the sting out of this one. The rock is sharp on this one so some tape on your digits might be a good idea.
80ft, 8 bolts to chains
FA Luke Evans, 2020

6. RAW 5.11a ★★★

Start on *Honeycomb* for the first two bolts then climb right up the fantastically featured face.
80ft, 7 bolts to chains shares anchor with Honeycomb
FA Luke Evans, 2020

7. WILD HONEY 5.7 ★

Climb the chimney to gain the first bolts. Follow the easy ridge to the top. Excellent views! Can be used to set a toprope on the previous routes.
80ft, 5 bolts to chains shares anchor with Honeycomb
FA Azaria, Maisie Evans, 2020

THE PAD

This shield of beautiful gray rock is perched on the upper portion of the north cliff band high above The Solution-al Cave and The Beach. An improbable wide ledge runs under this wall, making for airy single pitch routes. The climbing itself is high quality, but few routes exist at intermediate grades. The nature of the rock favors the 5.12 and above climber, but when things fill out there may be a handful of more moderate routes on the far right. While it is possible to reach this wall by wandering up the hill before the narrows, it is easiest to approach from the backside as for the Honey Wall. After reaching the saddle, follow the downstream side of the formation downhill and you should quickly see bolts.

1. SPUTNIK 5.13a/b ★★
Left most route on the upper ledge. Climb bouldery terrain through the left facing features to a much easier slap finish.
50ft, 6 bolts to chains
FA Jackson Wetherill, 2020

2. UNFINISHED PROJECT
Included for reference

3. UNFINISHED PROJECT
Included for reference

4. AQUARIUS 5.13a ★★★
First route on the main wall when hiking downhill. The business of the route is the first four bolts after which things ease to 5.12 to the jug below the chains
70ft, 7 bolts to chains
FA Kyle O'Meara, 2020

5. AQUARIES 5.13a ★★★
A shameless link up that adds length but not much dif-ficulty. After the 6th bolt on Aquarius, traverse right on neat edges past the ling bolt to then finish on Aries.
85 ft, 9 bolts to chains
FA Kyle O'Meara, 2020

6. ARIES 5.12d/13a ★★
Crank through long moves on a variety of nice holds. Amazing pitch!
70ft, 9 bolts to chains
FA Kyle O'Meara, 2020

7. GALACTIC CANNIBALISM 5.12d ★★★
Start with a long move right off the ground then contin-ue up easier terrain to the until things get steep. The crux is the final three bolts and packs quite a punch.
70ft, 7 bolts to chains
FA Jackson Wetherill, 2020

8. ALIEN SWAMP SNOT 5.9+ ★★ (Not Pictured)
Down and right of the other climbs. Very featured slab.
75 ft, bolts to chains
FA Jake Mergenthaler, 2020

PLATFORM 9¾

Like it's namesake from the Harry Potter novels, making your way to this hidden area can be a little tricky. While access does not require a leap of faith through a seemingly impassable brick wall, it does take some route finding. In fact even seeing the wall from the trail is difficult and requires standing in just the right place. The easiest approach is to rappel into the Room from the far end of the Pad (climbers right, see overview photo) . While working the route, climbers have been known to fix a line from the Pad through the room to the slope below to be able to jug directly to the Room. If you decide to take this option, seek to minimize visual impact and beware the resident wood rats that have a propensity to chew through ropes!

1. **ROOM OF REQUIREMENT** 5.13c/d ★★★
Bouldery climbing off the ground leads to a short but punchy arête that will keep you fighting til the end.
90ft, 9 bolts to chains
FA K. O'Meara

The Pad

Rap line from The Pad

x·x

①

Kyle O'Meara on *Room of Requirement 5.13c/d*
Photo by Ben Herndon

UPPER REFRIGERATOR CANYON

A maze of fins and towers sits to the west on the flanks of Sheep Mountain overlooking the canyon. While a few intrepid climbers have explored these features, this area's vast potential is mostly untouched.

1. CALL OF THE WILD 5.11b III

This climb ascends to the highest point of the largest outcrop above Refrigerator Canyon. From the summit the entire upper portion of Beaver Creek is visible, as is Helena. Established ground up on lead by Luke and Terry, it is a true adventure climb. During the first ascent a loose block broke Terry's leg high on the route. Despite the pain (not to mention the broken limb), they continued on to the summit and were rewarded by stellar climbing on great rock. Although this climb is bolted as a sport climb, the ground up establishment, route finding, and commitment, do not make climbing this route a trivial undertaking. This is high adventure sport climbing (bolt protected alpine climbing?) at its finest. Be aware that loose rock may be present, wear a helmet and protect your belays from rockfall when possible. To reach this climb begin bushwacking up the hillside in the gully just upstream of the upper Mustard Wall. Work right up the talus through a maze of towers and walls and eventually into a steep corridor after which you will see the first pitch in an alcove hidden at the end to the right. Look for bolts in a water grove. You can reach the wall in about 45 minutes to an hour, depending on fitness and route finding.

P1: Fun climbing through a well bolted grove leads to a single bolt belay, can be combined with the next pitch. Mossy with some loose rock in places. (50ft, 5.11b)

P2, P3: Cool stemming leads to easy scrambling and a two bolt belay in the "scoop". (200ft, 5.9)

P4: Climb out of the scoop. After a high crux, veer left on loose blocks over easy terrain (well bolted but use care). The scoop provides protection from any falling objects for the belayer. (120ft, 5.10)

P5: Short pitch of easy climbing leads to a bolted belay. (50ft, 5.4)

P6-8: Fabulous airy climbing on featured waves of blue limestone brings you to the top of the ridge. All belays bolted (2 bolts). Note there is a variation to P7 that goes left at 5.10R. (230ishft)

Descent: Walk off. Once you have gained the summit, downclimb the south side. Avoid the first gully, instead move up a ways before dropping down. Wander through the maze below and you will eventually end up somewhere above the Mustard wall.

600ft, 8 pitches, lots of draws & alpine draws, helmets, etc.

FA Luke Evans, Terry Cowen, 2014

2. BLUES TRAVELER 5.13 project

(Not Pictured)

Left of *Call of the Wild*, this project was bolted on rappel by Luke and may need some additional cleaning and bolts before it's completed. Crux pitch is the last one on great stone. It is possible to rappel this route to descend off back to the base.

Azaria and Maisie Evans on *Call of the Wild 5.11b*

POWERLINE BUTTRESS

A high voltage line skirts the base of this massive formation where it meets the road across from the Eye of the Needle formation. The buttress forms the eastern boundary of Refrigerator Canyon on one side and has a south face that curves to meet the road near the parking area for Eye of the Needle. The southwest face is split into two tiers by an expansive ledge. Two routes (Fried, Scarsft) provide access to the ledge and the Power Grid routes.

POWERLINE LOWER EAST FACE

Approach from main pullout across from the Eye of the Needle. Located on the north side of road.

1. **POWERLINE** 5.11c/d

This steep brown face on the east face of Powerline Buttress near the road starts in a grove of trees and pulls through several bulges.

85 ft, 10 bolts to chains

FA Randall Green, Martin McBirney, 1994

POWERLINE SOUTHWEST FACE

Can be approached by scrambling over some blocks than up a brushy hillside following the wall to the climbs. Alternatively park closer to the Refrigerator Canyon trailhead across from a grove of pine trees. Within this grove find a game trail that goes up and right across the slope, follow this for a bit than traverse directly to the climbs avoiding much of the brush.

2. PARTS IS PARTS 5.10c ★★

Climb is the farthest right on the wall. Start on a flat boulder/ belay pad, climb easier ground up and right then follow the black streak through several steep and sustained sections. Knot your ends as a 60m rope is just long enough to lower the climber back to the belay platform.

100ft, 13 bolts to chains

FA Jake Mergenthaler, Kim Mergenthaler, 2001

3. STICKER 5.10c ★

Just uphill from *Parts* on the corner of the main buttress. Steep and sustained.

90ft, 12 bolts to chains

FA Randall Green, Ted Simms, 2001

4. MEANS TO AN END 5.8

Short crack climb on left side of small slab that faces west. Slab is split by many cracks. Climb the cleanest one with a small mountain mahogany bush near top.

45 ft, gear to 3" chains

FA Randall Green, Ted Simms, 2001

5. INVITATION TO MADNESS 5.10a

Steep face route on pillar above *Means*. From *Means* anchors step right on ledge or from top of Sticker step left on ledge to belay bolt.

Descend with 2 single-rope raps.

50ft, 7 bolts to chains

FA Randall Green, Ted Simms, 2001

POWER GRID

See approach for the Powerline Southwest Face. Continue up the steep scree, and brush, covered slope following the buttress to a band of gray rock just right of center of the main south face that stands 60 yards from the obvious cracks of Means'.

6. SCARS MAKE THE BODY BEAUTIFUL 5.10d

Start 30' right of *Fried* and work up and left on puzzling light rock; surmount the right side of a toothy roof to cool but sharp rock above. Shares same chain anchor with Fried.

90ft, 12 bolts to chains
FA Randall Green, Ted Simms, 2001

7. FRIED 5.10b/c

This route serves as an approach pitch to ledge below the Power Grid but is a worthy endeavor all by itself. Start on a 15' high pedestal and slip up light gray rock on technical moves past several small roofs.

85 ft, 8 bolts to chains
FA Randall Green, 1994

8. WILLY WIRE HANDS 5.11a

The main Power Grid face stands above a 40' wide ledge; after climbing *Scars* or *Fried* it is safe to move around un-roped though caution is needed. Begin on the right side of the ledge; a light colored slab winds through bulges on sharp edges, near the finish the route bites back with steeper rock. Stay right off the start to avoid soft rock.

90ft, 8 bolts to chains
FA Randall Green, 1994

9. TRANSFORMER 5.12a/b ★

Left of *Wire Hands* and ascends steep rock to wavy, overhanging wall; pumpy with interesting technical sequences and fun finish.

95 ft, 12 bolts to chains
FA Randall Green, Kim Mergenthaler, 2005

10. BUDDHA BELLY 5.13b
Steep and exciting climbing up the belly of rock lead to a HUGE move and a redpoint crux.
90ft, 9 bolts to chains
FA Luke Evans, Liza Cabizares

11. BUDDHA FULL BLUE 5.13c/d
Start on Buddha Belly but break left into a steep mantle that leads to an arête and finishes on the slab.
90ft, bolts to chains
FA Luke Evans

12. BUDDHA'S DELIGHT PROJECT
Left of *Full Blue*.
Equipped by Luke Evans

13. POWER OUTAGE 5.11d ★★★
Starts left of the Buddha Routes. Although the rock is marginal at the beginning the rest of the route makes up for it. Climb the orange patina face, then pull the small roof (immaculate) to steep and very sequential moves to the anchors. Superb.
100ft, 12 bolts to chains
FA Jake Mergenthaler, Kim Mergenthaler, 2003

THE MITTEN

When driving past the trailhead, one small but prominent tower can be seen to the south. If viewed from the correct angle, it's summit resembles a mitten. Currently a single adventurous route has been established that reaches its summit. If you make it to the top, be sure to add your name to the register.

Getting There
Park at the Refrigerator Canyon Trailhead. Cross the creek and bushwack to the base of the feature avoiding the cliff band below the west face. A log crossing may be established near Dances With Roofs that will allow crossing with dry feet but add a bit to the hike.

1. THE MITTEN 5.8+ ★
Two pitch adventurous route that ascends the east face to the summit. This is more reminiscent of a true tower route rather than a closely bolted sport route and has seen relatively few ascents. Although the feature can be climbed in a single pitch, it is equipped to go in a long and a short pitch to reduce rope drag.
P1: Climb the east face on a mix of bolts and gear to an alcove below the summit. (80ft)
P2: A short pitch to reach the summit. (20ft)
Descent: Single rope rappel from summit anchors.
100ft, Alpine draws and an optional light rack of gear
FA Luke Evans, Terry Cowen, 2014

EYE OF THE NEEDLE

This impressive face of rock is found across the creek and upstream the Refrigerator Canyon trailhead. Currently its walls are home to the hardest multipitch routes on limestone and are among the hardest multipitch on any rock type within Montana. To reach the walls, park at the trailhead and hike up the road or continue and park at one of the pullouts directly below the formation.

NORTH FACE-LOWER TIER

The lower tier is directly above the creek across from the corner of the Powerline Buttress. As the base of the wall is in the creek during high water, climbing is best reserved for after spring runoff. Currently a single route has been established in the center of the wall.

1. DANCES WITH ROOFS 5.11a ★
Climb begins on the very edge of the creek, it is best to climb at low water stage. Grunt up and over roofs on blue- gray rock. Route easily seen from road.
60' 6 bolts to chains
FA Aaron Lefohn, 1996

Maiza Lima on *Whipstitch 5.13b*
Photo by Jules Jimreivat

EAST SIDE BOX CANYON

Cross Beaver Creek and ascend a steep game trail on the east side of the formation look for a path that cuts right and up the slope. Keep on this trail across the hillside under the support cable for the nearby power tower and up a steep slope. This eventually ends in a small box canyon the route is on the left.

1. WALK ON THE OCEAN 5.9+

Short right leaning crack climb on gray rock that starts out thin fingers then widens to hands.
60ft, gear to 3" chains
FA Aaron Lefohn, 1996

NORTH FACE-UPPER SLAB

Cross Beaver Creek and ascend a steep game trail on the east side of the formation look for a path that cuts right and up the slope. Keep on this trail across the hillside under the support cable for the nearby power tower and up a steep slope. This eventually ends in a small box canyon just above *Walk on The Ocean*. Scramble right (west) up a short gray face onto rocky shoulder and head up towards the now visible North Face. Routes listed right to left.

2. BATTERIES NOT INCLUDED 5.8 ★★★

Climb tackles the north face on a clean gray slab. The route is a bit sporty for the grade.
P1: From lower corner on right hand side of slab climb a broken corner (way easy) to gain a clean slab that surmounts a bulge at ¾ height. Belay on small stance from chains up and right of a cave with a tree growing from it. (5.8, 140ft, 10 bolts to chains)
P1 Bypass Variant: Go left at third bolt to gain a lieback flake follow this to a small cave with a tree growing from it. Continue up and right to Pitch 2 or rap from tree to base. (5.8, 120' 4 bolts, cams and nuts to 2"extra TCUs, to chains)
P2: From stance head up to the exposed shoulder tip toe up the razors edge and don't look right if you don't like heights (its 1000' to the creek) continue past the Eye of the Needle and step left into a cool recess with chains (5.8, 150ft) 9 bolts to chains
Descent: 2 double rope rappels the first going directly through the Eye (a 4x4' hole in the rock) from chains
290ft, bolts, gear (small TCUs to 3" cams) to chains.
FA Scott Payne, Randall Green, 1993

3. BASSACKWARDS 5.10 ★

Slab route 150' left of Batteries' that wanders up the north face. P1 offers more well-protected variant start for Batteries'.
P1: Traverse left on a ledge that begins down and left of the start of Batteries' tread left on ledge with trees for 150' and up a small gully until in a comfortable alcove. From alcove the line leans right on good rock to skirt bulges and then pad up a pretty slab to a cave with tree. (5.9, 80ft, tree belay)
P2: Step left from cave and ascend a steep left slanting line to the gully left of the summit block. (5.10, 90ft)
Descent: Single-rope rap from cold shuts (with a 60-meter rope) to tree in cave; from tree rap 80' to alcove.
170ft, bolts to chains
FA Randall Green, Scott Payne, 1994

[For Turbo and Wiener Dog, routes approach same as for Bassackwards alcove then continue traversing left and scrambling up ledges to 2-bolt belay below small overhang.]

4. WIENER DOG 5.8+ ★

Clip first bolt of Turbo Dog and continue scrambling right along broken ledge system past another bolt until it is possible to ascend steep face right of hole with small tree to same chain anchor as for Turbo.

80ft, 8 bolts to chains

FA Randall Green, Joe Bensen, 1998

5. TURBO DOG 5.11a/b ★

Leftmost of two routes that start from same bolted belay. Move slightly right under overhang and climb steep face to chain anchor at small ledge.

80ft, 8 bolts to chains

FA Randall Green, Joe Bensen, 1998

WEST FACE
The West Face is broken up into two areas. The upper part looms high over the canyon and holds a plethora of multipitch routes that are among some of the longest routes of their respective grades in the state. The lower area ranges in height from 65′ to 100′ and sports 3 fun climbs. Cross the creek near a large boulder and ascend a steep trail that follows the base of the wall. Routes are listed going uphill left to right.

1. BOOGER WOOGER 5.10b/c ★
This broken arête left of *Forearm Flambe'* has some distinct and fun climbing.
80ft, 8 bolts to chains
FA Randall Green, Theresa Green, 2000

2. FOREARM FLAMBE' 5.10b ★
Line ascends a clean gray face and utilizes horizontal breaks and crisp edges.
65 ft, 5 bolts and med gear to chains
FA Randall Green, 1995

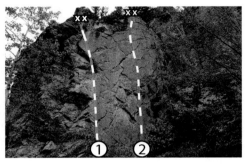

3. GIMPY 5.10d ★★
Climb this prominent corner about 100 yards above the creek where the lower tier intersects the upper part of the west face. Begin in a corner and slide up a layback crack step right onto committing face and gun for the top. Route was retrobolted by Randall in 2005.
100ft, 13 bolts to chains
FA Randall Green, 1995

4. THIS AIN' NOTHIN' 5.12c ★★
Ascends the west face to the summit.
P1: Begin in a V shaped notch about 200 yards above Gimpy to avoid rotten rock scramble about 25′ up into a cave and belay from a bolt there crank out left on insecure holds and up a well bolted headwall; step left as difficulty ends and head for the left edge of a nice ledge. (5.12c, 100ft)
P2: Ascend steep and sustained line that arches right toward an alcove dish high on face. Crux is directly above the chains. (5.11d, 130ft)
P3: From belay head up onto blunt arête tread right on sharp holds to the anchor. (5.11c, 80ft)
P4: Continue climbing up runnels; protected with medium gear to the summit.
(5.8, 80ft)
Descent: 3 double-rope raps down face to base.
310ft, bolts, optional gear chain and coldshut anchors
FA Bill Dockins, Randall Green 1995

5. WHIPSTITCH 5.13b ★★
P1: Shares a first pitch with *Nuthin'*, but instead of heading left through the last bolt, go straight up to an anchor. (5.12c/d, 90ft)
P2: The crux pitch. Immaculate, sustained climbing with a stellar slab finish. Climb straight up to a ledge. (5.13b, 120ft)
P3: A hard bouldery crux off the anchor leads through the blue streak to merge with the final two bolts of *Nuthin'.* (5.12d, 80ft)
Descent: 3 double-rope raps down face to base.
310ft, bolts to chains
FA Henry Schlotzhauer, 2018

6. PINTUCK 5.13c ★★
P1: Same start as for Nuthin', but continue straight up rather than beginning to traverse left as for both Nuthin' and Whipstitch. (5.12c/d, 90ft)
P2: Move up and left off of the belay to a more sustained pitch than it's neighbor to the left and wander up to the right of the ledge shared with *Nuthin'* and *Whipstitch.* (5.13c, 120ft)
P3: Up and right until the angle kicks back. Easy start leads to steep climbing and an exposed crux. Continue to summit and additional anchor if desired.
Descent: Rappel route with a single 70m (knot your ends!) or continue to summit and rappel alternative route. (5.13a, 70′ bolts to chains)
370ft, bolts to chains
FA Henry Schlotzhauer, 2020

7. THE THIMBLE 5.12d ★★

Same first pitch as for *Nuthin"* but continue straight up rather than beginning to traverse left as for both Nuthin'. Start off upper ledge and climb a steep blue streak through a technical crux that leads to absurd features and two finish options: left to the P2 anchor of Pintuck or right to finish on the access anchor to Humble Camel and pitch 3 of *Rich Man in Heaven.*

110ft, bolts to chains

FA Henry Schlotzhauer, 2020

8. RICH MAN IN HEAVEN 5.13c ★★

P1: Same start as for *Nuthin",* but continue straight up rather than beginning to traverse left as for both *Nuthin"* and *Whipstitch.* (5.12c/d, 90ft, bolts to chains)

P2: Shares start with The Thimble, but take the rightmost bolt line. (5.13a, 150ft)

P3: Climb up and right from the anchor to the top of the formation. (60ft, 5.13c?)

Descent: Rap the route

400ft, bolts to chains

Equipped by Henry Schlotzhauer, 2020

9. THE HUMBLE CAMEL 5.12c ★★

From the P2 anchors of *Richman* or *Thimble* take the left bolt line straight up the amazing shield of rock to an exposed finish.

60ft, bolts to chains

FA K. O'meara, 2020

Henry Schlotzenhauer on *Pintuck 5.13c*
Photo by Ben Herndon

PIKE CREEK

Pike Creek Canyon is a side canyon at the upper end of the Beaver Creek drainage. The lower reaches of the canyon have large slabby walls of good quality gray stone amongst the towering choss. Although this area is only a few minute hike from the road, it has a secluded feeling and it is almost surprising to hear vehicles pass. Depending on the time of year, Pike Creek may be running above or below ground. To approach the crags, start hiking up the creek following game trails or the creek bed. During the spring you will need to cross the creek several times which may be tricky during high water but things should be manageable by late May and dry by June. Once the valley opens up, favor the east side. In about 5 minutes you should pass Shangri La.

The canyon is 6.3 miles from Nelson and 1.75 miles past the Refrigerator Canyon trailhead. Drive past the aforementioned developed areas, continuing up the creek through an area without much rock. Once creek side cliffs reappear, keep an eye out for a narrow canyon on your right (south of the road 1.75 miles from the Refrigerator Canyon trailhead). If you reach the cattle grate before the private land, you have gone about 0.25 miles too far. Currently the USFS has a small sign noting the name of the creek beside the road. Park beside the creek. There are dispersed campsites adjacent to the road.

SHANGRI LA

A small and pleasant wall with easy access, well bolted routes on the shorter side, and a flat base near the seasonal creek. Perfect for a lazy morning or afternoon lapping moderate routes. These walls are south facing so they will get hot later in the day. The top of the cliff has loose rock and scree, so please lead all routes to get to the anchors. All-day sun.

1. RIGHT ON 5.9 ★
First line from the left. Climb thin edges under a small overlap.
55 ft, 7 bolts to rings
FA Dan Bachen, Danielle Noonan, 2019

2. GUILTY PLEASURES 5.8 ★★★
Second route from the left finishes on the crack. Climb goes on gear too if that's your thing.
55 ft, 7 bolts to rings
FA Dan Bachen, Danielle Noonan, 2019

3. BLISS 5.10a ★★
Third route from the left. A bit of a squeeze job, but the climbing is fun so we felt it was a worthwhile addition to the wall. Climb the increasingly steep slab through a techy crux to a fun juggy finish. Bolts where you need them if not quite where you want them.
55 ft, 7 bolts to rings
FA Dan Bachen, Danielle Noonan, 2019

4. ROSE-COLORED GLASSES 5.10b ★
Last route on the right, slab to an off-width crack. The bolting and movement are a little funky on this one due to the large hollow flake under the first half of the route. Some kneebar trickery helps at the end.
55,' 6 bolts to rings
FA Dan Bachen, Danielle Noonan, 2019

PIKE CREEK DOME

Looming above the gulch, Pike Creek Dome is a 400' high slab of weathered limestone. The climbing has a distinctly remote and alpine feel despite being a quick hike from the main road.

The rock is generally clean and high quality, but some choss and gravel are to be expected as route development is recent. Climbers should take care to stay on or near the bolt line and avoid loose looking features as they probably are. Remember it is always better to fly alone than to bring a "friend".

The approach to the dome is mostly moderate and should take no more than 20 minutes. Hike up the gulch just past Shangri La until you reach a small ridge that extends to the creek bottom on the same side. Ascend the downstream side of this until it is possible to walk over to the opposite side without being cliffed out (cairns). Sidehill across the scree, then cross a junky slab (3rd class but exposed). Follow the base of the cliffs until you see a carin marking a small gulley below the leftmost large pine tree. Work up the gulley crossing bands of stone (4th class some exposure). This should put you on a ledge by the tree and right of *Kelseya*.

1. KELSEYA 5.7 ★★

Put up on lead to access the top of the wall, this climb links slabs of good quality rock for the first two pitches then wanders up immaculate low angled stone to a slabby finish on the top of the formation. A long moderate route with a superb alpine feel.

P1: Start on a small ramp transitioning left to the clean face around the first bolt. Follow slab near the corner to a semi hanging belay. Some loose rock nearby so use care and follow the bolts. (5.6, 70ft)

P2: Move up and a little left from the belay then tackle the mini-roof straight on using the "tooth". Romp up the well featured and occasionally thoughtful slab of gray stone to a stance and anchor below the large ledge. Either rappel the route or continue on to the upper pitches. Can be combined with P1 for a long and fun pitch (5.7, 100ft).

P2 extension. 5.0

From the P2 chains, step right into the gully. Clip a bolt to keep your rope from rubbing on the choss and stem up to the large Ledge. There are several large and ominous looking blocks at the top of the gully. They appear to be stable, but it is best to avoid as much interaction with them as possible. Belay from rappel anchors. It is possible to reach the ledge from the start in a single very long pitch, however belaying from the top of P2 is recommended as it shields the belayer from any rock fall caused by climbing the gully.

15 ft. 1 bolt to bolt anchor

P3: Climb a short pitch up the beautifly featured slab to the next ledge. (5.5, 35 ft)

P4: Pad up the slab to the top of the wall. The pitch wanders a bit to avoid loose rock and a few alpine draws are nice. (5.7, 100ft)

Descent: Rap the route.

350ft, bolts with chains

FA P1-3 Dan Bachen, P4 Rob McVie, 2021

Andrew Schrader on *Tears of a Clown 5.7 R or 5.10+*
Photo by Bob Goodwyn

NORTH FORK TETON RIVER BY DAN FRAZER & MIKE PLANTE

WELCOME to the North Fork of the Teton River, the major drainage south of Blackleaf Canyon. This zone holds a few single-pitch routes and the gem of the area, *Tears of a Clown*. Park either in a large pullout on the road or in the dispersed camping area southeast of the Cave Mountain Campground Road.

DIRECTIONS

Drive to the forest service boundary on the North Fork of the Teton. Drive another 0.4 mile to the first pullout on the left side of the road (f you get to Clary Coulee you went too far). Walk back down the road 75 to 100 yds to a dirt bank with a trail on the left. Walk up the trail and trend to right a bit, but dont get below the cliffs. Follow the cairns up the hill for, give or take, 15 minutes until you come to two carins. Turn hard right and walk until you hit the top of a big cliff. Walk down to the right and around to the bottom of the cliff. The cliff is south-facing and gets sun most of the day. It is fairly wind protected from a north and west wind.

BORDER WALL

The wall just after the forest boundary offers some harder climbs. If you look up when you see the brown Lewis and Clark National Forest Sign, you are looking at the wall.

1. MEDIA CALLS THIS FIVE NINE 5.10d ★
The farthest left route with a crux at the bulge. It eases up above. Stick clip.
40 ft, bolts to chains
FA Dan Frazer

2. GRAB EM BY THE POCKET 5.11b ★
Another boulder problem at the bulge with easier climbing above. Stick clip.
40 ft, bolts to chains
FA Dan Frazer

3. COVFEFE 5.12a ★★
Ascend the crack feature. It is hard from the break and doesn't let up much.
50 ft, bolts to chains
FA Dan Frazer

4. MAKING AMERICA GREAT AGAIN 5.12- ★★★
This is the best route on the wall. Like its neighbors, it has a crux at the bulge but remains continuous.
50 ft, bolts to chains
FA Dan Frazer

There are chains on the crack on the right. The route is not bolted yet but goes around 11c and is mostly clean.

TEARS WALL/SLAB

1. TEARS OF A CLOWN 5.7 R or 5.10- ★★★
This slab on steroids is worth your while if you are in the area—an immaculate slab in a superblocation above the crystal-clear creek below!
P1: Two starting options exist: a 5.9 start from the creek bed, or a 5.7 start up the gully directly to the ramp.
P2/3. 2nd or 3rd pitch (depending on how you start the route) has a MEAN 5.7 roof—and by that, I mean that it has some 5.9 climbing with a hard roof pull-through. The second roof goes at 5.10-. The old book had it at 5.7 but that is a serious sandbag. There is, however, a 5.7R traverse to the right that wanders back on route. Pick your poison but be careful. It is possible to scramble and traverse into the top slab pitches but expect lots of loose scree and a sketchy entrance to reach the first protection on the route.
P3/4-6. Once on the upper slab you will be smiling ear to ear and your calves will be burning from top to bottom. Enjoy this treasure of a climb! There is also a 5.7 variation that goes left called *You're Gonna Die Clown*.
Descent: Rap the route.
500 ft, bolts 2 ropes required to rappel. Quickdraws.
FA Rob Hagler

2. SIXTH TIMES THE CHARM 5.10a (Not Pictured)
Two pitch west-facing slab up the mountain from *Tears of a Clown*. This can be climbed as a full 70 meter pitch, but requires two ropes to descend.

CHERT WALL (NOT PICTURED)

The Chert wall is found a few hundred feet downstream of Tears on the corner of the formation. The climbs share a start from a small ledge at head-height and diverge from there. Routes are listed left to right.

1. CHERT ON MY SHIRT 5.9 ★
Climb a cherty face through a few thin moves to the anchor. Best to stay right of the grungy gully.
80 ft, bolts to chains
FA Dan Frazer

2. CHERTY BUSINESS 5.10a ★★
Crimp up a chert-studded slab. More sustained and better climbing than *COMS*.
75 ft, bolts to chains
FA Dan Frazer

3. CHERTY KURTY 5.10a ★
Follow the right margin of the wall through some fun, if a little contrived, climbing. Finish back left. Watch for some loose rock toward the top.
70 ft, bolts to chains
FA Dan Frazer

CAVE MOUNTAIN CAVE ROUTES (NOT PICTURED)

Four to six easier routes to the left of the Cave Mountain cave that are all said to be 5.7 or easier.

Andrew Schrader on the 5.9 start of *Tears of a Clown 5.7 R or 5.10-*
Photo by Bob Goodwyn

Maiza Lima on *Zen and the Art of Bolting 5.12a*
Photo by Drew Smith

Welcome to Blackleaf Canyon. This place may change your life. The textured stone, gigantic buttresses and even the fickle weather make this a very special place. Unlike many cliffs along the Rocky Mountain front, the rock is solid and as beautiful as the scenery. It is unique for the massive amounts of bomber chert. The chance of spotting a Grizzly bear from high on a route also has its allure. With 70 individual lines composed of 145 pitches ranging in size from 50 to 600 feet high, Blackleaf is sure to please most everyone. If there is one variable to the area, it is the weather. The Front is infamous for wind. Even if it's 90 degrees along the Highline, the cliff will be 75 with a probable breeze. However, that wonderful breeze can quickly change to a tempest, bringing violent thunderstorms and snow. So, for high adventure sport climbing without tons of commitment bring your "ready for anything" attitude.

Photo by Damien Powledge

Main Wall

It's Only Money
by Randall Green

On our first few visits Blackleaf Canyon, we could only dream of climbing because the wind blew so hard we couldn't walk. We crawled to the base of the walls. We returned in the summer of 1999, during more favorable weather, and began to work. Due to copious amounts of loose rocks, precarious flakes on the wall, and the fact that our group consisted of "old but not bold climbers, " the first work began from the top down.

From the top of the wall, several false starts ended with ropes hopelessly dangling in space over huge overhangs. And even before one permanent rappel anchor was drilled a major mishap ended the day's exploration. The troubles began while we stood, unanchored, on a small sloping ledge at the top of the wall. A beloved canine companion ventured too close to the edge, setting off a chain reaction of events that resulted in a fate almost worse than death. The response to save the dog caused a dropped rope to nearly fall over the edge, which caused another reflexive response to save the rope. But the gallant idiot who saved the rope left the pack with the drill and bolts unattended. Without warning, the drill pack took a suicide leap off the edge. The group, dogs and all, froze until we heard the sickening sound of impact as the bag exploded like a watermelon at the base of the wall.

Sun Wall

The drill was on loan from a friend, who had just received it as a wedding present. We had no choice but to replace it. Two weeks and nearly $800 later we returned to Blackleaf with our tails between our legs. But we had a new drill, extra battery pack, and someone keeping the dogs out of harm's way. We began rapping and drilling our way down the 700-foot face of the black chert slab. For three months, usually on weekends, we worked on the route, set rap stations, cleaned, toproped, and drilled. Each trip we had to climb around the backside to the top and rap the route. More partners were recruited to help with the workload. On a good day when it wasn't too cold or the wind wasn't blowing too hard, we would get two pitches bolted. In September, we completed the upper pitches and were finally ready to lead the entire route in one push. But cold weather and the incessant winds eventually drove us home for the season. It wasn't until June, 2000 that the route was completed. With each subsequent trip to the canyon we've added other routes. We've only scratched the surface.

Blackleaf Canyon
Parking

Access
Since Blackleaf offers a trailhead into the Bob Marshall Wilderness, it is accessible by passenger car (with good tires—flats are common). As you approach the canyon, the range land past Bynum Reservoir springs to life with the yellow blossoms of Potentilla, which eventually give way to grassy hills of scrub juniper, pine and aspen all of which have a curious dwarfed appearance caused by nearly incessant winds. Wildflowers add a riot of color in spring and early summer. The wall on the south side of the canyon is the best quality stone, with layers of chert that offer some amazing edge climbing. With slabs, bulges, roofs, and ramps, Blackleaf has potential for dozens more high-quality routes up to six pitches or more.

Blackleaf Climbing History
Climbers from Haver, Butte, Helena, and Great Falls began realizing Blackleaf's potential in the early and mid-1990s. Although early forays on a couple crack-chimney systems had been climbed on both walls, it wasn't until the fall of 1998 that anyone actually explored the taller and more vertical faces. In winter of 1998, Jim Wilsom and Scott Payne discovered the glories of the canyon while scouting for ice climbs. They started talking about the canyon's potential. Cameron Burns, who lived in Great Falls at the time, started exploration independent of other groups. Randall Green, Chris Alke, and I put in the first multi-pitch lines. Randall's first visits to the canyon ended with frustration as gale force winds demanded him to crawl and stumble along the base of walls to check out the rock quality. I've experienced similar conditions where the wind accelerates through the narrows—strong enough to knock you down and throw golf-ball-sized rocks at you for good measure. Finally in 1999, with better weather, the real work began. Numerous people have contributed to the route development. In addition to Randall, Chris and my wife Kim, Rob Hagler has authored numerous new lines; Luke Evans has helped put finishing touches on some of the hardest pitches of several routes; Cameron Burns got things started on the east end of the face; Wayne Harney, Ted Sims, Paul Travis, Jim Semmelroth, Brandon Alke, Kevin Billington and others all have made great contributions to the overall effort. Kyle Perkins and Brad Maddock put a few routes on the north side of the canyon in 2010.

Establishing Routes
We only ask one thing of others who want to share in the fun of establishing new routes around Blackleaf: make them safe for climbers and invisible to non-climbers. We have camouflaged as much as we can. The first bolts on most routes are 10-20 feet off the deck. Unless you are really looking for routes, you probably won't see the protection. This is a touchstone wilderness gateway, so it is critical we do our part to minimize our impact. Small cairns often have been built at or near the base of the routes to help you locate them.

This is Grizzly Country
The law says if you are away from your campsite or car all bear attractants"must be kept in a hard-sided vehicle or hung from a support structure at least 10 feet off the ground and four feet out from the sides. Coolers alone are not bear proof unless IGBC certified and locks are used in the provided holes. Attractants include: food, garbage, beverages, cosmetics, or anything with a smell. These restrictions are a protection not only for us, but more importantly, to protect the bears themselves.

Car Camping at Blackleaf
Climbers from as far away as Bozeman and Missoula have been known to daytrip it, but most like to spend a few days. At the entrance to the canyon, limited undeveloped car camping sites are nestled in aspen and cottonwood groves just minutes from the main cliff. Do not do what bears do in the woods. EVERYONE must use the pit toilet!

NOTE: No camping is allowed within 200 feet of the trailhead; this includes the parking area near the kiosk.

The most popular sites fill up on the weekends but there's an alternate legal option: from the cattle guard near a stand of cottonwoods (about a half mile from trailhead) it is legal to pull off anywhere and park within 300 feet feet of the road. Set up your camp wisely and please use a leave no trace mentality.

Blackleaf Chert

Getting to Bynum, Montana

From the South
From Exit 226 (Wolf Creek) on 1-15, follow US Highway 287 to Choteau and continue north to Bynum (about 13 miles north of Choteau).

From the Northwest & East
If coming from Kalispell or near Glacier Park, follow US Highway 89 south from Browning to Bynum. If you are one of the few climbers in Great Falls, take the I-15 Exit 290 (Vaugn) north of town to Highway 89 leading directly to Bynum.

From the North (Canada)
Since all you Alberta hosers are familiar with the climbing Blackleaf offers, this is a great stop for anyone headed farther south on your bi-annual road trip. Take Exit 339 on 1-15 at Conrad (the next town south of Shelby) and follow State Route 219 to Pendroy near where it intersects Highway 89 just north of Bynum.

Bynum to Blackleaf Canyon

Take a left (west) at JD's Wildlife Sanctuary (a bar) and zero your odometer. Look for the signs to Bynum Reservoir and Blackleaf Road #145. Stay on the good gravel road and at 4.2 miles you will pass the Bynum Reservoir turnoff on the left. Continue heading west and northwest on the Blackleaf Road. At 13.5 miles you will cross a cattle guard with signs marking the route. Follow the signs for Blackleaf Road and the Blackleaf Wildlife Management Area. At 16.1 miles turn left at an intersection marked Blackleaf Canyon. You will cross Blackleaf Creek, sometimes dry, and eventually arrive at the trailhead about 20 miles from Bynum. Look west into the canyon. The wall on your left holds the treasures you are seeking. To date, there are only a few routes on the sunnier southeast-facing wall to the right.

Approach

From the parking area take the trail upcanyon for about a quarter mile until you see a climber's trail leaving the main trail and descending left towards the creek. Cross the creek—normally very shallow and easy to hop across on small rocks—and head up the obvious climber's trail towards the main wall. The trail will drop you off at the Prozac Zone near the base of *Sketched Out Fat Guy*. If heading to *Climbing 101* keep on the main trail for a bit longer and leave the trail closer to the base at the constriction in the canyon.

All routes described are from right to left as you face the cliff.

Kim Mergenthaler on *Prozac Moments 5.12a*
Photo by Jake Mergenthaler

Blow Hard
Wall

Dentist Area

Enlightnment Wall

Birdhead Buttress

68 66   64 60   57   52 51   50 48 47

Black Chert Slab

West Wall

Mojo Tower

Prozac Area

West End

42 41

28

10

1

Trail

West End

Gray buttress where the wall meets the creek near the constriction in the canyon on the extreme west end of the main wall. There are said to be two fun 5.10a's (Mosquito Cove) right of Climbing 101. They face West and get afternoon sun.

1. Climbing 101 5.7 or 5.9 ★★★

A beginner multi-pitch climb on wonderful chert and gray rock! Excellent adventure for the grade. Can be done as a three-pitch (5.7) or a five-pitch (5.9) depending on the climbing party's ability. The start can be a bit wet depending on where the spring runoff has routed the creek bed. Be conscious of rockfall if there are any parties below you, especially if you do the upper two pitches which have some ledges with lots of loose rock.

P1: Start below the large slab and pad up to a high first bolt which can be somewhat hard to find. Follow the bolts through large chert rails to a sloping ledge. 70m rope needed to lower or rap! (5.4)

P2: Begin on good rock to obtain grassy, rock-filled ledges. Head for a triangular tower up and left. Some parties stay roped up as this is exposed. Belay from one bolt at the good ledge. (5.4)

P3: Climb a steep wall on great holds (90 ft). Some parties choose to rap from here OR it is possible to carefully scramble off this ledge to the right (upcanyon). If you choose to walk off, be VERY careful of loose rock especially if other parties are below. (5.7)

P4: Climb the left-facing corner, exiting right around a small roof. (5.8)

P5: Continue straight up on thinner holds to a belay about 10 feet below the canyon rim. (5.9)

Descent: Rap the route and walk-off from top of P2. Some parties stay roped up for first 50' or so as it is exposed.

450 ft, bolts and fixed anchors. 14 draws needed for pitch 5 and a 70m rope needed to rap!

(P1-3) FA Rob Hagler, Mike Thompson, 2002
(P4-5) FA Dan Clark, Rob Hagler, Mike Thompson, 2004

2. Teachers Pet 5.6 ★★

Often confused with the start of of Climbing 101, this route is to the left.

85 ft, bolts to chains

Sarah Maddock on Climbing 101 5.7 or 5.9
Photo by Brad Maddock

INDOOR CLIMBING, GEAR, BETA

HILINECLIMBINGCENTER.COM

GREAT FALLS, MT

Info@hilineclimbing.com

406.315.1613

PROZAC AREA

This section is found on the far right side of the Main Wall. The area spans from the extreme western edge of the cliff to a 70-foot-high chossy pillar. This is the first spot you come to when hiking up the main trail. The rock here is varied and the routes are often memorable. The raps overhung so much that we spun like drunken spiders on our lines. Finally and miraculously we would touch back down and clumsily drill in an anchor. When we got to the ground we needed some Prozac, or at least a beer. Routes listed from right to left.

3. LOCO 5.10d
Starts at far western edge of cliff. Climbs up a sheer, thin shield. Ends on ledge.
75 ft, bolts to chains
FA Jake Mergenthaler, Kim Mergenthaler

4. MY PSYCHO GIRLFRIEND 5.10b ★★
A fun climb that ends on a prominent flake.
75 ft, bolts to chains
FA Jake Mergenthaler, Kim Mergenthaler

5. SEDATED 5.11a ★★
Good sustained climb. Move up through several bulges. Save some juice for the last bit.
95 ft, bolts to chains
FA Jake Mergenthaler, Kim Mergenthaler

6. CRAZY TRAIN 5.12a ★★★
P1: Nicknamed *Best 5.10d Ever,* this sustained climb is crazy fun. After a bouldery start (semi-high first bolt) cruise up on good holds then surmount a pair of small roofs. (5.10d, 90 ft)
P2: Move right off chains through desperate little roofs. (5.12a, 90 ft)
Descent: Rappel from chains.
180 ft, bolts to chains
FA Jake Mergenthaler, Kim Mergenthaler

7. SMURFS ON ACID 5.11c ★
Juggy start on steep good rock yields a few ledgy rests then the difficulty increases. Keeps you guessing to the chains.
90 ft, bolts to chains
FA Jake Mergenthaler, Kim Mergenthaler

8. SKETCHED OUT FAT GUY 5.11b ★★★
P1: Starts on super jugs then throws a short tricky crux at you. Hold on for some pumpy climbing to the chains. (5.10b, 85 ft)
P2: Exciting pitch that makes you think it ends on the pumpy arête. (5.11b, 90 ft)
Descent: Double rope rappel.
185 ft, bolts to chains
FA Jake Mergenthaler, Kim Mergenthaler

9. WHERE IS MY MIND? 5.10c
Romp up easy terrain to a small roof (some go slightly left) then scream through roof to chains.
85' bolts to chains
FA Jake Mergenthaler, Kim Mergenthaler, 2018

10. BROS BEFORE HOES (TOXIC MASCULINITY) 5.12b ★★
Beast of a climb through several steep roofs. The climb ends at the top of the cliff.
P1: Thought provoking climb that follows a prominent dull arête about mid-height. (5.11a, 85 ft)
P2 Right varient: Amazing climb! Starts on white letter slots then gets techy, then juggy! Ends in a steep dihedral. (5.11b, 90 ft)
P2 Left varient: Tread left through roofs and blocks. Ignore the poor man bolts and laugh in the face of rust. Like Butte sushi : a tiny bit spicy and funky. Double rope rap. (5.11b 90 ft)
P3: From ledge above the right varient, continue up super chossy but easy terrain to reach an arête out right. The crux is well-bolted on slightly better rock. Finish on a ledge below a roof. (5.10a, 80 ft)
P4: Tackle a steep boulder problem. The climbing eases off a bit to gain juggy roof, but it's still is no gimmie. (5.12b, 85 ft)
P5: From an OK stance continue up steep terrain to gain a bulletproof slab. Belay below steeper headwall. (5.12a, 100 ft)
P6: From the slab lurch into pumpy dihedral. Finish on great stone to a comfy ledge. (100 ft, 5.12a)
Name: This crass name comes from a messy break-up just before bolting the first pitch. Kim and I named the 5-pitch extension of this climb *Toxic Masculinity.*
Descent: rappel route using fixed draws to keep you from outer space.
600 ft, bolts to chains
P1. FA Wayne Harney
P2-6. FA Jake Mergenthaler, Kim Mergenthaler

11. SHIV. 5.11d ★★
Characterized by a car hood sized roof/ block at mid-height.
P1: Start on easier terrain to ledge, then whine up a slopey crimp tech fest. Once that nonsense is done, skirt a large block and continue up positive fun arête. Shares chains with 'Deep End'. (5.10c, 85 ft)
P2: If continuing at the end of pitch 1 head up and right to chains. from small stance head up on harder rock. Techy. (5.11d, 80 ft)
Name: For a girl who used to serve us pre-climb bagels. You never knew if you'd get service with a smile or the shiv!
165 ft, bolts to chains
FA Jake Mergenthaler, Randal Green

12. DIZZY WITH DANGER 5.11b ★★★

Shiv and *Deep End* all meet at same small ledge. This climb goes right up the middle. Unique movement on good stone.
85 ft, bolts to chains
FA Jake Mergenthaler, Kim Mergenthaler, 2018

13. DEEP END 5.11b ★★★

Fun and varied, but the third pitch is a tad chossy.
P1: Best pitch of the climb on clean rock. Start in an easy dihedral then move through a thin crux. Enter easier terrain only to get slapped by powerful moves to chains. (5.11b, 85 ft)
P2: Thin moves up and left help you gain a cool sharp corner. Worthwhile. (5.11b, 85 ft)
P3: Ok climbing on mid-grade rock through a bulge. We have plans to take this route to top, but there's just so many cool lines that we haven't gone back. (5.10b, 80 ft)
250 ft, bolts to chains
FA Jake Mergenthaler, Randall Green, Kim Mergenthaler

14. DELIRIUM TREMORS 5.10 ★★

Head up an easy short corner. Ends under a roof.
85 ft, bolts to chains
FA Jake and Kim Mergenthaler

15. PROZAC MOMENTS 5.12a ★★

A climb with some thin wild moves.
P1: Start in sa hallow corner, at third height, clip a bolt at bulge then step right to gain nice holds. Ends on a chossy ledge. (5.10b, 75 ft)
P2: Move up through moderate terrain, then scream through the intense crux. Keep your head about you while skirting the roof on good holds. (5.12a, 90 ft)
Descent: One double rope rap or two singles.
180 ft, bolts to chains
FA Jake Mergenthaler, Kim Mergenthaler

16. AMNESIA 5.11b ★

Start just right of a large boulder on a thin face; move up into a harder corner.
85' bolts to chains
FA Jake and Kim Mergenthaler

17. FLAKIN OUT 5.11c ★★★

Outstanding climb!
P1: Start on the six-foot boulder. Thin holds lead up to a surreal flake (don't worry, the bolt is just hidden). Crank to chains. Sustained. (5.11b, 90 ft)
P2: Follow bolts up a direct fun line. (5.11c, 85 ft)
175 ft, bolts to chains
FA Jake Mergenthaler, Kim Mergenthaler

18. QUESTION REALITY 5.11d ★★

Start just left of the large boulder. Boulder problem start (some stick clip) leads to a very technical steep slab. The upper bulges are easier. Helps to be tall.
85 ft, bolts to chains
FA Jake Mergenthaler, Kim Mergenthaler

19. PARANOIA 5.11b ★

Start left of *Reality* in a small corner. Climb interesting stone to a small roof high on the route.
90 ft, bolts to chains
FA Jake Mergenthaler, Kim Mergenthaler, 2020

20. BIPOLAR 5.11c ★

Fun climb on unique holds over several bulges. Start in an easy corner.
80 ft, bolts to chains
FA Jake Mergenthaler, Kim Mergenthaler, 2020

21. REST IN PIECES 5.10d ★

This is a funky climb with cool pinches and slopers. It follows a weakness of flakes, clipping bolts on your left (or just be a baller and climb up the gut).
75 ft, bolts to chains
FA Jake Mergenthaler, Kim Mergenthaler

22. WHY ASK WHY? 5.11c

Start on large ledge just right of a chossy pillar. A bouldery start on insecure moves leads to a distinct crux above a small roof. Memorable.
75 ft, bolts to chains
FA Jake Mergenthaler, Kim Mergenthaler

23. ONE JUG MOMMA 5.10d

Climbs the chossy pillar. Start on white rock then pull through a looser section. It ends on quality rock with one world class jug.
75 ft, bolts to chains
FA Jake Mergenthaler, Kim Mergenthaler

Justin Stewart on *Sketched out Fat Guy 5.11b*
Photo by Kim Mergenthaler

WEST WALL
Refers to the section of cliff just left of the chossy pillar all the way to the Fox Den area.

24. FEED THE RAT 5.12a ★
The first climb left of the chossy pillar. Battle up the initial bulge to more reasonable rock, then set sail in a sea of awesomeness. This thing is hard til the end.
105 ft, bolts to chains
FA Jake Mergenthaler, Kim Mergenthaler

25. SANDS OF TIME 5.11d ★
Two-pitch climb just left of the chossy pillar.
P1: Start under a small roof/flake on orange rock with a prickly bush just beneath it. Crimp out a bulge on sharp holds. (5.10d, 65 ft)
P2: Continue up a steep face on good but sustained holds, then power up over a thin bulge. (5.11d, 80 ft)
Descent: Rap the route.
145 ft, bolts to chains
FA Randall Green, Kyle Perkins, Brandon Alke, Jake Mergenthaler

26. NINE ROUNDS 5.11d ★
Long and continuous on good rock. Hang in for all nine rounds.
110 ft, bolts to chains
FA Jake Mergenthaler, Kim Mergenthaler

27. GARY COLEMAN 5.10c
Short weird route that shares anchors with *Paradigm*. Not a bad climb.

28. PARADIGM SHIFT 5.11d ★★
P1: Start just right of a broken crack—*Diablo*. Cool moves on great holds. (5.10c, 60 ft)
P2: Follow a steep and continuous line to a small ledge. (5.11c/d 100 ft)
P3: Follow the bolt line up and right to the ledge. (5.9, 100 ft)
P4: Follow bolts to a ledge. (5.9, 65 ft)
P5: Move left from the ledge and work up through a steep slot to a tiny ledge. Exciting. (5.10d, 100 ft)
P6: Wander up right then left on thin but good holds. (5.11b/c, 100 ft)
P7: Follow bolts to the top (5.11b, 100 ft)
Descent: Double rope rap the route.
625 ft, 15 bolts to chains
FA Randall Green, Kyle Perkins, 2005

29. BLANCO DIABLO 5.10a
Fun route up a broken crack. The bouldery, slippery start is crux. Start on a flat pad made of stacked rocks.
Name: An untethered, white, ornery mutt roamed the cliff and campgrounds for a weekend, causing trouble.
65 ft, bolts to chains
FA Jake Mergenthaler, Kim Mergenthaler, 2016

30. OFF LIKE A PROM DRESS 5.10c
Just left of *Diablo* lies this mellow-looking line on good rock. Careful or you'll be off…
70 ft, bolts to chains
FA Jake Mergenthaler, Kim Mergenthaler and Randall Green, 2003

31. BIG BROTHER IS WATCHING 5.10d
Begin at a nice flat spot. A precarious journey on a clean gray slab. Name: Bolted while being glassed by FWP.
70 ft, bolts to chains
FA Jake Mergenthaler, Kim Mergenthaler, Randall Green, 2003

32. GYM BRATS 5.10d ★
Eight feet right of a drafty cave lies this gymnastic climb. Huck and pray towards the top.
70 ft, bolts to chains
FA Jake Mergenthaler, Kim Mergenthaler, 2017

33. HIDING FROM GIANTS 5.11d ★ (Not Pictured)
Above a small cave in a huge corner climb up on a ledge to a very high first bolt (stick clip it). Start on vertical terrain to a ledge then scream through a steep toothy corner. Transfer out left and continue on sustained 5.11+ climbing. We plan taking this all the way to the top. Name: Lots of roofs and funky rock await above.
125 ft, bolts to chains
FA Jake Mergenthaler, Kim Mergenthaler, 2017

FUN ZONE

This good warm-up area consists of four routes 100 feet east, up the trail and around from the small cave after the West Wall. Routes go right to left.

34. **KYLE AND FRIENDS** 5.9 (Not Pictured)
A bit funky. Climb up broken rock past a bulge. The far-right route.
60 ft, bolts to chains
FA Kyle Perkins

35. **ITCHY AND SCRATCHY SHOW** 5.10a ★★
P1: Begin on a flat spot. Climb hrough a small roof on amazing rock just right of a corner. (5.10a, 70 ft)
P2 Right variant: Move up a broken corner and tread right on a techy journey. (5.10d, 70 ft)
P2 Left variant: Move up a broken corner, then step left and crank straight up on smaller holds. (5.10d, 70 ft)
140 ft, bolts to chains
FA Jake Mergenthaler, Clayton, Ben Alke, 2006
Varients FA Jake Mergenthaler, 2020

36. **DREAM KILLER** 5.10b ★★★
Start on nondescript rock then move into a corner. Commit out left on steep wonderful rock. In my dreams this would go on forever. Not a gimmie up top.
70 ft, bolts to chains
FA Jake Mergenthaler

37. **BEAD TIL YOU BLEED** 5.9 ★★
The easiest of the climbs in this area.. Nondescript rock to easy bulge to clean headwall.
Name: Kids making bead jewelry below.
Bolts to chains
FA Jake Mergenthaler, Kim Mergenthaler

Fox Den and Mojo Tower

The Fox Den is a good landmark to see where you are on the wall. It is a 20 feet deep recession in the wall marked by two small caves in the back. It also has a nice belay spot made of logs. Mojo Tower sits on the Den's left side.

38. **CRAZY LIKE A FOX** 5.11d ★★
P1: In back of the den climb this fun, steep, gymnastic route on decent rock. (5.10c, 75 ft)
P2: Move up on less-than-perfect stone to a short bulge crux. Not great. (5.11d, 75 ft)
Descent: Rap the route.
150 ft, bolts to chains
FA Jake Mergenthaler, Kim Mergenthaler, 2003

39. **MESSIN WITH MY MOJO** 5.11d ★★
P1: This route climbs on dark rock to reach the ledge. Shares anchors with *Workin'*. (5.10a, 80 ft)
P2: From the top of the tower climb this excellent sustained pitch with a very thin crux. (5.11d, 90 ft) ★★
Descent: Rap the route.
170 ft, 12 bolts to chains
FA Jake Mergenthaler, Kim Mergenthaler, 2003

40. **GOT MY MOJO WORKIN'** 5.12a ★★
P1: Down left and around the corner is this good climb that gets steeper towards the top. (5.10a, 80 ft)
P2: From the chains work up and left on techy terrain to finish on a steep slab. (5.12a, 90 ft)
Descent: Rap the route.
170 ft, bolts to chains
FA Jake Mergenthaler, Kim Mergenthaler, Randall Green, 2003

Jackson Wetherill on *Dream Killer 5.10b*
Photo by Jake Mergenthaler

BLACK CHERT SLAB

This wide dark-colored slab can be seen from the parking lot. It features some of the oldest routes at Blackleaf. The rock quality is generally good. Routes are listed right to left.

41. MR. SHARPIE 5.11b ★

P1: Rightmost line on the slab. Head up nondescript rock. (5.10c, 90 ft)
P2: Move up on steeper sharper rock. (5.11b, 80 ft)
P3: Eases off to a beautiful gray slab with chert. (5.10a, 90 ft)
Descent: Rap the route.
260 ft, 11 bolts to chains
FA Jake Mergenthaler, Kim Mergenthaler, Randall Green, Kevin Billington, Paul Travis

42. IT'S ONLY MONEY 5.11c ★★★

This is the one that began it all. Randall's vision. It's good and sustained.
P1: Begin in small corner then up through a bulge on good rock. (5.10a, 90 ft)
P2: Start cranking up the steep headwall. The crux comes quickly and eases slightly towards top. (5.11a, 90 ft)
P3: After pitch two, this one might calm you down a bit. Cruise up the fun gray slab. (5.8, 80 ft)
P4: Climb an arching line that slithers between formidable roofs. Take care to minimize rope drag. (5.9, 95 ft)
P5: Gasp and claw straight up wishing I would have bolted it a bit better, then trend right on an airy ramp. (5.11c, 95 ft)
P6: This exposed pitch rewards you with big moves on good holds. (5.11a/b, 90 ft)
Name: Randall spent over a grand on this route: one chopped rope, one dropped Bosch, and all the hardware.
Descent: Rap the Route
540 ft, 13 bolts to chains
FA Randall Green, Jake Mergenthaler, 2000

43. SPARE CHANGE 5.10c ★★

This variation to *Money* comes in from the left on good rock with techy slab towards top.
90 ft, 10 bolts to chains
FA Paul Travis, Randall Green, Theresa Green 1999

Truck Stop

Walk east on flat ground past the left edge of Black Chert Slab. If the trail starts going up, you've gone too far. The routes are fun but the rock is not good. Unless your bored with the other routes I'd pass these by.

44. BEER GOGGLES 5.11a

Go up a chossy corner to a steep bulletproof finish.
65 ft, bolts to chains
FA Jake Mergenthaler, Kim Mergenthaler, 2016

45. EURO TRASH GIRL 5.10c

Chossy start through fun bulges. The best of the three.
65 ft, bolts to chains
FA Jake Mergenthaler, Kim Mergenthaler, Jackson Weatheral, 2016

46. GEAR JAMMIN 5.11b

P1: It's chossy and a tad easier, but not as well bolted. Bolts to chains. (5.10a, 65 ft)
P2: Interesting stemming on funky rock, but not great. (5.11b, 75 ft)
140 ft, bolts to chains
FA Jake Mergenthaler, Kim Mergenthaler, 2016

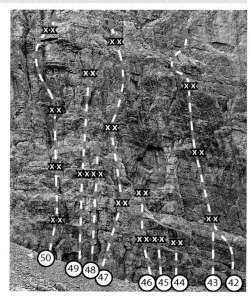

BIRD HEAD BUTTRESS

Walk east along base of the wall past Black Chert Slab and Truck Stop. When the trail angles right and steepens look for a 30-feet-tall feature that loosely resembles a bird head. There's also a distinct chimney and a belay spot made of stacked rocks. Listed right to left.

47. SUPER 8 5.10c ★★

A good climb with unexpected moderate climbing on steep rock and great belay ledges.

P1: Start just right of a chimney. At mid-height step right and continue up to a nice ledge. (5.8, 80 ft)

P2: Start with a tricky boulder problem to a sustained and exciting face. (5.10c, 105 ft)

P3: Go up and right, eventually stepping back left to a ledge. (5.10a, 80 ft)

P4: Upward on nondescript pitch. (5.9, 80 ft)

P5: So good! Trend up and right to a break in the large roof. After this obstacle step left and reach high for good holds. (5.10c, 90 ft)

P6: Work straight up a steep broken face to gain a curving crack on the slab. The rock isn't great, so some people don't do this pitch. But the reward is a cool hanging rappel.

(5.10c, 80 ft)

Descent: Rap the route carefully with one 70m or two shorter ropes.

505 ft, bolts to chains

FA Jake Mergenthaler, Kim Mergenthaler Dave Sturn, Dave Brummond, 2016

48. SHOTGUN WEDDING 5.10d ★★

P1: Start in a chimney and move left through a steep section. Belay under a roof—or better, combine pitch one and two. (5.8, 60 ft)

P2: Crank through a white roof on good holds to gain a choss ledge (watch what you grab on this easy part) then follow a clean slab. (5.10d, 95 ft)

P3: Grip through a vertical face on crimps to gain a unique chert-filled face. Belay in an exposed right facing corner. (5.10d, 95 ft)

Descent: Rappel the route carefully with one 70m rope or two shorter ropes.

250 ft, bolts to chains

FA Jake Mergenthaler, Kim Mergenthaler and Randall Green, 2005

49. ORIGINAL SIN 5.10d

P1: Climb through the beak on slightly fragile rock.

P2: Angle up and right to meet *Shotgun's* anchors.

155 ft, bolts to chains.

FA Jake Mergenthaler, Kim Mergenthaler, 2004

50. HOME BOYS ON SOY 5.11b ★★★

This is a justifiably popular climb with fun climbing and good belay ledges. The crux is short, stout, and steep on good holds. The crack climbing is easy. Like other big rigs in Blackleaf a lot of people helped get this one done. My vote for best climbing name of all time. Name credit goes to Ted Sims.

P1: A steep bouldery section (hard!) leads to good rock and chains. (5.9, 65 ft)

P2: Move up the steep slab to a good belay ledge. Sustained. (5.9, 95 ft)

P3: Layback up a cool steep corner then step left to a slab.

(5.9, 85 ft)

P4: Trend left to the belly of the bulge and prepare to pull the roof. As difficulty eases, be sure to follow an easy crack up and RIGHT (medium gear) to chains. Some have gone left and it ain't pretty. (5.11b, 95 ft)

P5: Jam straight up a hand-to-finger crack, passing a bolt along the way. (5.9)

P6: Move up and slightly left past bolts and through a small bulge.Continue to a ledge at the top of a large chimney. (5.10, 75 ft)

Descent: Rap the route.

580 ft, bolts and gear to chains

FA Randall Green, Jim Semmelroth, 2001 Equipped by Randall Green, Jim Semmelroth, Jake Mergenthaler, Kevin Billington, Ted Sims

On Randall Green
By Jake Mergenthaler

Randall Green has been contributing to climbing in North America since 1978. He established dozens of first ascents in North Idaho, the Bugaboos and, of course, right here in Montana. Randall has written three guidebooks and edited many others.

Randall moved to Montana in 1989 to finish a degree at University of Montana and in 1992 took a job with Falcon Publishing in Helena. He quickly began exploring the area crags. In his search for the few established routes, he explored the limestone in Hellgate Gulch and tried, sometimes in vain, to climb routes done by Bill Dockins and Kristen Drumheller. He dragged many a beginner to the granite crags at Sheep Mountain and Blue Cloud. But the limestone of Hellgate, and eventually Avalanche Gulch and Blackleaf Canyon, captured his interest and sharpened his eye to all the unclimbed possibilities.

With few climbing partners in Helena, Randall established climbs that had a broad appeal since they often were moderate in difficulty, but safe and enjoyable to climb again and again. He truly crafted his routes, from thoroughly cleaning them to thoughtfully placing bolts. He taught me a lot about craftsmanship and respecting the rock.

He was also a visionary. He convinced me that the rock under the roof at Hellgate was "not that bad" and that we should begin bolting it on lead. That lead to "Devils Highway" and opened the way for some of the more popular routes in the area.

His tenacity made him a driving force— opening lines at Blackleaf, as well. For over two decades he would envision a line, then make many arduous hikes to the top of the 600' formation and finally clean, bolt, and link all the pitches together. He was seldom competitive about climbing difficulty, but he wanted to be the one to equip the best lines up there. I'm just glad he let me tag along and even left a few lines for me.

Eventually he quit climbing for health reasons and began competitive road bike racing. He charged into that pursuit with great enthusiasm and discipline. I miss climbing with him but know that whatever he does he goes all out or not at all. I owe a debt to Randall for his mentorship and friendship. All of us owe him for the countless hours of work spent putting up routes that we all can enjoy.

Randall Green on Flakin Out 5.11b
Photo by Jake Mergenthaler

ENLIGHTENMENT WALL

East of the Birdhead you encounter a steep short trail. When the terrain flattens out look up and right. This is Enlightenment—home to some amazing lines. Routes described right to left.

51. Bodhisattva 5.12d ★★★

A fantastic voyage up broken corners and steep slabs. Most people bail after the fourth pitch. **P1:** A broken easy slab leads to a steep corner. Feels like 5.10 to me. (5.9, 90 ft)

P2: Follow bolts on a continuous journey up a steep prow. (5.10, 90 ft)

P3: Meander left up a face. Free your mind and your feet will follow. Belay on a huge grassy ledge. (5.10, 90 ft)

P4: Step right to encounter delicate face climbing on a gorgeous slab. Can be toprroped or rapped with one 80m rope. (5.10+, 140 ft)

P5: Hard climbing to a runout 5.11 slab. Some strong climbers have mentioned that this runout pitch isn't great. (5.12d, 100 ft)

Descent: Rap the route using one 80m or two shorter ropes.
510 ft, bolts to chains
FA Rob Hagler, Luke Evans, 2002

52. YUAN CHI 5.10d ★

One route right of *Zen* in open corner. Start with a boulder problem with an Esher-esque rock spike. Can be a variation start to *Zen*. Possible to climb second pitch variation.
70 ft, bolts to chains

53. ZEN AND THE ART OF BOLTING 5.12a ★★★

Many consider the fourth pitch of this rig the best pitch in Bleaf—amazing moves throughout, good rock and nice belay ledges. Look for an easy slab first pitch left and up from *Bodhi*.

P1: Climb this easy slab to a ledge. (5.6, 60 ft)

P2: An amazing half-moon shaped line with a crux right in the middle. (5.11b, 80 ft)

P2 Variation: Instead of stepping left, go straight up and right on quality rock. Ends near the original pitch. (5.11d, 80 ft)

P3: Walk right on a ledge (15 feet) to the second anchor. This allows you to climb up the good strenuous pitch. (5.10b, 50 ft)

P4: Laugh up the steep white face to a pumpy crack on wonderful holds. End on the grassy ledge. (5.10a, 95 ft)

P5: Chimney, stem and face climb up a leaning pillar. (5.10a, 65 ft)

P6: Scream up this bouldery crimpy line on good rock. (5.12a, 100 ft)

Descent: Rap the route.
450 ft, bolts to chains
FA Randall Green, Rob Hagler, 2004, 2009

THE DENTIST AREA

This exciting area lies just left of Enlightenment on a flat spot. Look for toothy roofs at half height and a 20-feet-high prominent flake on good rock. Threre is a band of suspect rock in the first third of some of these routes. Routes described right to left.

54. LAUGHING GAS 5.11a ★★★

P1: Find first high bolt in an easy corner. Crank up through bulges. (5.11a, 80 ft)

P2: Continue up to a committing technical corner. Easy to combine both pitches with 80m rope. (5.11a 40 ft)

Descent: Rap the route.
120 ft, bolts to chains
FA Jake Mergenthaler, Kim Mergenthaler, 2010

55. BRACES 5.10d

Look for a roof at ¼ height. Climb through the right side of the roof on sharp holds. Shares anchors with *Laughing*.
80 ft, bolts to chains
FA Jake Mergenthaler, Kim Mergenthaler, 2010

56. GAP TOOTH GIRL 5.12a ★★

P1: Up a broken slab to a white corner that ends in a fun roof. (5.11a, 90 ft)

P2: Shriek up sharp techy bulge to nice ledge. (5.12a, 60 ft)

Descent: Rap the route.
150 ft, bolts to chains
FA Jake Mergenthaler, Kim Mergenthaler, 2012

57. AIN'T DEAD YET 5.12a ★★

This is a great climb that keeps getting better as you climb higher.

P1: Start on a triangular boulder. Travel across a chossy easy ledge. Pull through toothy blocksto a hanging belay. (5.11a/b, 90 ft)

P2: Pull over a tricky bulge to a shallow scoop, then up immaculate rock to a large ledge. (85 ft, 5.11a/b)

P3: Continue up the steep wall on the left using great jugs. Encounter ten feet of choss that's not gonna kill anyone, but isn't fun to climb (10a). Try avoiding it by trending left. Uneventful climbing leads to large ledge. Bolts to chains (5.10a, 75 ft)

P4: Charge up to a very high first bolt (5.9) then a cool chimney. Exit the chimney and head right on good flakes, staying right as long as you can. Head left in an arch to reach a sloping semi-comfy hanging belay. (5.11a, 105 ft)

P5: Step right and it begins. Bouldery start then good holds through a roof on a pretty gray streak. Wander over several bulges (mostly 11c). Well bolted, airy and fun. End on small ledge. (5.12a, 105 ft)

Descent: Rap the route.
500 ft, bolts to chains
FA Ted Sims, Jake Mergenthaler, Kim Mergenthaler, 2015

58. DRILL EM FILL EM 5.11b ★★
P1: Climb up distinct 20' tall flake then through fun roof like blocks. (5.11b, 90 ft)
P2: Follow bolts up techy ground. (5.11b/c, 70 ft)
Descent: Rap the route.
160 ft, bolts to chains
FA Jake Mergenthaler, Kim Mergenthaler, 2012

59. MORPHINE 5.12a ★★
Just right of 6' high boulder lies this immaculate face climb. Very technical.
80 ft, bolts to chains
FA Jake Mergenthaler, Kim Mergenthaler, 2012

60. DIRTY MERG AKA NO PAIN WITH NOVICAIN 5.10d ★★
P1: Start just left of 6" high boulder. Head up on good stone to encounter a ledge, step right up arête. (5.10b, 80 ft)
P2: From ledge move up and left surmount bulge and then move into burly chimney crack. (5.10d, 80 ft)
P3: From good ledge scurry up easy but broken terrain, at the top dive right into a dusty corner. (5.9+ 95 ft)
P4: From a great ledge move up and left around a corner. Steep climbing on good rock leads to an exciting slab, then easier corners. (5.10a, 80 ft)
P5: Continue on brilliant steep face to gain a well bolted but chossy bulge (2 moves), then slab it out to chians and small stance. (5.10c, 80 ft)
Name: I climbed this route with my broken arm in a cast. It actually jammed pretty good.
Descent: Rap route with a 70m rope
160 ft, bolts to chains
FA Jake and Kim Mergenthaler 2021

BLOW HARD WALL

This popular area lies on the far east side of Main Wall. It is characterized by a beautiful 90-feet-tall slab covered with chert. Routes described right to left.

61. SURFACE TO AIR 5.8 ★
Farthest right and shortest of the routes in this area. White-gray slab.
45 ft, 4 bolts to chains
FA Wayne Harney, Luke Evans 2003

62. G-FORCE 5.10b ★
Second route from the right.
90 ft, 8 bolts to chains
FA Wayne Harney, Kriston Griffon, 2003

63. PULL OR EJECT 5.10a ★
Starts just left of the "nose" in the slab.
90 ft, 10 bolts to chains
FA Wayne Harney Mary McKennery, 2003

64. THE VENTURI EFFECT 5.12a ★★★
A sustained line to the top of the wall on good rock.
P1: Climbs great chert edges to a blank slab. (5.10+, 90 ft)
P2: Steep and pumpy climbing through a bulge to a hanging belay. (5.11b, 90 ft)
P3: Fun climbing on the great chert slab. (5.10b, 85 ft)
P4: Extra-long and strenuous pitch that ends above a roof. (5.12a, 110 ft)
P5: Crimp up a techy slab with hidden holds. Toward the top there's a bolted variation featuring a harder direct finish up the prow. You cna also move right on 5.10 ground. (5.11d, 85 ft)
P6: Nice slab finish. (5.10a, 80 ft)
Descent: Rap the route with an 80m or two shorter ropes.
540 ft, bolts to chains
FA Luke Evans, Rob Hagler, 2002
Equipped by Randall Green, Kim Mergenthaler, Jake Mergenthaler, Luke Evans and Rob Hagler

65. BLOW HARD 5.10d ★
Fun climb in the middle of the chert face. Capped by tricky smooth slab.
85 ft, 10 bolts to chains
FA Jake Mergenthaler, Randall Green, Kim Mergenthaler, 2000

66. TOP GUN 5.10d ★★★
P1: Second route right of choss chimney. Climb a great face on chert of every size toa lieback flake. Belay on a ledge. Shares anchors with *Fly Boys*. (5.10a, 85 ft)
P2: Continue up the large chimney on jugs. Step left around the corner and continue on featured rock. In the chimney do not go up right to an abandoned aid line. (5.10d, 85 ft)
P3: Follow the bolt line up a steep fun slab. (5.10c, 85 ft)
255 ft, bolts to chains
FA Jake Mergenthaler, Kim Mergenthaler, Randall Green, Wayne Harney, 2002, 2012

67. FLY BOYS 5.10a ★
Just right of a chossy chimney. Climb up vertical rock on cherts. A bit heady at the second or third bolt.
Name: This couple was stationed at the Air Force base.
85 ft, 9 bolts to chains
FA Christine and Cameron Burns, 2000

68. PISSIN' IN THE WIND 5.11a ★★
P1: Start down and left from a nice slab on easy ground. (5.6, 90 ft)
P2: Surmount a huge roof/flake corner on fun large holds. Ends on a nice slab. (5.11a, 70 ft)
P3: From the ledge go straight up the steep face (crux) to gain an arête. Follow the left side to the top. (5.11a, 90 ft)
Descent: Rap the route.
250 ft, bolts to chains
FA Jake Mergenthaler, Kim Mergenthaler, Randall Green, Theresa Green, 2015

Damian Mast on *The Venturi Effect 5.12a*
Photo by Damien Powledge

RAINY DAYS AREA
This area resides down and about 100 yards east of all other climbs. The four routes sit in a little alcove. Routes are described right to left.

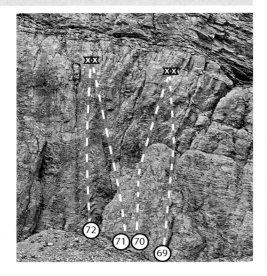

69. JAWS OF LIFE 5.11a ★
Climb up the chimney high and right of *Beer*. The first bolt is past the chimney section. Shares the last three bolts and chains with *Beer*. Heady lead for me.
85 ft, 10 bolts to chains
FA Jake Mergenthaler, Rob Hagler, 2004

70. BEER RUN 5.10a ★
Far up the gully, commence in a corner and finish with a tricky slab.
85 ft, bolts to chains
FA Jake Mergenthaler, Rob Hagler, 2004

71. TRAD CLIMBERS BEWARE 5.12a ★★
Up the gully to the right of *Rainy*. The crux is in a steep shield with tricky clips.
95 ft, 12 bolts to chains
FA Rob Hagler, 2004

72. RAINY DAYS AND BAD BELAYS 5.11d ★★
Start just left of a gray streak and pull up this very contin-uous sustained line. Name: Done rope solo in the rain.
95 ft, 12 bolts to chains
FA Rob Hagler, 2002

Sun Wall
A southeast-facing wall that gets great sun most of the day and currently holds only a single six-pitch route, but with potential for many more. This is a great route to climb on a colder day! Approach via the main trail, just past *Climbing 101* and what looks like an old glacial moraine on your right. Head up and right up the scree field toward the wall to a prominent corner with a cave. Uplift is 50 feet right of this cave.

73. Uplift 5.10c
P1. A well-bolted, very steep pitch ascends crumbly and textured rock to a belay station beneath the roof.
The crux is a traverse across a crack near end of the pitch. It's not great, but keep going as it gets better! (5.9)
P2. Mixed, crack. Dodge the roof by climbing right from the belay station. Stay in the crack or use the crack when neccessary. Clip bolts left and place pro in the crack when needed.
P3. Great immaculate friction slab. Pull over the bulge from the second belay station and chase bolts. At the third belay station, traverse right across the scree field ledge to the the back chimney. You will see a pair of anchor bolts on the right side before the chimney. (5.8)
P4. Super fun! Head up the chimney, clipping bolts on the right face. Once the chimney ends, rotate 180 de-grees to head onto the left face. Use the bolts and a thin crack to guide you to a nice ledge. (5.10b)
P5. Climb a small dihedral to the face traverse right after a mini-roof. Crimps and balance moves lead to the next good ledge. (5.10c)
P6. Climb the face and pull over a large bulge. Traverse right and up after the bulge, on slightly runout, easy terrain. Finish at a good standing belay. (5.8/9)
Descent: Rappel from top anchors, double rope rappels to the large scree ledge. Backtrack your route to the third belay station. A single-rope rappel from third belay and a double-rope rappel from second belay will get you to the bottom.
A dozen draws, some alpines, cams .75-3 for pitch 2.

Kyle O'Meara on *Pintuck 5.13c* in Beaver Creek
Photo by Henry Schlotzhauer

Routes and Areas by Name

Routes By Grade

ONE MOVE TOO MANY

By Volker Schoeffl, Thomas Hochholzer & Editor Sam Lightner, Jr.

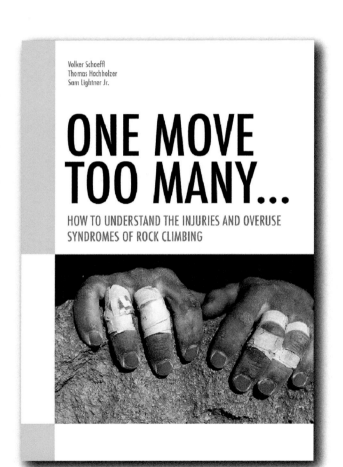

For those of us who've made one move too many, esteemed German sports medicine doctors Dr. Volker Schoeffl and Dr. Thomas Hochholzer provide an in-depth examination of common climbing injuries, treatments, and prevention. From the mildest case of belayer's neck to a complete finger pulley rupture, get the information you need to avoid injury or to get back on the rocks as soon as possible.

Curious about our latest books? Follow us:

⊙ 🛟 @sharpendpublishing

www.sharpendbooks.com

women of climbing

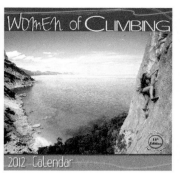
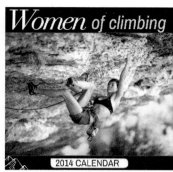
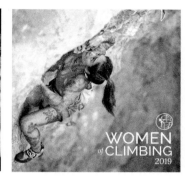

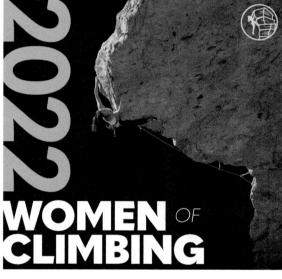

For over 20 years our Women of Climbing calendar has adorned the walls of climbers' homes, offices, and gyms. We represent women in our community showcasing strength and boldness. Whether wedged in a desert crack or poised on granite granules, we strive to collect the most inspiring images of women climbers in their element.

Sharp End

VERTICAL MIND

By Don McGrath & Jeff Elison

In Vertical Mind, Don McGrath and Jeff Elison teach rock climbers how to improve their mental game so they can climb better and have more fun. They teach how the latest research in brain science and psychology can help you retrain your mind and body for higher levels of rock climbing performance, while also demonstrating how to train and overcome fears and anxiety that hold you back. Finally, they teach climbing partners how to engage in co-creative coaching and help each other improve as climbers.

With numerous and practical step-by-step drills and exercises, in a simple to follow training framework, your path to harder climbing has never been clearer. If you are a climber who wants to climb harder and have more fun climbing, then Vertical Mind is required reading. Well, what's stopping you? Pick it up and get training today!

Curious about our latest books? Follow us:

⊙ f @sharpendpublishing

American Alpine Club

Climbing injuries happen. Club members benefit from backcountry rescue coverage, adventure grants, and gear discounts, while supporting our policy, advocacy, and community work. Explore all that the American Alpine Club has to offer climbers by scanning the QR code or by visiting: americanalpineclub.org

United We Climb.

ROCK CLIMBS OF
SOUTHWEST UTAH &
THE ARIZONA STRIP

By Todd Goss

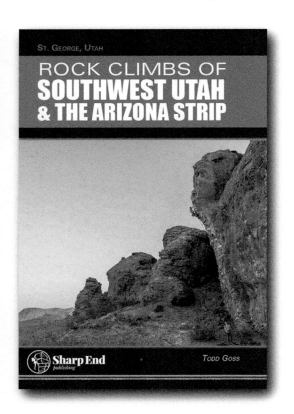

This full-color guide will make you want to pack up and buy real estate in St. George, Utah. With eight rock types, 50+ areas and many renowned crags, the St. George region has become the West's premier sport climbing venue. Routes run the gamut from novice to expert, and scenery from red rock to alpine. This diverse area boasting nearly a thousand climbs truly has something to satisfy any climber's taste.

Curious about our latest books? Follow us:

 @sharpendpublishing

www.sharpendbooks.com